Economic Integration and National Economic Policy

Olaf Münster

# Economic Integration and National Economic Policy

PETER LANG
Frankfurt am Main · Berlin · Bern · Bruxelles · New York · Oxford · Wien

**Bibliographic Information published by the Deutsche Nationalbibliothek**
The Deutsche Nationalbibliothek lists this publication in the Deutsche Nationalbibliografie; detailed bibliographic data is available in the internet at http://dnb.d-nb.de.

Zugl.: Passau, Univ., Diss., 2010

Cover Design:
© Olaf Glöckler, Atelier Platen, Friedberg

D 739
ISBN 978-3-631-61817-2



www.peterlang.de

To my parents

# Acknowledgements

This dissertation was written during my time as research and teaching assistant at Darmstadt University of Technology and Passau University. I thank the many people who have guided me throughout the development of this work.

In particular, I am indebted to my teachers for sharing their knowledge in economics with me and for their consistent encouragement. Especially, I am deeply grateful to Michael Pflüger (Passau University) who was my principal advisor. I am also obliged to Hans Fehr (Würzburg University) – my second advisor – and Irene Lurie (State University of New York at Albany) who both guided me into the field of public finance while I was a student.

Eventually, I also benefited from numerous insightful and stimulating discussions with friends and colleagues at conferences and at seminar classes of the Bavarian Graduate Program in Economics (BGPE). Notably, I want to thank Andreas Röthig, Ralph Scheicher, Gerald Csipek and Jens Rubart.

Finally, I am deeply grateful to my family for constant moral support.

Augsburg,
Mai 2011

*Olaf Münster*

# Table of Contents

# 1 Introduction

## 1.1 Motivation and Precursory Thoughts

Analyzing the fiscal implications of economic integration among independent countries occupies a large number of researchers today. The elementary roots for this research area, however, date to the late 1950s.[1] Since that time the fundamental question about the optimal provision and funding of public goods and services has been vividly debated in the closed economy setting.[2] Today, many of the implications of fiscal federalism discussed earlier are being debated in the field of international economics with the goal of highlighting the various aspects of public sector organization in an open economy.

This is mainly owed to the rapid pace at which globalization took place especially within the last two decades. Two factors have mostly been responsible for this development: (1) technological progress tends to reduce the spatial distance between countries – examples include declining costs of transportation and enhanced communication/ data transmission technology, and (2) political actions such as free trade agreements (e.g., the WTO that originated from the GATT) or economic unions (e.g., the European Union).[3]

The effects of enhanced economic integration become visible in trade of goods and services and increasingly manifest themselves in factor mobility, predominantly concerning the footloose character of capital.[4] On the following pages we shall therefore turn to the prominent example of capital mobility to illustrate the particular problems and complexity of the interaction between economic integration and public policy and to motivate the approach of this thesis.

Capital mobility materializes in foreign direct investments (FDI) and portfolio investments. The former comprise, for instance, investments in new firms or equipment, mergers and acquisitions, retained earnings from affiliated companies or loans provided to affiliated companies and the latter describe pure financial transactions that are usually not asset backed. These both expressions of capital mobility are strategic foreign investment devices primarily used by mul-

1 Cf. Tiebout (1956).
2 Cf. Wildasin (2003).
3 Cf. Andersen (2003) and OECD (2007a).
4 Though labor is far less mobile, the spread of multinational firms supports the notion that jobs are mobile, which finally influences labor markets.

tinational enterprises (MNE) to increase their economic success. According to these thoughts, there is a close conceptual relationship between capital and corporate income which we account for by using these two terms in the sense of synonyms throughout the remaining chapters.

The topic of capital mobility has attracted considerable attention in the contemporary literature on open economy public finance, establishing the wide research area of so called capital tax competition.[5] In an open economy setting, capital becomes a very mobile factor of production across borders and national governments find themselves in strategic interaction with other governments in setting up their national rules of taxation for capital income. With capital mobility, the tax burden on capital income becomes a criterion in the investment decisions of firms.[6] National governments are thus concerned not to lose their capital tax base when they set capital tax rates without taking other governments reactions into consideration. Therefore, capital mobility is made responsible for potentially restraining the tax setting behavior of a national government: capital will leave high-tax countries and sail into tax havens. A national government that seeks to avoid losing its tax base consequently takes this likely reaction of capital owners into consideration and finally adjusts its capital tax rate to the level of the low-tax country. In the extreme case this approach will leave capital completely untaxed.

This so-called race-to-bottom scenario is the reason why the ongoing European integration combined with the experienced progress of global economic integration has stirred up a widespread apprehension in the public that national governments will lose their independence in economic policy. Consequently, capital mobility is usually related to tax base mobility. National governments commonly use their overall tax revenues to finance all kinds of public welfare services and public goods, such as infrastructure[7]. Therefore, the fear that national governments in a globalized world would be incapable to independently collect tax proceeds in the course of economic integration finally becomes manifest in the notion of a decline in the provision of public services.

---

5 For a survey of the theoretical research in this area consult Wilson (1999) and Fuest et al. (2005) for a more recent analysis which puts the focus on multinational firms and financial arbitrage.

6 Devereux and Maffini (2006) provide an extensive survey on the empirical literature on the investment decisions of multinational firms and capital taxation. Ernst & Young (2007a) deliver survey results of selection criteria for investment decisions.

7 The term infrastructure will be used in a very broad sense comprising ‘soft’ infrastructure as, for example, property rights or legal security as well as ‘hard’ infrastructure as, for instance, roads or bridges.

The critics of economic integration (esp. in terms of capital mobility) underpin their claim that capital mobility has harmful implications on the public policy of independent countries by referring to the development of tax rates. Figure 1.1 illustrates the development of the statutory tax rates on corporate income in the European Union in the recent past.

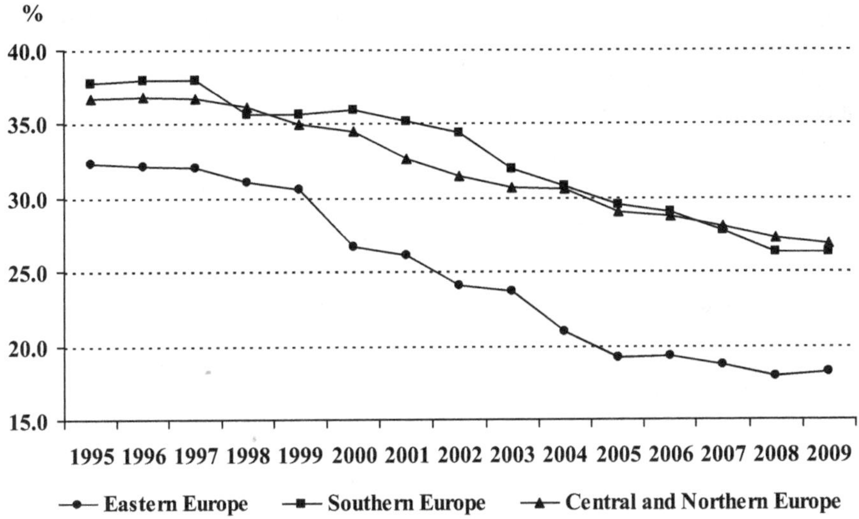


*Figure 1.1: Statutory tax rates on corporate income; Eastern Europe: unweighted average of Bulgaria, Czech Republic, Estonia, Hungary, Latvia, Lithuania, Poland, Romania, Slovenia and Slovakia. Southern Europe: unweighted average of Cyprus, Greece, Italy, Malta, Portugal and Spain. Central and Northern Europe: unweighted average of Austria, Belgium, Denmark, Finland, France, Germany, Ireland, Luxembourg, Netherlands, Sweden and United Kingdom; Source: COM (2009), Table II-4.1*

It clearly shows that the statutory corporate income tax rates within the European Union have tremendously declined over the years, especially between 1999 and 2005. While the gap between Southern Europe and Central and Northern Europe became smaller in the most recent past, the overall decline in the statutory tax rates across Europe was very strong. Since statutory tax rates in Eastern Europe declined sharply, the tax rate gap between Eastern Europe and the rest of Europe increased. However, since the determination of the tax base varies significantly across different countries, the statutory corporate tax rate is only a weak measure for a comparison of the corporate tax burden across different countries. Therefore Devereux and Griffith (2003) proposed to calculate effective tax rates which determine the tax burden of a hypothetical investment by taking the underlying applicable tax code into consideration.

Taking differences in each country's tax base into consideration, the derived effective average tax rates on corporate income which are illustrated in figure 1.2 show the same trend as the time series of the statutory tax rates. The decline in the effective average tax rates shows the same pattern as the decline in statutory tax rates, however the downward movement of the statutory tax rates is much sharper. Additionally, in both figures the gap between tax rates in Central and Northern Europe and Southern Europe declined over the recent past so that these two groups maintain roughly the same tax rates.

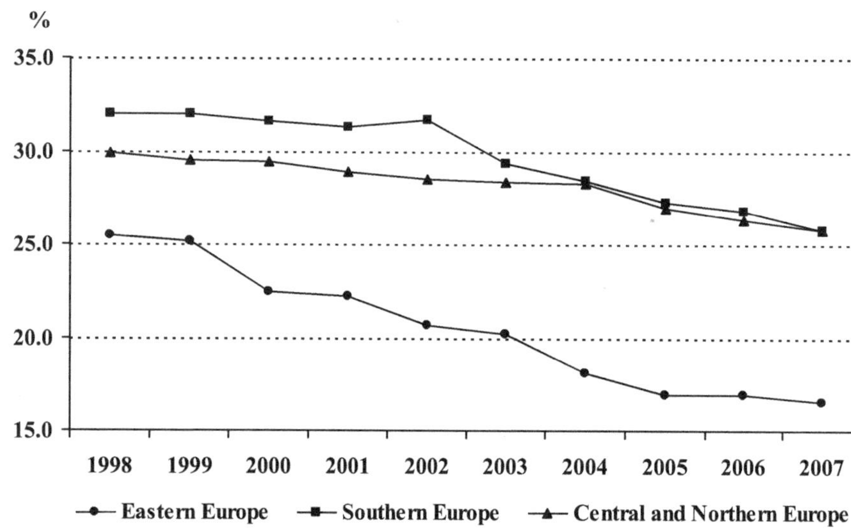


*Figure 1.2: Effective average tax rates on corporate income;*
*For country groups cf. figure 1.1;*
*Source: Elschner et al. (2009), Table 4*

However, the tax rate gap between these two groups and Eastern Europe increased over the observed period in time while the tax rates in Eastern Europe have almost remained unchanged since the year 2005. Beside, the general tendency of declining corporate tax rates illustrated in figure 1.1 and figure 1.2 it is important to recognize that the overall decline in statutory tax rates is much sharper than the decline in effective tax rates. The reason why the decline of the effective tax rate in percentage points is distinctively smaller than the decline in the statutory tax rates can be found in the efforts of governments to not just lower statutory tax rates but to also broaden the tax base on the other hand (e.g., cancellation of exemption rules, changes in depreciation rules and valuation principles, etc.).[8] So finally, both figures may well support the fears expressed by the critics of capital mobility.

Turning to tax measures based on tax revenues however delivers quite a different picture. The figures 1.3 and 1.4 report the share of taxes on corporate income as percentage of GDP and total tax revenues respectively. Figure 1.3 reveals an increasing trend in the share of corporate income taxes of GDP for Southern Europe as well as for Central and Northern Europe, and an almost stable development of this share for Eastern Europe for the period of observation.

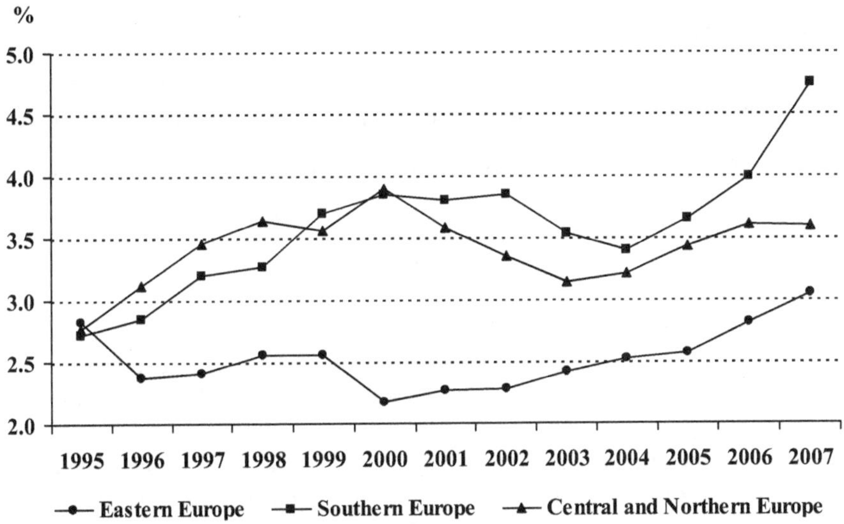


*Figure 1.3: Revenues from taxes on corporate income as % of GDP;*
*For country groups cf. figure 1.1;*
*Source: COM (2009), Table C.3.1.1_G*

Figure 1.4 shows that the share of corporate income taxes as percentage of total tax revenues increased for all country groups and that corporate income taxes still play a role for a country's total tax bill. Haufler (2006) suggests that the development of tax receipts from corporate income mainly rests on two factors: (1) the tax base became larger (e.g., more companies become incorporated) and (2) corporate profits rose.

8 Cf. Devereux et al. (2002).

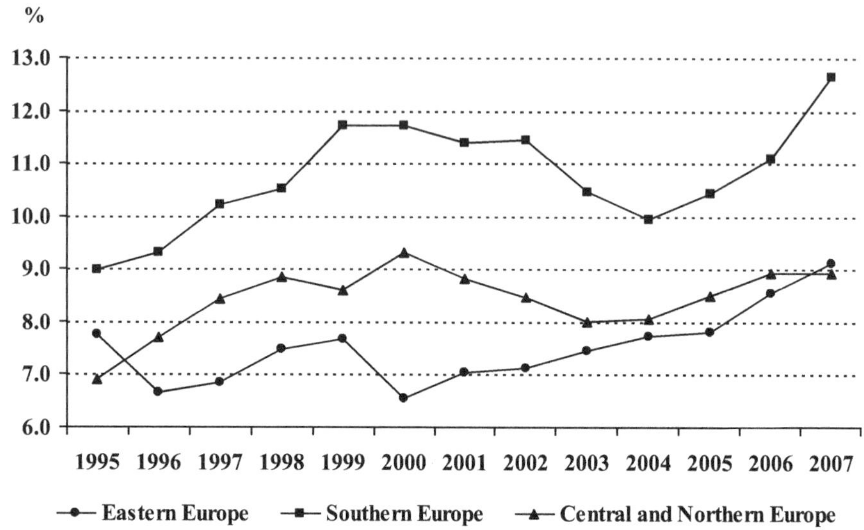


*Figure 1.4: Revenues from taxes on corporate income as % of total tax revenues;*
*For country groups cf. figure 1.1;*
*Source: COM (2009), Table C.3.1.1_T*

This illustration of stylized facts on corporate income taxation revealed that the race-to-bottom scenario the critics of international economic integration usually refer to obviously falls too short to explain the interaction of capital mobility and fiscal policy.[9]

Contrasting the past tendency of rising corporate income tax receipts and declining corporate income tax rates, the prominent example of international capital mobility and national tax policy therefore clearly exemplified that it is hardly possible to deliver short and simple answers to the question of the interaction of economic integration and public policy.[10]

## 1.2 Scientific Approach

The following chapters contribute to the understanding of the interaction of economic integration and public policy by analyzing and discussing specific fiscal

9 Devereux et al. (2002) analyze the development of corporate income taxation in the EU and G7 for the 1980s and 1990s and deliver similar results.

10 Appendix 4.C delivers some information on capital mobility referring to foreign direct investments/ multinational firms.

topics subject to the current debate of economic integration. All of these topics deal with questions concerning the scope and limits of national fiscal policy that come along with economic integration. The examination of different aspects of fiscal competition under economic integration offers a broad access to the numerous research topics in this area. And since open economy public finance is a theoretical as well as an empirical research area, this work deals with both of these fields.

We start from a very basic perspective on independent public policy under economic integration using a very simple and general model. The line of argument illustrates in a very convincing way the basic mechanism that supports the race-to-bottom hypothesis commonly used by critics of economic integration. For this purpose, the following chapter on income redistribution and migration adopts the perspective of the standard public finance literature on tax competition and demonstrates that economic integration in terms of labor mobility limits the methods and the scope of a government's redistribution activities. It synthesizes and augments existing literature to illustrate welfare effects of migration when government interferes with market forces. By analyzing the implications of different redistribution tools on the welfare of an integrated economy (i.e. an economic union) with independently acting governments, the employed model demonstrates that changes in the way governments redistribute income influence the welfare level of the overall economic union. This illustrates that economic integration alone does not increase the welfare of the economic union if the different member states insist on pursuing different approaches to or systems of income redistribution. Allowing for free labor force migration between the members of an economic union such as in the EU can create burdens for the member states that maintain income redistribution systems as well as for the economic union as a whole. Though the inefficiency that becomes visible when migration is allowed stems from the income redistribution itself, the model draws an important point. Labor mobility affects an existing nation state's income redistribution policy in two ways: (1) the type of its income redistribution system and (2) the choice of its income redistribution level. In this scenario a policy approach allowing for free migration of workers must be accompanied by further adjustments in public policy to be welfare increasing. Due to different systems of basic social security, migration imposes an additional burden on social support systems that can easily lead to an overall loss in welfare for the economic union regardless of how the system is designed.

Additionally, the model shows that merely analyzing the welfare position of one nation state simply fails to consider the main goal of an economic union, namely the improvement of the overall welfare of the entire union. Thus, the results that have been obtained support the notion demonstrate that social redistribution policies should be carried out at the level of the economic union with a common social transfer system and not at the level of the single member states. Such an approach will prevent welfare losses for the entire union.

This basic model strongly supports the reasoning of the race-to-bottom scenario, namely the loss of fiscal power of a government due to economic integration. An outstanding feature of this chapter is the simplicity of the employed model. It's an application of the factor proportions theory with two factors and one good in a perfect market environment which always produces efficient equilibria. As soon as there is any interference with the price setting mechanism (here: an income redistributing government) inefficiencies will be obtained (here: a loss in welfare) and made visible by migration. Therefore, the model presented in chapter 3 relaxes some of the assumptions made in the second chapter to show more precisely what exactly drives the results obtained in the simple framework before. The use of a more sophisticated model shows that the plain race-to-bottom scenario has to be qualified. Assuming that tax proceeds are taken to finance public infrastructure which is necessary to run a business, taxation of mobile factors in an open economy setting reaches a new quality: it's not solely the tax rate that determines a firm's location decision but also the level of public infrastructure provision in a country. To illustrate this channel the model in the third chapter on regional public infrastructure and tax competition is embedded in the analytical framework of the economic geography literature. It analyzes the relationship between public infrastructure, taxes and the location decision of firms. Implementing separate factor taxation additionally enables a refining of each government's budget mix. The applied model shows that differentials in the capital tax rate across locations indeed have strong (de-) location effects that favor the low (capital) tax country. This effect is even magnified as trade integration of goods' markets between two countries proceeds and when a critical level of trade integration is reached, full agglomeration of the industrial sector in the low-capital-tax country occurs. However, the size of a country (i.e. the market size in this setting) can mitigate the degree of industrial relocation. For governments that are concerned about their national share of industry the analysis additionally teaches the lesson that separate factor taxation as, for example, realized with dual income taxation, can also deter firms from leaving a region. Increasing the tax rate on the immobile factor can increase the tax receipts that the government uses to provide public infrastructure that, in turn, attracts additional firms. Though this change in the structure of a government's budget seems unfortunate for immobile factors, consumers may benefit from the increased tax burden. Since an improvement of public infrastructure may attract additional firms, consumers save on transportation costs they incur when buying consumer goods from foreign industrial firms. Increasing trade integration induces firms to be more responsive to differences between the two regions making firms' location decisions more unstable. But since lower transportation costs make goods less expensive, the location of a firm is less crucial for the consumer so that the degree or level of tax competition declines with trade integration of goods markets. However, the results confirm the view that solely focusing on plain tax rates such as in the present capital tax harmonization efforts of the EU is highly misleading.[11] Public infrastructure influences the location decisions of firms and thus, a harmonization of capital tax rates across the EU may simply open the gates for the EU member states to engage in public infrastructure competition financed via taxes on immobile factors, though the model shows that this approach becomes more significant the less integrated the countries are.

The integration of goods and factor markets has also influenced the organization structures of firms. Especially in the last decade firms with several affiliated companies in different countries, so-called multinational firms have become a distinctive characteristic of economic integration. A network of affiliated companies makes it easy for international corporations to shift profits between the different affiliates with the aim to minimize the overall company tax burden. Profit shifting implies a virtual displacement of production factors which saves the company the costs of a physical relocation of factors. The easy and costless dislocation of the tax base also causes governments to become concerned about losing their taxable assets and, therefore, proposals to handle this issue have been worked out. Relying on a game theoretical background, the fourth chapter thus analyzes the implications on optimal transfer pricing under two different approaches to taxing the profits of multinational firms that are engaged in Bertrand competition with perfect substitutes. The analysis demonstrates that multinational enterprises have strong incentives to use transfer pricing for profit shifting, regardless of whether they were taxed according to a capital taxation system that treats affiliates of multinational firms as separate entities (i.e. separate accounting) or a capital taxation system that uses a common consolidated tax base for the entire multinational firm (i.e. formula apportionment). Furthermore, the analysis reveals a crucial insight concerning the effects of economic integration (reflected in declining spatial market separation) on the way the multinational firm conducts transfer pricing: with enhanced economic integration, the market power of the multinational firm in one region declines and thus, the strategic effect of the transfer price also declines. Therefore, the higher the market inte-

11 Devereux (2004) offers a draft historical overview, showing the proposals for corporate tax co-ordination. A more recent overview of EU tax harmonization efforts is presented by Nicodème (2009).

gration, the lower the transfer price implemented by the multinational enterprise. Besides, it could be seen that the taxation effect on the transfer price only declines in the separate accounting taxation scheme while it remains almost stable in the formula apportionment taxation scheme. Hence, with market integration, multinational firms engage more actively in transfer pricing under the formula apportionment taxation scheme than they do under taxation according to separate accounting whenever the tax differential between the two different regions increases. Governments, that are concerned about losing their profit tax base because of enhanced profit shifting due to transfer pricing, should therefore be very careful about relying on formula apportionment as the right means to retain multinational firms from using transfer pricing for profit shifting. Besides, shifting profits from one jurisdiction to another, firms can additionally use transfer pricing also to exert the market power of their affiliates.[12] This strategic device should be carefully taken into consideration while talking about an optimal method for taxing profits of multinational companies.

Finally, all theoretical considerations stated before have to be proven in reality. Thus, the obtained results of the preceding theoretical essays will be amended by a survey of the empirical work that has been done on the issue of economic integration and fiscal competition in chapter 5. This chapter provides a survey of the most recent literature that empirically investigates the interaction of economic integration and capital or corporate tax competition with a special focus on tax competition in the presence of agglomeration economies.

This comparative survey essay on empirical studies casts doubt on the existence of an unambiguously negative and robust impact of globalization on fiscal policy. The apparent deduction from basic theoretical economic considerations that indicate a race-to-bottom scenario (e.g., illustrated in the second chapter) cannot explicitly be identified in the data used in the various empirical models. These findings are, for example, carried by a meta-analysis on the interaction of capital taxation and firms' location decisions by De Mooij and Ederveen (2008). Their study can show that the scope of the 'relocation elasticity' of corporate or capital taxation strongly depends on the underlying data and empirical model. Though their results deliver some support for a negative interaction of economic integration and corporate taxation they also show that the results of tax competition models are very sensitive to their underlying assumptions and thus the theoretical background of each model. Eventually, it is crucial to take the specific context in which jurisdictions 'compete' for mobile factors of production into consideration. Therefore, the second part of chapter 5 summarizes the results of further studies that empirically investigate the role of additional forces influenc-

12 Cf. Choi and Day (1998).

ing the interaction of mobile factor taxation and economic integration. It illustrates the most recent empirical literature on the interaction of economic integration and capital tax competition in the presence of agglomeration economies. These studies cast additional doubts on the plain race-to-bottom assessment delivered by the model in chapter 2. Agglomeration on the level of a specific industry (i.e. localization economies) or on the general level of economic activity (i.e. urbanization economies) could strongly qualify the outcome delivered by the basic tax competition model. Depending on the degree of goods market integration, industrial structure and market size, the strength of agglomeration forces varies differently influencing the tax rate setting behavior of jurisdictions. Strong agglomeration forces in a jurisdiction shelter its government from tax competition pressure from other jurisdictions so that the effects of economic integration on corporate taxation are not the same for all countries. In some cases the results of tax competition under agglomeration forces indicate a broad scope for governments to set their tax rates that may even reverse the results of a race-to-bottom scenario.

The following chapters all contribute to the broad subject of open economy public finance. They build on each other and show that the fears attached to economic integration need to be qualified. Since the underlying assumptions vary significantly across different countries, the effects of economic integration on public policy will not be the same for every country indicating that different theoretical models have to be employed and generalizations have to be used with caution.

# 2 Does Economic Integration Eliminate a Government's Ability to Independently Redistribute Income ?

All Member States of the European Union (EU) maintain different systems of social security to support their needy people and to change the overall distribution of income in their economy. These systems vary in the scope and the design of their support mechanisms. Since some of these social support systems have an influence on the labor supply, the European Commission's demand to allow free labor market access for all EU citizens within the EU by 2011 at the latest raises concerns and stimulates debates about the effects of labor force mobility on social policy within the EU member states. These concerns of the EU member states are the reason why the vast majority of EU member states have chosen to exercise their right to protect their labor markets from immigration of workers from the Eastern European accession countries. In the present chapter the effects of labor mobility on the social policy of a country are analyzed. The effects of labor migration on the welfare of the target and the origin country of workforce migration are contrasted and the effects on an economic union that consists of two countries is studied. A partial equilibrium model is used to illustrate the welfare outcome of two different approaches to income redistribution within a country that allows workforce immigration. We find that allowing for labor force mobility between a country that conducts income redistribution and a country that does not provide transfers leads to excessive emigration from the latter. This leads to welfare losses in the target country and welfare gains in the origin country. Depending on the overall level of redistribution within the target country workforce migration, this can lead to an overall loss in welfare of the entire economic union, whether the income redistribution tool influences the labor supply in the origin country or not.[♣]

---

♣ This chapter has partially been presented at the 10th Conference of the "Association for Public Economic Theory", June 2009, Galway, Ireland and has been accepted for presentation at the 65th Annual Congress of the "International Institute for Public Finance", August 2009, Cape Town, South Africa.

## 2.1 Introduction

Mobility of workers is one of the primary pillars of the European Community (EC) along with free trade in goods and services as well as capital mobility.[1] Recent developments in the European Union (EU), however, show that the mobility of labor force is the one most intensely and controversially discussed, especially during the course of EU eastern enlargement which began in 2004. Several EU member states (including Germany and Austria) have demanded exemptions from the requirement to allow free labor market entry to citizens of the new accession countries and still exercise exemptions to the rule of labor force mobility.[2]

Since many of the western European states operate extensive social security systems to support needy people, they were concerned about incurring welfare losses as a result of the EU eastern enlargement. The social security systems maintained by EU member states often differ in how they are financed, in their range of beneficiaries and their type of the financial support that is granted. Factor mobility may influence the sustainability of the maintained redistribution system in two ways. First, there may be a direct attraction of welfare beneficiaries if transfer payments can be demanded by immigrants.[3] Second, there can also be indirect immigration into the welfare system if migrants are willing to work for a wage rate lower than the reservation wage of native citizens maintained by the transfer payments of the welfare system. Thus, international labor force may place pressure on a country's government to adjust its transfer system to allow that economic integration (in terms of factor mobility) does not impose an additional financial burden but instead enhances the welfare of the host country.

---

1 These "Fundamental Freedoms" of the European Community are codified in the "Treaty Establishing the European Community": Art. 18, Art. 39, Art. 43 (workers), Art. 23, Art. 25, Art. 28 (goods), Art. 49 (services), Art. 56 (capital and payments), cf. CVT (2002).

2 Treaty on the Accession of the Czech Republic, Estonia, Cyprus, Latvia, Lithuania, Hungary, Malta, Poland, Slovenia and Slovakia. Ireland, Sweden and the UK were the only member states that allowed for free labor market access also for the 'new' eastern accession countries. Exemptions can be applied for a maximum of seven years, i.e. until 2011. Presently, restrictions for labor market access are applied in Germany, Austria, Denmark, Belgium, France, The Netherlands and Luxemburg.

3 This may be the case in Germany, where the basic social transfer payments ("Sozialhilfe" and "Arbeitslosengeld II") are also available for foreigners living in Germany, cf. SGB II, SGB XII and AsylbLG.

This issue is embedded in the broader context of literature that deals with the question of providing public goods in federal states. This literature dates back to the well known model of public expenditures by Tiebout (1956), a model that triggered an extensive branch of literature that also examines the topic of raising the financial means for public spending and it established the vast field of tax competition literature that is mainly linked to Zodrow and Mieszkowski (1986).[4]

This chapter is closest in spirit with literature focusing on income redistribution in an economic union or federal state as, for example, illustrated in Wildasin (1991, 1994) and in Sinn (2004). Cremer and Pestieau (2004) survey the theoretical treatment of the effect of factor mobility on the ability of a government to raise revenues and redistribute income.

Wildasin (1991, 1994) illustrates the fiscal externality of labor migration that arises among jurisdictions in which redistribution among factors of production takes place. He uses a model similar to that used by Sinn (2004) to show that a system of jurisdictions that is linked by a common labor market can improve the welfare effects of redistribution by coordinating the independent redistribution policies of each jurisdiction through a higher-level government.

Sinn (2004) analyzes the effects of labor migration on a welfare state that uses social replacement incomes and labor standards to reach certain redistribution goals within its territory. He uses a model very similar to Wildasin (1991) in which a homogenous good is produced in a competitive economy comprised of two countries (domestic and abroad). In both countries labor is the only variable input factor. The costless tradable good is produced with a 'well-behaving' production function that exhibits a declining marginal product of labor.[5] Laborers are mobile between the two countries, earning the marginal product of labor $f'(L)$ while the reminder $f(L)-f'(L)L$ is earned by the owners of some immobile (fixed) factor such as land. Accounting for migration costs, Sinn (2004) compares the different welfare levels of labor migration in terms of joint GDP net of migration costs. On the background of social replacement incomes and labor standards, Sinn (2004) investigates the welfare effects of different policy alternatives as reaction to labor migration from a poor to a rich country. He shows that a government that protects social replacement incomes and social standards incurs strong welfare losses. This should induce the government to

4 Wilson (1999), for instance, surveys the literature on tax competition. Wellisch (2000) as well as Haufler (2001) deal with the implications of federalism on fiscal autonomy of the member states.

5 This implies $y = f(L)$ with $f'(L) > 0$ and $f''(L) < 0$ (i.e. decreasing marginal product of labor).

change its approach to welfare policy by granting wage subsidies that are most effectively available only to domestic residents.

The goal of this chapter is to examine the welfare effects of economic integration (i.e. labor mobility between two regions that make up an economic union) in a region that redistributes income between two factors of production. It also illustrates the implications of this redistribution policy on the income of the entire economic union and it highlights the consequences of an uncoordinated redistribution policy within an economic union.

We develop the main findings within a simple partial equilibrium model of a competitive economy (i.e. factor proportions model) similar to the model illustrated in Wildasin (1991, 1994). In this model, the world comprises two regions. In both of them a homogenous good, which can be traded costlessly, is produced using land and labor input. While landowners are immobile, workers are allowed to move between the two regions when both regions economically integrate. For simplicity reasons we abstract from migration costs and assume that workers settle down spontaneously, that is, they instantly move from one region to another as soon as there is any difference in the wage level between the two regions. The supply of both production factors is inelastic and income redistribution takes place in region 1 from the immobile factor (i.e. landowners) to the mobile factor (i.e. workers).

The chapter highlights two different aspects of labor market integration (i.e. full mobility of workers) on national social policies. Therefore, the main section (2.4) of this work consists of two parts. The first part (2.4.1) complements the above mentioned literature by synthesizing the basic considerations of Wildasin (1991, 1994) and Sinn (2004). It analyzes the welfare effects of migration within an economic union where one region redistributes income between the different factors of production in a stylized and very intuitive way. This scenario compares the welfare results of different income redistribution tools, when two asymmetric regions integrate their labor markets (i.e. allow for full geographic mobility of workers). The government in region 1 maintains income redistribution through either a direct transfer or a wage subsidy respectively, while the government in region 2 is not engaged in income redistribution. An independent social policy may now exert influence on the migration decision of workers who react to differences in the wage rates between the two independent regions when migration is allowed. With differences in the wage rates between the two regions due to variations in the relative size of the two regions (i.e. the relative factor proportions of land and labor) social policy instruments may eventually create inefficiencies by disturbing migration equilibrium.

The second part (2.4.2) augments the existing literature by focusing on the welfare effects of an independent change of the income redistribution patterns within a region that is part of an economic union. In this scenario we ask how changes in the social system (i.e. changes in the transfer level) of a region show up in the economic welfare of this region and the economic union where migration between the two regions is allowed. We examine the welfare effects of labor market integration between two identical regions with respect to their relative size (i.e. the relative factor proportion of land and labor). In this scenario there is no incentive to migrate before the government in region 1 decides to change (here: increase) the level of income redistribution. The fact that migration incentives are triggered after changes in a country's preferences for income redistribution are made indicates that a 'redistribution externality' exists.

Both approaches highlight the two ways an independent social policy of a government is affected by labor market integration, namely the choice of its redistribution scheme (illustrated in 2.4.1) and the determination of income redistribution levels (illustrated in 2.4.2).

We find the following result: first, when two regions with differences in their wage rates (region 1 has a larger land-labor-ratio since it is equipped with relatively less workers than region 2) economically integrate by allowing for labor migration, social policy instruments like income redistribution tools lead to distortions in the migration decision that may manifest in welfare losses for the entire economic union. A system of direct transfer payments creates a loss in welfare in the region that provides this kind of redistribution system (region 1) as well as for the entire economic union. Analyzing the welfare effects of integration under the wage subsidy instead of a direct transfer payment, we will see that region 1 also incurs a loss in income. However, aggregating the welfare changes over the two regions shows that the wage subsidy need not necessarily imply a welfare loss as long as the wage subsidy is not too large. The reason why the wage subsidy may lead to a gain in welfare is that it does not interfere with the overall labor supply in the integrated economy. Hence, since a direct transfer influences the overall labor supply, integration of the two regions affects the wage rate and thus prevents some workers form offering their labor and to instead rely on transfer payments. This implies that a region that economically integrates can mitigate the welfare effects of labor market integration by changing its system of redistribution prior to integration. This indicates that allowing for factor mobility may force nation states to adjust their public policy due to globalization.

Second, departing from migration equilibrium (i.e. identical regions with respect to their relative size which articulates in equal wage rates), a unilateral change in the level of income redistribution in an integrated region leads to a loss in the welfare of region 1 as well as an overall loss in the entire economic union. The distortions of the transfer payment on the labor market are again so severe that the gain in welfare of region 2 is outweighed by the loss in welfare in region 1. Considering the case of the wage subsidy also reveals losses for the overall economic union. This result suggests that even in the case of identical regions an independent social policy creates a welfare loss under economic integration.

Therefore, both results show that a region's independent redistribution policy is accompanied by a decline in welfare in this region that might be so large that the overall welfare of the economic union may decline eliminating any net gains from migration. Hence, economic integration may influence a region's choice between different social systems as well as its preferences about the degree of redistribution.

The chapter is structured as follows: the basic model will be presented in the next section, section 2.3 then analyzes the benchmark case of redistribution under autarky. Finally section 2.4 studies the welfare effects of redistribution under economic integration. In the first part of this section the welfare effects of economic integration of the two regions that differ in size are decomposed. The second part of this section then delivers the analytical results of the welfare effects of an increase in transfer payments within the two integrated regions (i.e. redistribution externality). Section 2.5 finds a conclusion.

## 2.2 The Model

The implications of redistribution in an integrated economy are illustrated in a stylized fashion, using a simple partial equilibrium model of a competitive economy.[6] There are two regions $i$ $(i=1,2)$ in which a homogenous good is produced under constant returns to scale using two factors of production $f_i(l_i,r_i)$. Labor $(l_i)$ is homogenous and mobile between the two regions and land $(r_i)$ is immobile and thus fixed in supply. In the following we assume that $r_i$ is normalized at unity. The production technology is identical in both regions with the usual assumptions about the mobile input: $f_i'(l_i)>0$ and $f_i''(l_i)<0$ (i.e. decreasing marginal product of labor).[7] Each worker's wage rate $w_i$ is equal to the marginal product of labor $f'(l_i)$. $n_i$ is the number of mobile households (= workers) in region $i$ which is exogenous. Note that this number can differ from the actual number of employed workers in region $i$ denoted by $l_i$. There

6 Appendix 2.A illustrates the graphical intuition of this model.

7 $f_i'(l_i)$ denotes the first partial derivative of the production function with respect to labor, i.e. $f_i'(l_i)=\partial f_i(l_i,r_i)/\partial l_i$.

can be two reasons for that: one may be a social transfer income $b_i$ which exceeds the marginal product of labor and thus creates unemployment, or secondly, due to labor force mobility, workers may leave one region and settle in the other region where the wage rate is higher than in the region of origin. Within a region each government can redistribute income between the two factors of production, labor and land. We also assume budget neutrality of income redistribution indicating firstly that redistribution is lump sum and secondly that the government budget is always balanced. To keep the model simple we also abstract from migration costs. These can comprise monetary costs of moving but also the social costs of leaving family and friends behind or the difficulties of adjusting to a new environment. The existence of those costs works against migration so that the wage gap has to reach a certain level before it triggers migration. All kinds of transfer measures discussed in the following however increase the wage gap and thus work in favor of migration. As a result, neglecting migration costs is a minor issue here.

Since the objective of the following analysis is to illustrate the loss of welfare due to redistribution within an economically integrated area, we will first display the effects of redistribution under autarky before analyzing the open economy case.

## 2.3 Redistribution under Autarky

The autarky scenario is equivalent to a situation in which the labor force is immobile between the two regions $i$ $(i=1,2)$ so that the number of workers is fixed in both areas. For simplicity reasons we focus in this section on region 1 only.[8] With an immobile labor force, the number of workers available in region 1 is equal to $n_1$. As indicated in the introduction we will investigate two different redistribution schemes in the style of a Beveridge system, i.e. a redistribution system financed through the tax system where welfare benefits are not tied to prior contributions.[9]

In the first case, redistribution takes place through a direct transfer of income (e.g., the basic transfer system "Sozialhilfe" or "Arbeitslosengeld II" in Germany). The government in region 1 offers a grant to those households who don't work. This grant serves as a reservation wage, since rational workers

8 A graphical illustration of this section is presented in appendix 2.A.1 using the figures 2.A.1 and 2.A.2.

9 Cf. Cremer and Pestieau (2003) for a comparative analysis of redistribution systems in Beveridge and Bismarck style.

would never work for a wage rate $w_1$ that is below the direct transfer $b_1$. Depending on the level of the grant, the number of active workers $l_1$ may now differ from the number of available workers $n_1$. The means to finance the transfer income are taken from the landowners by lump-sum taxing their income in a way that the government budget is always balanced. Total receipts from the landowners are labeled $T_1$ and total outlays for transfer payments are denoted by $B_1$ so that $T_1 = B_1 = [n_1 - l_1]b_1$ always holds. With the transfer acting like a wage floor the labor supply becomes a function of this reservation wage, so that $l_1 = l_1(b_1)$ holds and

$$l_1 \begin{cases} < n_1 & \text{for} \quad b_1 > f_1'(n_1) = w_1 \\ = n_1 & \text{for} \quad b_1 \leq f_1'(n_1) = w_1 \end{cases}$$

i.e. labor supply solely depends on the transfer payment $b_1$. Accordingly, we can derive the aggregated income of the factor land $(r_1)$ in region 1

$$R_1 = f_1(l_1) - f_1'(l_1)l_1 - b_1[n_1 - l_1] \tag{2.1}$$

and correspondingly the total income of the factor labor $(l_1)$

$$W_1 = f_1'(l_1)l_1 + b_1[n_1 - l_1]. \tag{2.2}$$

The number of workers who draw on public transfers will be denoted as transfer recipients $t_1 = [n_1 - l_1]$.

Assuming that the factor income serves as a measure for welfare, we will now analyze the welfare effects of changes in the transfer income $b_1$. We depart from an equilibrium in which $b_1 = f_1'(n_1)$, i.e. a full employment equilibrium, and investigate the effects of an income redistribution from landowners to workers. Differentiating the income equations (2.1) and (2.2) with respect to $b_1$ and evaluating the result at the initial equilibrium gives us the change in total income for landowners

$$\frac{\partial R_1}{\partial b_1} = -n_1 + \frac{f_1'(l_1)}{f_1''(l_1)} < 0$$

and for workers

$$\frac{\partial W_1}{\partial b_1} = n_1 > 0$$

respectively, so that the overall change in total income

$$\frac{\partial R_1}{\partial b_1}+\frac{\partial W_1}{\partial b_1}=\frac{f_1'(l_1)}{f_1''(l_1)}<0$$

indicates an overall loss in welfare. This loss in welfare increases with the transfer payment $b_1$

$$\frac{\partial l_1}{\partial b_1}=\frac{1}{f_1''}<0, \tag{2.3}$$

showing that increases in the transfer rate decrease the workforce and thus the overall income of the economy since less output is produced.

Contrasting the results of the direct transfer, we now demonstrate the welfare effects of a wage subsidy (e.g., the Family Income Tax Credit in the U.K.). Now let the government offer a per capita wage subsidy $s_1$ for workers. The basic idea of a wage subsidy is to raise the income of each worker so that the government reaches certain income distribution goals. Again, the government taxes income of the landowners lump sum to finance the wage subsidy. The total amount of tax receipts $T_1$ is set to pay for the total amount of wage subsidies $S_1$ so that the government budget is balanced, indicating that $T_1 = S_1 = l_1 s_1$. Under the wage subsidy the total income of the factor land $(r_1)$ in region 1 is

$$R_1 = f_1(l_1) - f_1'(l_1)l_1 - s_1 l_1 \tag{2.4}$$

and correspondingly the total income of the factor labor $(l_1)$ is

$$W_1 = f_1'(l_1)l_1 + s_1 l_1 . \tag{2.5}$$

Note that the subsidy is paid to all workers and thus there is no influence of the subsidy on the labor supply. Differentiating the income of landowners with respect to the subsidy delivers

$$\frac{\partial R_1}{\partial s_1} = -l_1 < 0 .$$

The change in income of workers due to a variation in the subsidy amounts to

$$\frac{\partial W_1}{\partial s_1} = l_1 > 0,$$

so that the overall welfare in region 1 does not change. In comparison to the direct transfer $b_1$ income redistribution does not create any distortions in the labor supply. This reveals that as long as redistribution does not interfere with labor supply, there will be no loss in welfare due to a government's social policy. Hence, variation in the way the government redistributes income between the factors of production (here: support of the factor labor) does not result in any adverse welfare effects.

## 2.4 Redistribution within an Integrated Economy

Economic integration between the two regions shall take place in the next step. This occurs by allowing for worker mobility. Workers in both regions can now choose where to live and settle down. Based on the wage rate workers will instantly move from one region to another as long as there are differences in the wage rate between the two regions. Since workers' compensation depends on the relative factor proportions within the region in this model, moving from one region to another will alter the wage rates, that is increase the wage rate in the origin region and depress the wage rate in the destination region (i.e. wage rates between the regions are set endogenously). Again, $n_i$ denotes the number of native workers in region $i$ and $l_i$ quantifies the number of employed workers in region $i$. To analyze the welfare effects of an independent social policy under labor market integration two different scenarios are illustrated in the following two sections. We first look at the welfare effects of labor market integration between two different regions, where one region redistributes income between the different factors of production. We then investigate the welfare effects of labor market integration between two identical regions, where one region changes its redistribution efforts.

The reason for this two-stage approach is to highlight two different impacts of labor market integration on independent social policy. With the first section we address the question how economic welfare is influenced by labor market integration when a region sticks to its social policy. The second section addresses the question how economic welfare is influenced by labor market integration when a region alters its social policy variables.

### 2.4.1 Welfare Effects of Labor Mobility on Redistribution Systems

In the following, we will assume that both regions are equally equipped with land but differ in their initial labor supply $n_2 > n_1$, i.e. region 2 has more workers than region 1. With a decreasing marginal product of labor, this indicates $f_1'(n_1) > f_2'(n_2)$, that is the wage rate in region 1 is higher than in region 2. Allowing workers to migrate between the two regions, this scenario implies an incentive for workers in region 2 to move to region 1 until the differences between the wage rates disappear.

We begin with the welfare analysis of the direct transfer.[10] Before allowing for worker mobility there is full employment in both regions. The government of region 2 does not offer any kind of income redistribution while the government of region 1 offers a direct transfer $b_1$ at a level that does not distort its labor market, i.e. $b_1 = f_1'(n_1)$. Allowing for labor mobility, migration equilibrium will be attained when $f_2'(l_2) = f_1'(l_1) = b_1$ holds and thus labor market equilibrium is given by $l_1 + t_1 + l_2 + t_2 = n_1 + n_2 \equiv \bar{n}$, with $t_1\,(t_2)$ indicating the transfer recipients from region 1 (region 2). Since region 2 is not offering any redistribution of income, there are two ways to address the case of 'foreign transfer recipients'. In the first possible approach, one can assume that natives from region 1 as well as migrants from region 2 can draw on transfers. In a second possible approach, one can visualize an indirect type of immigration into the transfer system. While native workers from region 1 would not be willing to work for a wage rate lower than the transfer $b_1$, immigrants from region 2 would be likely to work for a wage rate lower than the transfer rate $b_1$, as long as it exceeds the prevailing wage rate in region 2 which is $f_2'(l_2) = w_2$.[11]

As illustrated before we depart from labor market equilibrium in both regions and then allow workers to migrate. Since such a situation is characterized by $b_1 = f_1'(n_1) > f_2'(n_2)$, opening borders unleashes migration pressure from region 2 to region 1 implying a decline in the wage rate in region 1.[12] However, the above mentioned line of argument demonstrated that the transfer acts like a wage floor that prevents wages from declining in region 1 below the transfer guaranteed by the government. The government's budget in region 1 is always balanced and to finance the transfer income to workers, the government taxes

10 Appendix 2.A.2 provides the graphical intuition of the analytical results (cf. figures 2.A.3 and 2.A.4).

11 Cf. Sinn (2004).

12 The analysis departs from cleared labor markets in both regions, i.e. $l_1 = n_1$ and $l_2 = n_2$.

the landowners. $T_1$ describes total tax receipts collected lump sum from landowners and $B_1$ denotes the transfer payments to workers so that $T_1 = B_1 = [n_1 - l_1]b_1$.

The welfare analysis rests again on the income associated with the two factors. The total income of the (immobile) landowners in region 1 is now

$$R_1 = f_1(l_1) - f_1'(l_1)l_1 - b_1\left[\underbrace{n_1 - l_1}_{t_1} + \underbrace{n_2 - l_2}_{t_2}\right] \quad (2.6)$$

while the total income of (mobile) workers in region 1 is

$$W_1 = f_1'(l_1)l_1 + b_1[n_1 - l_1], \quad (2.7)$$

since we first only focus on the income of the region 1 natives. Note, that the number of employed workers in region 1 will not change due to the wage floor. Thus, allowing for free migration induces workers to leave region 2 and settle in region 1. This would not increase the number of workers but only the number of transfer recipients. Here we assume that the migrants from region 2 can claim welfare benefits, so that a change in $t_2$ is analyzed.[13] Hence, if the borders between the two regions are open and if a worker from region 2 decides to move into region 1, the income of the immobile landowners in region 1 declines

$$\frac{\partial R_1}{\partial t_2} = -b_1 < 0. \quad (2.8)$$

Since the transfer marks a wage floor, the additional worker migrates into the welfare system, drawing on the transfers $b_1$ in region 1, indicating that the wage rate of the mobile workers in region 1 does not change

$$\frac{\partial W_1}{\partial t_2} = 0. \quad (2.9)$$

13 According to the above considerations this is equivalent to an indirect immigration in the welfare system.

Therefore, adding up (2.8) and (2.9) shows that the overall welfare in region 1 declines by the additional transfer that has to be paid and which reduces the landowners' income.[14]

Finally, we want to examine the overall welfare of the integrated economy – that is the welfare changes in region 1 and region 2. Therefore, we would have to calculate the change in income in region 2 due to emigration. As indicated before, emigrants from region 2 cannot find a job in region 1 due to the wage floor and thus directly migrate into the social system. The income of landowners in region 2 is

$$R_2 = f_2(l_2) - f_2'(l_2)l_2 \tag{2.10}$$

and the income of workers in region 2 is

$$W_2 = f_2'(l_2)l_2 + b_1\underbrace{[n_2 - l_2]}_{t_2}. \tag{2.11}$$

To assess the welfare effects of migration from region 2 to region 1 due to economic integration of the two regions, we again evaluate the change in income in region 2 due to emigration of a single worker (transfer recipient) into region 1.[15] The change in the income of the landowners in region 2 is

$$\frac{\partial R_2}{\partial t_2} = f_2''(l_2)l_2 < 0 \tag{2.12}$$

and the change in the income of the workers is

$$\frac{\partial W_2}{\partial t_2} = -f_2''(l_2)l_2 \underbrace{-f_2'(l_2) + b_1}_{\substack{>0 \\ \text{since } b_1 > f_2'(l_2)}} > 0\,. \tag{2.13}$$

Emigration of a worker from region 2 reduces the productivity of land so that land rents decline, reducing the income of the landowners. The income of

14 In accordance with the proceeding line of arguments it is not relevant who gets the transfer payments. If migrants from region 2 are not eligible to receive benefits, they may well be willing to work for an infinitesimal lower wage rate than a worker in region 1 (i.e. an amount above the wage rate offered in region 2 but below the wage rate in region 1) squeezing out this worker in the welfare system.

15 Note that labor market equilibrium in region 2 implies $l_2 = n_2 - t_2$.

workers in region 2 increases, since their productivity increases, with fewer laborers working with the unchanged amount of land in region 2. Adding up (2.12) and (2.13) provides us with a positive change in welfare in this region – that is, if a worker emigrates from region 2 into region 1 the overall income of regions 2's citizens increases.

Eventually, we can now generate the overall change in welfare of the integrated economy by aggregating the changes in income of the workers and landowners in the two regions. The sum of (2.8), (2.9), (2.12) and (2.13) yields $-f_2'(l_2)<0$, so that the integrated economy (i.e. economic union) incurs a loss in welfare. This shows that migration can have adverse welfare effects for the economy as whole when there are income redistribution tools that distort markets indicating inefficiencies. It can be seen that the change in welfare depends on the wage rate that is prevalent in region 2 (which depends on the employment in this region) so that with equally equipped regions there would be no welfare effects resulting from migration at all. As illustrated, pure labor market integration of two economies can very well have adverse effects on the overall welfare, depending on the types of the social systems that prevail in the two regions that integrate.

We now seek to contrast the preceding impacts of a transfer payment with the outcome of a wage subsidy which is modeled as a surcharge on the wage rate of each worker employed in region 1.[16] With a subsidy, migration equilibrium will be reached when $f_1'(l_1)+s_1=f_2'(l_2)$ holds. The equilibrium allocation of workers will then be $l_1+l_2=n_1+n_2\equiv\overline{n}$.[17] The aggregated wage subsidy $S_1$ is funded by the landowners whose income is taxed lump sum with $T_1$ denoting the total tax receipts. The government's budget is balanced, indicating that $T_1=S_1=l_1s_1$ always holds.

The welfare analysis departs from labor market equilibrium in each of the two regions, where $f_1'+s_1>f_2'$ so that there is again an incentive for workers to move from region 2 to region 1 as soon as migration is allowed. The total income of landowners in region 1 is

$$R_1=f_1(l_1)-f_1'(l_1)l_1-s_1l_1 \tag{2.14}$$

and the total income for the native workers of region 1 is

---

16 Appendix 2.A.2 contains the graphical illustration of the analytical results (cf. figures 2.A.5 and 2.A.6).

17 Cf. Wildasin (1994).

$$W_1 = f_1'(l_1)n_1 + s_1 n_1. \qquad (2.15)$$

If an additional worker from region 2 immigrates into region 1, the income of workers in region 1 declines

$$\frac{\partial W_1}{\partial l_1} = f_1''(l_1)n_1 < 0,$$

while the implications for landowners' income is ambiguous

$$\frac{\partial R_1}{\partial l_1} = -f_1''(l_1)l_1 - s_1 \gtreqless 0.$$

The resulting overall change in welfare in region 1 is

$$\frac{\partial W_1}{\partial l_1} + \frac{\partial R_1}{\partial l_1} = f_1''(l_1)[n_1 - l_1] - s_1 \gtreqless 0,$$

indicating that whether the economy in region 1 incurs a welfare loss or not depends on the level of the subsidy. If a worker from region 2 enters region 1, the labor income declines so that the productivity of labor declines resulting in a lower income of workers. The effect of labor migration into region 1 on the income of the landowners is ambiguous: the additional worker in region 1 increases the output (productivity of land increases), however it may be possible that the labor productivity of this additional worker in region 1 is in total lower than its productivity would be in region 2. The higher the wage subsidy, the higher this productivity loss will be and the more likely is a loss in overall welfare. Since the landowners in region 1 have to bear the costs of the wage subsidy, it finally depends on the level of the wage subsidy whether migration delivers an increase or a decline in the welfare of the landowners and finally for the entire economy.

To assess the overall welfare effects of migration, we first analyze the change in income in region 2. Total income of landowners in region 2 is

$$R_2 = f_2(l_2) - f_2'(l_2)l_2 \qquad (2.16)$$

and total workers' income in region 2 is

$$W_2 = f_2'(l_2)l_2 + f_1'(l_1)[l_1 - n_1] + s_1[l_1 - n_1].^{18} \tag{2.17}$$

Emigration of a worker from region 2 into region 1 decreases the total income of immobile landowners in region 2

$$\frac{\partial R_2}{\partial l_1} = f_2''(l_2)l_2 < 0$$

and the change in total income of mobile workers in region 2 is

$$\frac{\partial W_2}{\partial l_1} = -f_2''(l_2)l_2 + f_1''(l_1)[n_1 - l_1] + f_1'(l_1) + s_1 - f_2'(l_2) > 0,$$

so that the overall change in welfare in region 2 is

$$\frac{\partial R_2}{\partial l_1} + \frac{\partial W_2}{\partial l_1} = f_1''(l_1)[n_1 - l_1] > 0.^{19}$$

This implies an increase in the overall welfare of region 2. With workers leaving region 2 for region 1 the productivity of the factor land declines so that the land rents also fall. On the contrary, workers experience an increase in income since their productivity rises and the emigrated workers additionally benefit from the wage subsidy. Since the transfer payments are paid by the landowners in region 1, the overall effects for the citizens of region 2 are positive.

Finally, an aggregation of welfare effects in both regions is

$$\frac{\partial R_1}{\partial l_1} + \frac{\partial W_1}{\partial l_1} + \frac{\partial R_2}{\partial l_1} + \frac{\partial W_2}{\partial l_1} = 2 \cdot f_1''(l_1)[n_1 - l_1] - s_1 \gtreqless 0.$$

That demonstrates that the impact of allowing migration may have a positive or negative effect on the overall welfare depending on the level of the wage subsidy. The higher the wage subsidy paid in region 1, the more migration from region 2 into region 1 takes place. With a wage subsidy a worker earns a higher compensation than its marginal product in this region. However, with every

18 Note that without migration $n_1 = l_1$ and so the last two terms of (2.17) are 0.

19 Remember that migration stops when $f_1'(l_1) + s_1 = f_2'(l_2)$ holds (i.e. migration equilibrium).

worker leaving region 2 the marginal product of labor increases in this region and declines in region 1, which is the origin of a loss in welfare. Even though the marginal product of an additional worker in region 2 is higher than its marginal product of labor in region 1, this worker decides to leave region 2, since the wage rate in region 1 is higher than the wage rate in region 2 due to the wage subsidy. However, note that in the case of a negative wage subsidy (i.e. redistribution from workers to landowners) welfare will always increase.

This contrasts the result of the transfer payment which resulted in a decline in welfare. Since the transfer payment influences the labor supply, the decline in welfare originates from the distortions in labor markets and migration amplifies these distortions. Even though there might be no distortions in equilibrium before migration is allowed, the integration of the two regions shows the negative effects of this specific feature of a welfare system that redistributes income through a transfer payment. Therefore, economic integration may very well exercise pressure on governments to remodel their welfare systems – thereby tending to restrict public policy. However, the overall analysis has also demonstrated that redesigning a social system can increase the overall welfare of the integrating economy. Therefore, allowing for integration is only beneficial if it is accompanied by appropriate adjustments in public policy.

*Result: To prevent welfare losses of independent social policy due to globalization forces, governments need to adjust their income redistribution systems prior to economic integration. This limits the scope of public policy for a nation state if regions with different social policy objectives integrate.*

### 2.4.2 Welfare Effects of Labor Mobility on Redistribution Preferences

The preceding section illustrated the welfare effects of economic integration on different income redistribution schemes in one of the two regions. We could see that social policy can disturb migration decisions leading to inefficiencies. Depending on the scope and the way social policy is conducted the disturbances could be so severe that economic integration would lead to an overall loss in economic welfare for the economic union. The transfer payment, for example, distorted the migration decision due to variations in the overall labor supply and it produced a welfare loss for the integrating regions. In contrast, the wage subsidy did not influence the overall labor supply allowing the integrating economy to reap some of the migration gains. However, this redistribution tool also disturbs the migration decision and thus, it may also bear economic costs leading to losses in overall welfare.

As illustrated before, income redistribution between the different factors of production in one region influences the migration decision in the other region. The remainder of this chapter will thus be devoted to analyzing this redistribution externality.[20] To isolate this welfare effect of redistribution from the welfare effects of redistribution due to migration as illustrated before, we depart from a slightly modified situation: before a change in redistribution levels there is no incentive for workers to migrate. Thus, we analyze the welfare effects of migration triggered solely by the redistribution system. Again, the government of region 1 can either use a transfer payment or a wage subsidy to manage income redistribution.

We first consider the effects of an increase in the transfer payment in region 1, starting form an international equilibrium with $f_1'(l_1) = f_2'(l_2) = b_1$ and $l_1 + t_1 + l_2 + t_2 = n_1 + n_2 \equiv \bar{n}$, as well as allowing for labor mobility. The government in region 1 imposes a lump sum tax on landowners' income to fund the transfer income paid to unemployed workers in region 1 so that total tax receipts $T_1$ equal total outlays $B_1$. The total income of the landowners in this region is

$$R_1 = f_1(l_1) - f_1'(l_1)l_1 - b_1\left[\underbrace{n_1 - l_1}_{t_1} + \underbrace{n_2 - l_2}_{t_2}\right], \tag{2.18}$$

while the native workers in region 1 earn

$$W_1 = f_1'(l_1)l_1 + b_1[n_1 - l_1] \tag{2.19}$$

which is equivalent to (2.2). An increase of the transfer in region 1 decreases the total welfare of landowners

$$\frac{\partial R_1}{\partial b_1} = -n_1 - n_2 + l_2 + b_1\left[\frac{1}{f_1''(l_1)} + \frac{1}{f_2''(l_2)}\right] < 0$$

and increases the total income of the workers

20 Again there will be a graphical illustration of the line of arguments in appendix 2.A.3 using figures 2.A.7 and 2.A.8.

$$\frac{\partial W_1}{\partial b_1} = n_1 > 0,$$

leading to an overall decline in the income of region 1[21]

$$\frac{\partial R_1}{\partial b_1} + \frac{\partial W_1}{\partial b_1} = [l_2 - n_2] + b_1 \left[ \frac{1}{f_1''(l_1)} + \frac{1}{f_2''(l_2)} \right] < 0.$$

The transfer payment sets a wage floor that prevents wages from declining in region 1. Therefore, an increase of the transfer induces workers to leave their positions and rely instead on transfer payments. The productivity of the landowners declines so that they lose income, while the workers gain income because their productivity grows while some workers now become transfer recipients. In total, the welfare of the economy declines: with less production, less income is generated.

Since we allow for migration, the increase of the transfer in region 1 has an impact on the migration decision of workers in region 2. That influences the income of the landowners and workers in region 2. Again, it does not play any role whether the migrants from region 2 are eligible for transfer payments or whether the migrants form regions 2 drive workers in region 1 out their jobs by accepting jobs that pay a little less than the transfer payment offered to region 1 workers. The increase of the transfer payment creates an incentive for workers of region 2 to move into region 1. The total income of the landowners is

$$R_2 = f_2(l_2) - f_2'(l_2) l_2 \tag{2.20}$$

and the total income native region 2 workers is

$$W_2 = f_2'(l_2) l_2 + b_1 [n_2 - l_2]. \tag{2.21}$$

The increase of transfer payments in region 1 attracts workers from region 2 to immigrate into region 1. The change in income of the landowners is negative

---

21 Note, that $b_1 = f_1'(l_1) = f_2'(l_2)$ and thus there is an implicit function $F(b_1, l_1) = b_1 - f_1'(l_1)$ or rather $F(b_1, l_2) = b_1 - f_2'(l_2)$. The implicit function theorem then shows $\partial l_1 / \partial b_1 = l_1' = 1 / f_1''(l_1) < 0$, respectively $\partial l_2 / \partial b_1 = l_2' = 1 / f_2''(l_2) < 0$.

$$\frac{\partial R_2}{\partial b_1} = -l_2 < 0$$

and the workers of region 2 realize a welfare gain

$$\frac{\partial W_2}{\partial b_1} = n_2 > 0$$

so that the overall welfare of region 2 increases, since $n_2 > l_2$ (i.e. there are now less laborers working in region 2 than were born there). The welfare of the landowners declines, since productivity of land falls with fewer laborers at work, while the income of the workers increases.

Eventually, the welfare effects for the integrated economic area is the sum of welfare effects in the two regions, implying an overall loss of

$$\frac{\partial R_1}{\partial b_1} + \frac{\partial W_1}{\partial b_1} + \frac{\partial R_2}{\partial b_1} + \frac{\partial W_2}{\partial b_1} = \frac{b_1}{f_1''(l_1)} + \frac{b_1}{f_2''(l_2)}.$$

Again, the origin of this loss is the effect of the transfer on the labor supply: the transfer induces workers to no longer offer their labor and, instead, rely on the welfare system. This loss in welfare has to be borne by the region that engages in redistribution. Since labor supply depends on the transfer payment, the loss in welfare increases as the level of the transfer payment increases.

Increasing the transfer payment also caused a welfare loss in the closed economy case. However, we could show that the wage subsidy had neutral effects on the overall welfare in this setting. Therefore, the results of the transfer payment will again be contrasted by the subsidy. We depart from an international equilibrium, i.e. $f_1'(l_1) + s_1 = f_2'(l_2)$ and there is again the assumption about employment and size of the regions, namely $n_1 = l_1 = n_2 = l_2$. This implies that the production functions must now be different between the two regions. But since we are departing from labor market equilibrium, this assumption does not constrain the obtained results. The government in region 1 imposes a lump sum tax on landowners' income to fund the wage subsidy paid to workers employed in region 1 so that total tax receipts $T_1$ equal total outlays $S_1$.

The total income of landowners in region 1 is

$$R_1 = f_1(l_1) - f_1'(l_1)l_1 - s_1 l_1 \tag{2.22}$$

and workers' total income in that region is

$$W_1 = f_1'(l_1)n_1 + s_1 n_1. \tag{2.23}$$

Increasing the wage subsidy, decreases the income of the (immobile) landowners in region 1

$$\frac{\partial R_1}{\partial s_1} = \frac{s_1}{f_1''(l_1) + f_2''(l_2)} - l_1\left[1 - \frac{f_1''(l_1)}{f_1''(l_1) + f_2''(l_2)}\right] < 0$$

and increases the income of the (mobile) workers

$$\frac{\partial W_1}{\partial s_1} = \left[1 - \frac{f_1''(l_1)}{f_1''(l_1) + f_2''(l_2)}\right] n_1 > 0,$$

so that the overall change in welfare in region 1 is[22]

$$\frac{\partial R_1}{\partial s_1} + \frac{\partial W_1}{\partial s_1} = \frac{s_1}{f_1''(l_1) + f_2''(l_2)} + \left[1 - \frac{f_1''(l_1)}{f_1''(l_1) + f_2''(l_2)}\right]\underbrace{\left[n_1 - l_1\right]}_{\text{since } n_1 < l_1} < 0.$$

The welfare effects of increasing the wage subsidy are negative indicating a loss in welfare for region 1. The increase of the wage subsidy induces workers form region 2 to immigrate into region 1, so that employment in region 1 rises. This expands the workforce in region 1 so that productivity of the landowners rises, expanding land rents and productivity of the workers declines, pushing down their wage rate. In contrast, the higher wage subsidy redistributes income from the landowners to the workers, so that in total the workers of region 1 experience an increase of their income, while the landowners lose income. In total, however, the landowners of region 1 lose more than the workers of region 1 gain. The reason for that outcome can be found in the opportunity that region 2 workers gain from migrating. Increasing the wage subsidy attracts workers from region 2 so that there is too much migration, i.e. beyond the optimal level.

22 Note, that $f_1'(l_1) + s_1 = f_2'(l_2)$ and thus there is an implicit function $F(b_1, l_1) = f_1'(l_1) - f_2'(l_2) + s_1$ with $l_2 = n_1 + n_2 - l_1$.
The implicit function theorem then shows $\partial l_1 / \partial s_1 = -1/\left[f_1''(l_1) + f_2''(l_2)\right] > 0$, respectively $\partial l_2 / \partial s_1 = 1/\left[f_1''(l_1) + f_2''(l_2)\right] < 0$.

Finally, the overall welfare effects in the economic union will be assessed, analyzing the change in income in region 2. The total income of landowners in region 2 is

$$R_2 = f_2(l_2) - f_2'(l_2)l_2 \tag{2.24}$$

and the total income of native workers in region 2 is

$$W_2 = f_2'(l_2)n_2 . \tag{2.25}$$

An increase of the wage subsidy in region 1 depresses the total income of the (immobile) landowners

$$\frac{\partial R_2}{\partial s_1} = -\frac{f_2''(l_2)}{f_1''(l_1) + f_2''(l_2)} l_2 < 0$$

and increases the total income of the (mobile) workers

$$\frac{\partial W_2}{\partial s_1} = \frac{f_2''(l_2)}{f_1''(l_1) + f_2''(l_2)} n_2 > 0$$

so that the total change in welfare in region 2 is positive

$$\frac{\partial R_2}{\partial s_1} + \frac{\partial W_2}{\partial s_1} = \frac{f_2''(l_2)}{f_1''(l_1) + f_2''(l_2)} [n_2 - l_2] > 0 ,$$

since migration from region 2 into region 1 implies $n_2 > l_2$.

As mentioned, increasing the wage subsidy triggers migration of workers from region 2 into region 1. Thus, the landowners in region 2 will lose income, since their productivity declines, while workers incur a rising income, due to the increased wage subsidy. In sum, the aggregated income of region 2 increases, because the burden of income redistribution is carried by the landowners of region 1.

Finally, the change in welfare over the integrated economy (i.e. economic union), evaluated around the symmetric equilibrium is given by

$$\frac{\partial R_1}{\partial s_1} + \frac{\partial W_1}{\partial s_1} + \frac{\partial R_2}{\partial s_1} + \frac{\partial W_2}{\partial s_1} = \frac{s_1}{f_1''(l_1) + f_2''(l_2)} < 0 .$$

This implies a loss in aggregate welfare due to redistribution through a wage subsidy, the amount of which depends on the level of the subsidy. Increasing the wage subsidy in region 1 distorts the workforce allocation in the economic union. Workers from region 2 are attracted by the wage subsidy. In region 1 their productivity however is less than in region 2 so that economic output in the entire economic union declines compared to the situation before the wage subsidy was increased. The loss in welfare in the economic union is thus due to the distortions in workforce allocation.

Regardless of the income redistribution scheme used by a national government, increasing income redistribution in an economically integrated region causes a loss in welfare not only for the region that maintains redistribution, but also for the overall economy. Even though the wage subsidy does not directly influence the labor supply (as the transfer payment does), increasing the level of income redistribution triggers migration flows that, in turn, cause welfare distortions because there are now too many workers migrating into region 1. Note that changes in both redistribution mechanisms create welfare losses when we depart from a situation where migration equilibrium exists. Therefore, an independent national social policy generates a burden that cannot be circumvented by a change in the style of its welfare policy. This contrasts the result of the preceding section where a change in the redistribution system could alleviate the welfare burden of redistribution that come along with economic integration. Again, economic integration exerts pressure on governments to remodel their welfare systems, thereby causing a restriction of public policy. In this case, however, both income redistribution schemes carry a welfare burden while both regions economically integrate. This suggests that sovereign action of the region that maintains a system of income redistribution is not enough to prevent welfare losses. Consequently, a unilateral redesign of a social system cannot be the right response strategy. Referring to the analysis of the autarky case thus highlights the fact that common action by the entire economic union is necessary to prevent welfare losses due to income redistribution.

*Result: Changing the levels of income redistribution under migration equilibrium in a region that economically integrates with another region creates welfare losses for the entire economic union. This indicates that a change in the redistribution levels should not be done unilaterally but in a common action. This limits the scope of action for nation states that are pursuing an autonomous income distribution program for their own territory.*

## 2.5 Conclusion

This chapter analyzed the implications of different redistribution tools on the welfare of an integrated economy with independently acting governments as it occurs in the EU, for instance: the European Commission (EC) supports the idea of an "Open Method of Coordination" concerning social policies of the member states.[23] Thus, the EC does not have a common social policy for all member states in mind but the "adoption of common principles" fully acknowledging autonomy of the member states in designing their system of social policy (i.e. applying the principle of subsidiarity).[23]

We have found that changes in the way governments redistribute income influences the welfare level of the overall economic union. This indicates that migration per se does not increase the welfare of the economic union if the different member states pursue different approaches to or systems of income redistribution. In this case, migration, which is supposed to enhance efficiency in production (i.e. optimizing product factor allocation), shows severe adverse effects on the overall welfare of the economic union since prevailing income redistribution systems interfere with the labor market.

Allowing for free labor force migration between the members of an economic union such as the EU can create burdens for the member states that maintain a system of income redistribution as well as for the economic union as a whole. Thus, labor mobility affects a nation state's social policy in two ways: (1) the type of its income redistribution system and (2) the choice of its income redistribution level. However, solely analyzing the welfare position of one nation state simply misses the main target of an economic union, namely the improvement of the overall welfare of the entire union. Thus, the preceding results demonstrated that social redistribution policy should be carried out at the level of the economic union and not at the level of the single member states. Such an approach will prevent welfare losses for the entire union. Allowing for free migration of workers alone is not automatically accompanied by increases in welfare. Due to different systems of basic social security, migration imposes an additional burden on social support systems that can easily lead to an overall loss in welfare for the economic union regardless of how the system is designed. These results hinge on the inefficiencies that are carried into the model by the implementation of redistribution systems. The nature of these inefficiencies is not addressed while it is acknowledged that these redistribution systems have

23 Cf. COM (2007a) and COM (2007b).

usually manifest themselves over decades and are eventually the outcome of political decision making processes.

Therefore, the model implies that the incentives for migration into the social security system can only be circumvented by a common social security policy concerning basic financial care. However, the issue of an indirect migration into the social security system reveals that moral hazard is a player in this game, too. Therefore, it is clear that proposals simply applying different transfer schemes linked to the nationality of the citizen and the rules that apply in the citizen's country of origin cannot solve the problem.

# Appendix 2.A Graphical Illustrations

The aim of appendix 2.A is to deliver a more intuitive understanding of the analytical results of the main section of this chapter. It therefore translates the analytical results of the main section in figures as it has, for instance, been done in Sinn (2004).

## 2.A.1 Basic Model

The total amount of workers available in region 1 is $n_1$. Output is produced using labor and land. With land being fixed in supply, the marginal product of labor declines. The area under the line $f_1'(l_1)$ is equivalent to overall output. The labor market is cleared when all workers are employed, that is the total amount of employed workers in region 1 $l_1$ is equal to the total amount of workers available $n_1$. Each worker in region 1 earns the wage rate $w_1 = f_1'(l_1)$. Total income of workers and landowners in each region is given by the differently marked areas in the figure. The rectangle in the lower part of figure 2.A.1 shows the total income of workers (i.e. the area with horizontally dashed lines) and the triangle shows the income of landowners (i.e. the area with vertically dashed lines).

In figure 2.A.1 the government offers a transfer income $b_1$ to redistribute income from the landowners to the workers. To assure that workers will earn a specific level of income, the government chooses to offer a transfer income $b_1$. Whenever this transfer income is larger than the equilibrium wage rate $w_1$ the transfer income manifests a wage floor as, for example, illustrated by the dotted black line labeled $w_1^* = b_1$. Rational workers would now choose to receive the transfer income (i.e. transfer recipients $t_1$) instead of working whenever they would earn a wage rate that is lower than the transfer income $b_1$. Since some workers decide to receive the transfer income instead of working labor market equilibrium is reached when the wage rate is again equal to the transfer income (i.e. $w_1^* = b_1$ in figure 2.A.1). Total income of laborers is now the rectangle filled with horizontally dashed lines plus the rectangle surrounded by the solid black line. Note that there is a total loss in aggregated welfare (i.e. income) compared to a situation without income redistribution that stems from losses in output (the number of employed workers declined) shown by the area surrounded by the dashed black line which is born by the landowners who have to pay for the aggregated transfers.

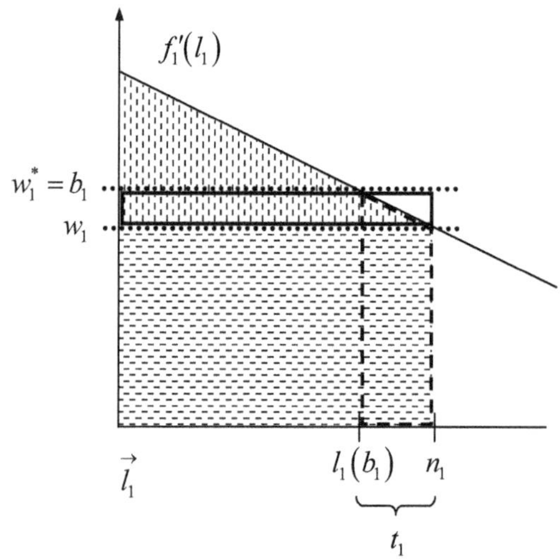


*Figure 2.A.1: Illustration of the basic model: transfer payment*

In figure 2.A.2 the government uses a wage subsidy $s_1$ (i.e. the wage rate is augmented by a certain amount of money) to guarantee workers a certain income level. Augmenting the wage rate of each worker with a certain amount of money does not interfere with the labor market, since workers are not influenced in their decision to work or not as they were in the case of a transfer income $b_1$. In comparison to the transfer income the wage subsidy does not interfere with the number of employed workers. The area surrounded by the solid black line indicates the redistributed income from landowners to workers compared to a situation where there is no redistribution. With a wage subsidy workers get the wage rate $w_1$ plus the wage subsidy $s_1$ indicated by the dotted black line labeled $w_1 + s_1$.

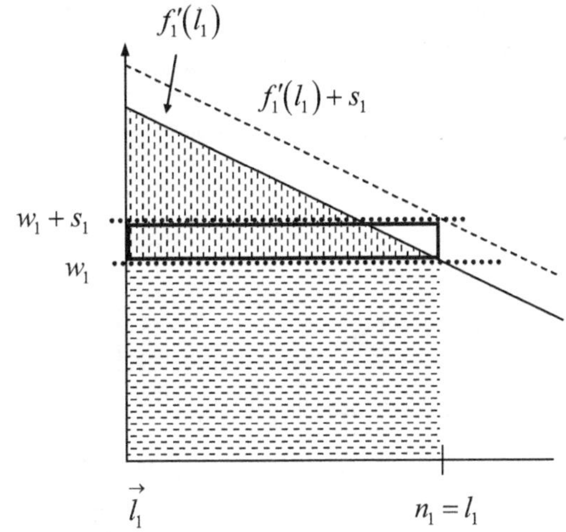


*Figure 2.A.2: Illustration of the basic model: wage subsidy*

## 2.A.2 Welfare Effects of Labor Mobility on Redistribution Systems

The following figures (figure 2.A.3 through figure 2.A.6) deal with the issue of redistribution in an integrated economy as analytically explained in section 2.4.1 (Welfare Effects of Labor Mobility on Redistribution Systems). The analysis only handles the overall welfare effects but the welfare effects within the regions can also be inferred.

We begin with the scenario of a transfer payment. Figure 2.A.3 illustrates the situation before migration between the two regions is allowed. The two regions have the same production technology and differences in the wage level stem from differences in the relative size of the regions: both regions have the same amount of land but region 2 is relatively larger in terms of available workforce.

The marginal product of labor declines so that the areas under the line $f_1'(l_1)$ and $f_2'(l_2)$ indicate output in each region. In region 1 $n_1$ workers are available and the total amount of available workers in region 2 is $n_2$. Labor markets in both regions are cleared so that the total amount of employed workers in region 1 $l_1$ equals $n_1$ and the total amount of workers employed in region 2 $l_2$ equals

$n_2$. Therefore, each worker in region 1 earns the wage rate $w_1$ and each worker in region 2 earns the wage rate $w_2$.

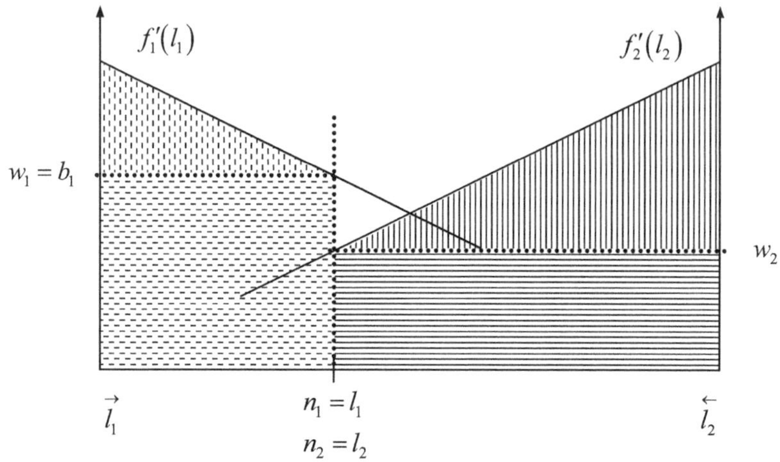


*Figure 2.A.3: Income redistribution: transfer payment*

Total income of workers and landowners in each region is given by the differently marked areas in the figure. The rectangles show the total income of workers (dashed horizontal lines show aggregated income of workers in region 1 and solid horizontal lines indicate aggregated income of workers in region 2) and the triangles show the income of landowners (dashed vertical lines show aggregated income of landowners in region 1 and solid vertical lines indicate aggregated income of landowners in region 2).[24] In region 1 the government offers a transfer income to unemployed workers $b_1$, while the government in region 2 does not redistribute income.

The level of the transfer income in region 1 $b_1$ does not interfere with the labor market so that all workers in region 1 are employed. Figure 2.A.4 illustrates the welfare effects of migration, when region 1 offers a transfer payment $b_1$. Due the transfer payment there is a wage floor in region 1 that prevents wages from declining in this region. With this wage floor, the aggregated output of the economy declines under migration and now $l_1^*$ and $l_2^*$ indicate the number of employed workers in each region. Due to the transfer payment there are workers who do not work but instead rely on transfer income. These transfer recipients

24 These graphical income specifications are used for all the following figures.

are labeled $t_2$ indicating that former workers from region 2 are eligible for transfer payments in region 1.[25] With fewer workers employed, the aggregated output declines compared to the situation before migration was allowed. This is indicated by the area surrounded by the broken black line. The rectangle marked with the crossbred black lines marks the total transfer payments to the unemployed workers. If we allow for migration in this setting, there will be an overall loss for the economic union shown by the area surrounded by the broken black line (i.e. production inefficiency).

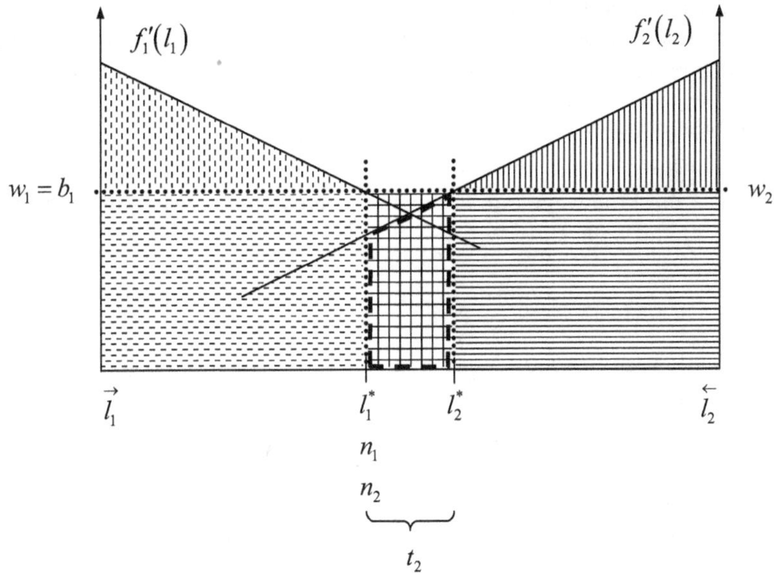


*Figure 2.A.4: Income redistribution: welfare effects of the transfer payment*

Figure 2.A.5 and figure 2.A.6 analyze the welfare and migration effects when region 1 offers a wage subsidy. The analytical part showed that things look quite different for the wage subsidy. Figure 2.A.5 illustrates the situation before migration between the two regions is allowed. The government in region 1 now uses a wage subsidy to reach its income distribution goals. Both regions have the same production technology and differences in the wage level stem from differences in the relative size of the regions: again both regions have the same amount of land but region 2 is relatively larger than region 1 in terms of

25 In the analytical part a way of indirect immigration into the welfare system of region 1 is also explained.

workers available. The marginal product of labor declines so that the area under the line $f_1'(l_1)$ and $f_2'(l_2)$ indicates output in each region. In region 1 $n_1$ workers are available and the total amount of available workers in region 2 is $n_2$. Labor markets in both regions are cleared so that the number of employed workers in region 1 $l_1$ is equal to $n_1$ and the total amount of workers employed in region 2 $l_2$ is equal to $n_2$.

The government in region 1 provides a wage subsidy $s_1$ to each worker while the government in region 2 does not redistribute income. Each worker in region 1 earns the wage rate $w_1$ augmented by the subsidy rate $s_1$ and each worker in region 2 earns the wage rate $w_2$.

The area surrounded by the solid black line indicates redistributed income from landowners to workers. Note that there is no loss in welfare under autarky for every level of $s_1$. Figure 2.A.6 shows the welfare effects of migration, when region 1 offers a wage subsidy. Due the wage subsidy, the wage rate in region 1 will be augmented by the amount $s_1$. Workers from region 2 will now migrate into region 1 until the wage rate in region 2 is equal to the wage rate in region 1 augmented by the wage subsidy.

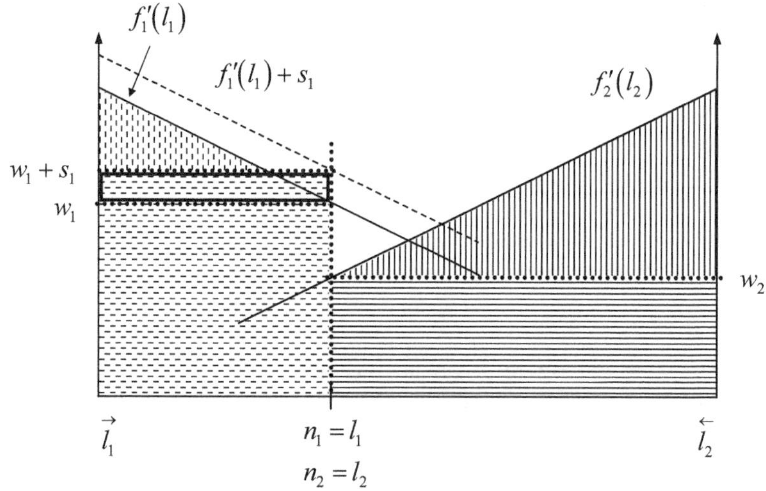


*Figure 2.A.5: Income redistribution: wage subsidy*

Compared to a situation without any government intervention in income distribution, there is too much migration so that there will be a loss in welfare illustrated by the area surrounded by the solid black line.

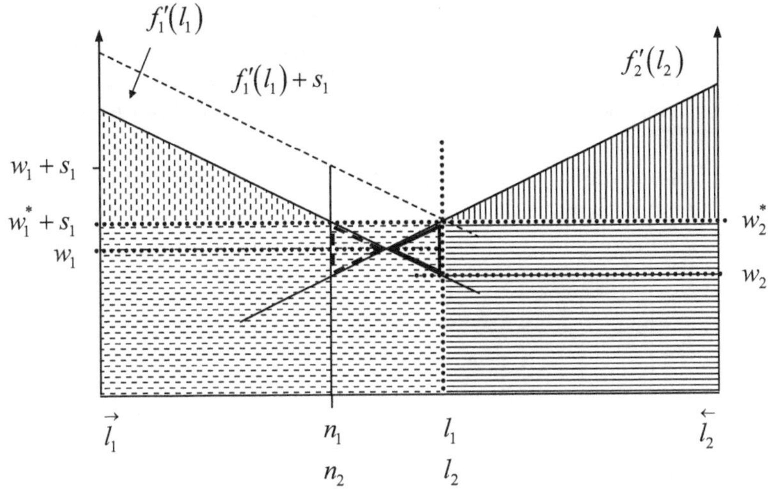


*Figure 2.A.6: Income redistribution: welfare effects of the wage subsidy*

The marginal product of a worker remaining in region 2 would be higher than its marginal product of migrating into region 1, i.e. the wage subsidy creates an incentive for too much migration (i.e. productivity inefficiency). Since all factors of production are employed under a wage subsidy it does not interfere with labor markets. The loss in welfare is therefore not due to a loss in output but due to inefficient allocation of workers between the two regions. Note that compared to a situation without migration there is also a gain in welfare which is marked by the area surrounded by the broken black line. Thus, the overall welfare effects depend on the relative size of these two areas (i.e. as long as the size of the subsidy is not too large, there might be a gain in the overall welfare).

### 2.A.3 Welfare Effects of Labor Mobility on Redistribution Preferences

The remaining figures 2.A.7 and 2.A.8 deal with the issue of redistribution in an integrated economy as analytically explained in section 2.4.2 (Welfare Effects of Labor Mobility on Redistribution Preferences). We therefore graphically analyze the aggregated welfare effects of migration triggered solely by the redistribution system.

Figure 2.A.7 illustrates the situation under the transfer income $b_1$. It highlights the welfare effects of migration that is triggered by changes in the transfer level of region 1. We now assume that both regions are identical with respect to relative size and production technologies so that there is no incentive for workers in both regions to migrate which is illustrated in the upper panel of figure 2.A.7. A transfer income $b_1$ for unemployed workers is offered by the government in region 1, however, in the equilibrium situation the transfer rate is equal to the equilibrium wage rate so that there is no distortion on the labor markets. The government in region 1 then decides to increase the transfer rate $b_1$.

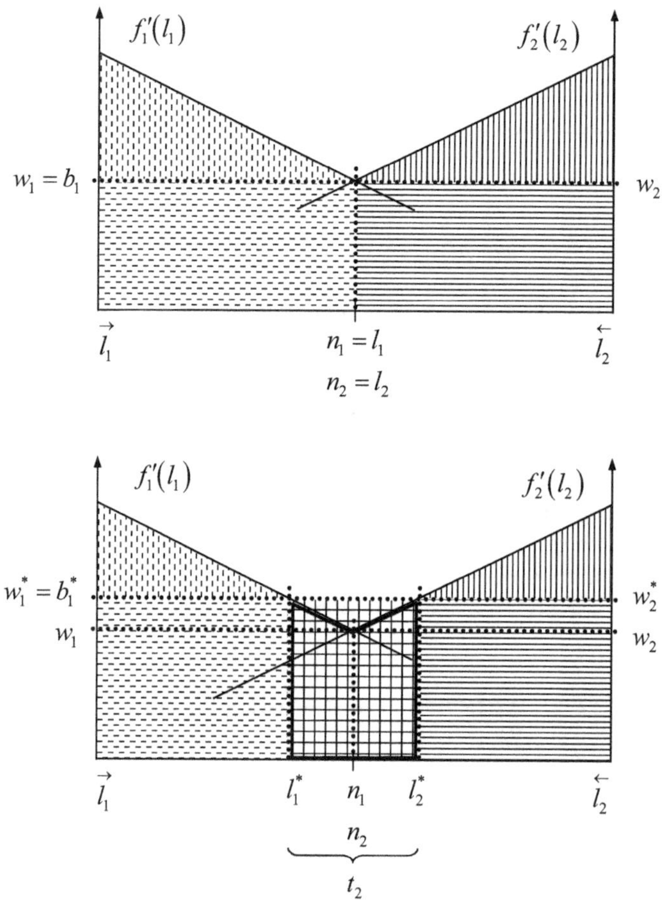


*Figure 2.A.7: Income redistribution: transfer payment*

This distorts the labor markets and triggers emigration from region 2 into region 1, leading to unemployment. The area marked with black crossbred lines (in the lower panel of figure 2.A.7) indicates the total amount of transfer paid and $t_2$ the number of transfer recipients. With workers deciding to receive the transfer income and not to work, output in the economic union declines leading to a decline in overall welfare. This is illustrated by the area surrounded by the solid black line with the black crossbred lines indicate the total amount of redistributed income between landowners and workers.

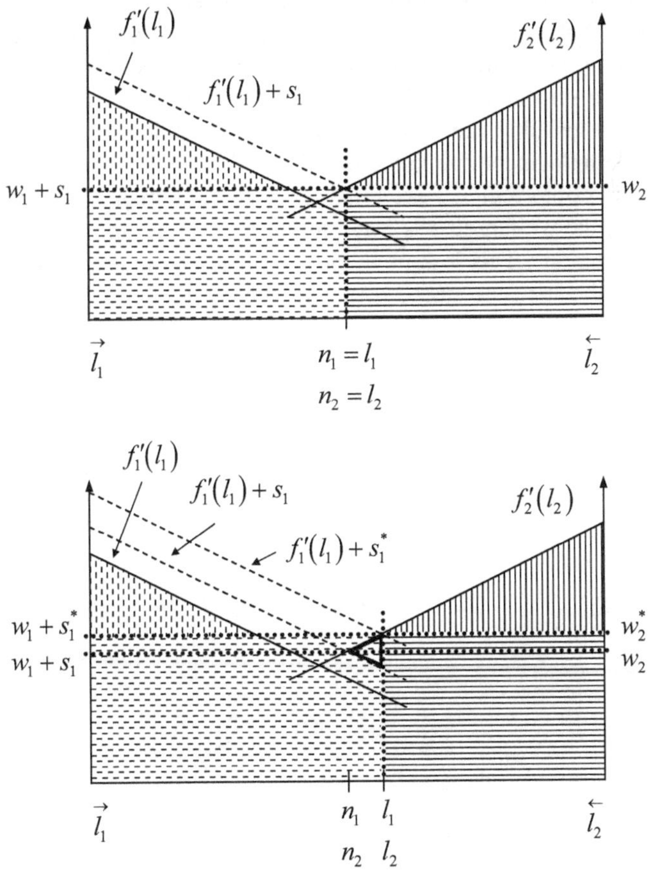


*Figure 2.A.8: Income redistribution: wage subsidy*

The last figure 2.A.8 illustrates the welfare effects of increasing the wage subsidy. Again, we depart from a migration equilibrium indicating that before the government increases the wage subsidy there is no incentive for any workers to migrate from one region into another, shown in the upper panel of figure 2.A.8.

Both regions are identical with respect to the relative size. However, $f_1'(l_1)+s_1=f_2'(l_2)$ with $l_1=n_1$ and $l_2=n_2$ implies that there must be differences in the production functions between both regions.

This assumption shall not constrain the obtained results since we depart from labor market equilibrium. Increasing the wage subsidy to $s_1^*$ increases the total compensation for workers in region 1 and thus creates an incentive for workers in region 2 to immigrate into region 1. This causes a loss in welfare denoted by the area surrounded by the solid black line. In comparison to the transfer scenario this loss does not come from idle production factors (i.e. workers that choose unemployment due to the transfer). Workers from region 2 who decide to immigrate into region 1 are less productive in region 1 than they are in region 2 and so the welfare loss is owed to inefficient allocation of workers between the two regions. This loss in welfare is illustrated in the second panel of figure 2.A.8 by the area surrounded by the solid black line.

# 3 Regional Infrastructure and Tax Competition with Two Instruments

Especially since the enlargement of the European Union (EU) to the East in 2004, the issue of tax competition is extensively discussed in the EU, mainly addressing claims for a harmonization of corporate tax rates. This debate primarily focuses on statutory tax rates on capital income, highlighting the burden of taxes only. However, tax receipts are usually taken to finance public infrastructure, directly or indirectly influencing the way business is conducted. The contribution of the following chapter is to analyze the interaction of taxes and public infrastructure on the location decision of firms. From the perspective of the new theories of trade and economic geography the following chapter draws on a 'footloose capital model' in which the two factors of production are taxed at different rates. The model reveals that taxes on the immobile (mobile) factor have strong positive (negative) location effects with capital favoring the low capital and high labor tax country. In contrast to standard tax competition theories, this effect is strongly magnified as trade integration between two countries proceeds. The relative market size can shelter a high capital tax region from the loss of firms. Finally, a Nash tax game reveals that identical regions impose a tax on labor income and subsidize capital income. With rising economic integration the subsidy on capital will be reduced, as well as the tax rate on labor income.[♠]

♠ A strongly modified version of this chapter has been elaborated in collaboration with Michael Pflüger and been presented at the 8th Conference of the "Association for Public Economic Theory", July 2007, Nashville, TN, USA, at the 63rd Conference of the "International Institute of Public Finance", August 2007, Warwick, UK and the BGPE Conference "Incentives in Economics", November 2007, Nuremberg, Germany. Financial support from the German Research Foundation (DFG) (KON 859/2007 MU 2882/1-1) is gratefully acknowledged.

# 3.1 Introduction

With ongoing economic integration in the European Union (EU), especially after the EU enlargement of 2004, the issue of tax competition is intensely debated, mainly on the background of a harmonization of corporate tax rates.[1] Primarily, this debate focuses on statutory or at best effective tax rates on capital income, highlighting the burden of taxes only. However, tax receipts are usually taken to finance public infrastructure which directly or indirectly influences the way business is conducted. These policy instruments are usually left aside in the political debate. However, different firm level surveys like Ernst & Young (2007a) reveal that firms looking for investment location do very well value all kinds of 'soft' and 'hard' infrastructure.[2] The ranking of selection criteria for investment locations in Ernst & Young (2007a) shows that some infrastructure topics (e.g., transport and logistic infrastructure, telecommunication infrastructure) clearly dominate corporate income tax matters. This supports the idea that high corporate tax rates may materialize in a well-developed public infrastructure fostering the conduct of business and thus easing the net corporate tax burden. The purpose of this chapter is therefore to shed some light on the interaction of taxes and infrastructure on the location decision of firms.

To do so, a model of the new theories of trade and economic geography is used in which capital and labor income is taxed at different rates and the tax receipts are taken to finance public infrastructure.[3] Specifically, we envision a world consisting of two regions which are tied up by international trade and capital mobility: using a footloose capital model, illustrated in Martin and Rogers (1995) or Baldwin et al. (2003), trade is of the intra-industry nature based on increasing returns and product differentiation and capital is physical in nature. Particular attention is paid to the relocation of firms which is induced by a process of trade integration. The model allows for differences in the market size of the regions and the government of each region imposes separate taxes on labor and capital income to provide public infrastructure.

Splitting up tax rates for different sources of factor income is been practiced by the Nordic countries since the beginning of the 1990s. The defining characteristics of a so-called Dual Income Taxation (DIT) are the combination of a

1 Devereux (2004) provides a historical overview on this issue.

2 'Soft' infrastructure comprises, for instance, property rights, while 'hard' infrastructure applies to roads and bridges, for example.

3 In appendix 3.B a different version of the model will be presented in which the tax receipts are taken to finance a public consumption good.

progressive tax on labor income with a flat tax rate on capital income which is (significantly) lower than the top marginal tax rate on labor income. Elements of such separate factor income taxation have meanwhile been developed for a number of European countries and have finally been implemented as illustrated, for instance, in Eggert and Genser (2005), Sørensen (2005) or Sachverständigenrat (2005). Boadway (2005) and Sørensen (2005) have shown that the basic case for the dual income tax usually rests on pragmatic considerations involving efficiency, equity and political economy aspects. The reasoning to tax capital income at a lower rate than labor income is largely based on the so-called basic tax competition model (BTCM). This model delivers the insight that it is not optimal for a small open economy operating in a world of constant returns to scale and perfect competition to levy a source tax on capital. However, once it is acknowledged that capital is not perfectly mobile or a region is relatively larger than the other a positive, yet low, tax rate on capital is indicated.[4]

The following analysis first highlights that labor taxes have a strongly positive location effect when proceeds are used to finance public infrastructure. Second, differentials in the capital tax rate across locations have strong location effects favoring the low (capital) tax country. Third, in contrast to standard tax competition theories, this effect is strongly magnified as trade integration between two countries proceeds. If a critical level of trade integration is reached, there is full agglomeration of the manufacturing sector in the low-tax country. Fourth, a relocation of industry does not obtain when the high-tax country under consideration is large enough in relation to the low-tax country. Finally, in a Nash tax game identical regions only put a tax on labor income and subsidize capital income. With rising economic integration the subsidy on capital will be reduced as well as the tax rate on labor income indicating that tax competition will be weaker with increasing trade integration.

Models of new trade and geography have been used in a couple of previous works to study industry location effects of taxes, tax differentials and tax competition and they have challenged some of the insights revealed by the BTCM. The footloose capital model is used, for example, by Pflüger (2001) to study environmental taxes and by Haufler and Pflüger (2004) to study commodity tax competition.

The contribution closest in spirit to the following analysis is Forslid (2005) who studies capital tax competition in the model used in this chapter. However, in contrast to the following analysis, his work assumes that there is no tax on labor and that the capital tax revenues are spent according to the average private consumption basket rather than used to provide public infrastructure or a public

4 Cf. Sørensen (2005) and Wilson (1999).

good. He points out that due to the existence of agglomeration forces two different cases of tax competition need to be distinguished. With two symmetric regions differences in the tax rate of this factor induce the mobile factor to move to the region with the relative lower tax burden. In contrast, whenever the mobile factor agglomerates in one region, this agglomeration creates rents that can be taxed without leading to a relocation of the mobile factor.

Andersson and Forslid (2003) analyze (possibly differentiated) taxes on capital and labor income which are used to provide a public consumption good. In contrast to the following analysis, they use an endogenous agglomeration model, a footloose entrepreneur model, to study tax competition. They show that taxes may destabilize a symmetric equilibrium and, in line with Baldwin and Krugman (2004) and the previous authors mentioned, they find that industrial agglomeration, once established, produces taxable rents.

The notion of taxable rents due to agglomeration of a mobile production factor is also confirmed by Ludema and Wooton (2000). They can show that it's optimal for the government of a region to set a positive tax rate on mobile factor income as long as this factor agglomerates in this region. In opposite to the following analysis, they model regional integration not only as a variation of trade costs (i.e. consumer market integration) but also as differences in the mobility of labor between the two regions. Additionally, the tax receipts in this model are used as lump-sum transfers for immobile workers. Contrary to popular notion as captured by the BTCM, they find that tax competition is weakened with increasing freeness of trade. This finding is in line with the results obtained in this chapter.

Using a so-called vertical linkage model elaborated in Krugman and Venables (1995), Kind et al. (2000) can show that a country which hosts the industrial core can gain from imposing a source tax on capital that exceeds the capital tax rate of the other region. However, with industry equally spread over the two countries, each government will subsidize capital, a result that can be confirmed with the present model, too.

Bénassy-Quéré et al. (2007) use a standard tax competition model to quantitatively estimate the relationship between the tax and public infrastructure nexus. In their estimations they also control for geography, country/ market size so that agglomeration effects are also considered. They reveal that increasing public infrastructure attracts firms. However, the empirical results show that an increase of the capital tax rate induces firms to relocate to the region with the relatively lower capital tax rate, a result that can be supported with the following model. Also in line with the theoretical results presented here is their empirical observation that tax receipts on the immobile factor can be taken to finance the necessary level of public infrastructure to keep business from leaving the region due to differences in the capital tax rate.

This chapter is set up as follows. The basic model will be outlined in section 3.2. Section 3.3 then studies the location effect of public infrastructure under separate factor income taxation. Section 3.4 performs the analysis of optimal factor taxation under increasing trade freeness, while section 3.5 concludes. Appendix 3.B provides a modification of the model, substituting public infrastructure with a public consumption good.

## 3.2 The Model

### 3.2.1 Basic Structure

The theoretical considerations on the following pages build on the footloose capital model as, for instance, illustrated in Martin and Rogers (1995) or Baldwin et al. (2003) which exhibits intra-industry trade in differentiated products and capital mobility. The economy examined here consists of two regions called home and foreign (characterized by an asterisk *) which are assumed to have identical preferences, technologies and trade costs. There are two types of productive factors, physical capital $(K)$ and labor $(L)$, each in fixed supply. The number of households (labor) in both regions is normalized at unity and $s_L$ denotes the domestic share. Households are immobile across regions. The world capital stock is also normalized at unity and $s_K$ is the share of this stock which is owned by domestic households. Physical capital is mobile across regions and moves in response to differentials in rate of returns. However, the capital owners (i.e. the households) are immobile. Hence, capital installed abroad generates a stream of repatriated capital earnings.

There are two private sectors: a manufacturing sector $(X)$ characterized by increasing returns, monopolistic competition and iceberg trade costs produces a composite of manufactures as well as a perfectly competitive outside sector $(A)$ which produces a homogeneous good with constant returns to scale. This good is assumed to be produced in both regions and traded without costs. The $A$-good is taken as the numéraire, i.e. its price is normalized to one.

The government taxes labor and capital income with proportionate and possibly different rates. Tax proceeds will be used by the government to provide public infrastructure which facilitates the setup of manufacturing firms.[5]

For brevity, the exposition of the model focuses on home and omits the analogous expressions which pertain for foreign.

## 3.2.2 Utility and Demand

Domestic preferences are depicted by a quasi-linear utility function given by

$$u = C_A + \mu \ln C_X \left[\mu(\ln \mu - 1)\right] \text{ with } C_X = \left[\int_0^M x_i^{\frac{\sigma-1}{\sigma}} di\right]^{\frac{\sigma}{\sigma-1}} \tag{3.1}$$

where $\sigma > 1$ and $\mu > 0$.[6] $C_A$ denotes consumption of the outside numéraire good, $C_X$ represents the consumption of the manufacturing composite as in Dixit and Stiglitz (1977), $x_i$ is the quantity of variety $i$, $M$ is the mass of varieties produced in manufacturing and $\sigma$ is the elasticity of substitution between any two manufacturing varieties. The aggregate household budget constraint of home is

$$C_A + \int_0^M p_i x_i di = y \tag{3.2}$$

where $p_i$ is the consumer price of variety $i$ and $y$ denotes aggregate private income in home. Utility maximization leads to the demand functions $x_i$, $C_X$, $C_A$ and indirect utility $v$:

$$C_A = y - \mu, \qquad C_X = \frac{\mu}{P}, \qquad x_i = \mu \frac{P^{\sigma-1}}{p_i^{\sigma}} \tag{3.3}$$

$$v = y - \mu \ln P, \tag{3.4}$$

5 In appendix 3.B we analyze the case where the government takes the tax receipts to provide a public consumption good.

6 $\sigma$ denotes the elasticity of substitution between different variants of the industrial good and $\mu$ stands for the share of income spent on industrial goods.

where $$P \equiv \left[ \int_0^M p_i^{1-\sigma} di \right]^{\frac{1}{1-\sigma}} \tag{3.5}$$

is the perfect CES price index for the manufacturing composite. It is assumed that $\mu < y$ always holds, to ensure that the consumption of the outside good is positive.

### 3.2.3 Production

The numéraire good is produced with labor as the only input factor under a linear technology: $X_A = N_A$, where $X_A$ is output and $N_A$ is the input of labor. Perfect competition implies that this good is priced at marginal costs. Hence, the wage equals labor's marginal product (i.e. one). Costless trade implies the equalization of the wage across regions at unity.

Each variety of manufactures is supplied by a single firm $i$. Each firm requires one unit of physical capital to be able to produce at all. One unit of each variety is then produced with $c$ units of labor. Total costs of a domestic firm $i$ are therefore given by $R + cX_i$, where $R$ denotes the compensation of a unit of capital and $X_i$ is total output. Trade costs $\tau \geq 1$ are of the iceberg type: only $\frac{1}{\tau}$ of a unit bought in the foreign region arrives for consumption there. With producer prices indicated by a hat, we have $p_i = \hat{p}_i$ for domestic products. For imported varieties, $p_j = \tau \hat{p}_j$ where $j$ denotes varieties produced in foreign. Mill pricing is optimal in the Dixit-Stiglitz model of monopolistic competition. Profits of firm $i$ in the domestic region are

$$\Pi_i = [\hat{p}_i - c] X_i - g(I) R \qquad \text{where} \qquad g(I) \equiv \frac{1}{1+\beta I}. \tag{3.6}$$

If the government supplies public infrastructure, $I > 0$, it becomes cheaper to set up business, i.e. public infrastructure increases the number of firms and thus, the variants produced in this region. $\beta > 0$ is a parameter which indicates how efficient domestic institutions are in implementing a given amount of public infrastructure expenditures to the private sector's benefit.[7] The maximization of profits gives the optimal producer price of each variety:

7 This way of modeling public infrastructure follows Egger and Falkinger (2006).

$$\hat{p}_i = \hat{p} = \frac{c\sigma}{\sigma - 1}. \tag{3.7}$$

Normalizing marginal costs to $c = \frac{(\sigma-1)}{\sigma}$ implies $\hat{p} = 1$. Hence, the consumer price index of the manufacturing composite in the domestic region is

$$P = \left[ \frac{s_N}{g(I)} + \phi \frac{(1 - s_N)}{g^*(I^*)} \right]^{\frac{1}{1-\sigma}} \tag{3.8}$$

where $s_N$ is the share of firms (≡ capital invested) in the domestic region and where $0 \leq \phi \equiv \tau^{1-\sigma} \leq 1$ stands for the degree of trade freeness. Since each firm requires one unit of physical capital, the number of varieties produced in the domestic region is $s_N$.

In the framework of monopolistic competition, competition drives pure profits down to zero and the reward to capital is then equal to the operating profit $\frac{X_i}{\sigma}$, amended by a positive effect originating from public infrastructure. Hence, using (3.6), (3.7) and the normalization of marginal costs, the following relationship between capital's rate of return in home and the output of firm $i$ is obtained

$$R = \frac{1}{g(I)} \frac{X_i}{\sigma}. \tag{3.9}$$

Aggregate demand for variety $i$ from home and foreign (which includes indirect demand associated with the iceberg trade costs) can be derived from (3.3), (3.7), (3.8) and their foreign analogues. This yields

$$X_i = \mu \left[ \frac{s_L}{\frac{s_N}{g} + \frac{\phi(1-s_N)}{g^*}} + \frac{\phi(1 - s_L)}{\frac{(1-s_N)}{g^*} + \frac{\phi s_N}{g}} \right]$$

where the total endowment of labor across the two regions has been normalized at unity (i.e. $L^W = 1$).[8] Substituting this market clearing condition into (3.9) yields

8 The quasi-linear utility function implies that the aggregation of demand basically amounts to a head count.

$$R = \frac{\mu}{\sigma}\left[\frac{s_L}{s_N + \phi(1-s_N)\frac{g}{g*}} + \frac{\phi(1-s_L)}{\phi s_N + (1-s_N)\frac{g*}{g}}\right]. \tag{3.10}$$

## 3.2.4 The Government

The government levies a tax $t_L$ on labor income and a source tax $t_K$ on capital. The domestic government's tax receipts then amount to $T = t_L s_L + t_K s_N R$ and aggregate net income of the private sector in home is given by $y = (1-t_L)s_L + (1-t_K)s_K R$, assuming that the international arbitrage condition (3.12) holds.

Government takes the total tax receipts to finance public infrastructure

$$g(I) = \frac{1}{1+\beta I} \qquad \text{with} \qquad I = T = t_L s_L + t_K s_N R \tag{3.11}$$

which has an immediate impact on the business sector by making it cheaper to set up business. $\beta$ is used to characterize the efficiency at which the government transforms the tax receipts into public infrastructure.

## 3.2.5 International Equilibrium

The international equilibrium in the manufacturing sector can be represented by a system of five equations which are put together below for convenience. For a given allocation of firms across regions $s_N$, the rate of return of capital in home $R$, is determined by (3.10) together with (3.11). An analogous expression pertains for the rental rate in foreign, $R^*$ (cf. (3.10$^*$) and (3.11$^*$) below). Arbitrage ensures that physical capital and thus firms move between the two regions until the after-tax rate of returns are equalized (cf. (3.12)) in an internal location equilibrium. These five equations jointly determine the five variables $s_N, R, R^*, g$ and $g^*$:

$$R = \frac{\mu}{\sigma}\left[\frac{s_L}{s_N + \phi(1-s_N)\frac{g}{g*}} + \frac{\phi(1-s_L)}{\phi s_N + (1-s_N)\frac{g}{g*}}\right] \tag{3.10}$$

$$R^{*}=\frac{\mu}{\sigma}\left[\frac{\phi s_{L}}{s_{N}\frac{g^{*}}{g}+\phi\left(1-s_{N}\right)}+\frac{\left(1-s_{L}\right)}{\phi s_{N}\frac{g^{*}}{g}+\left(1-s_{N}\right)}\right] \tag{3.10*}$$

$$g=\frac{1}{1+\beta\left(t_{L}s_{L}+t_{K}s_{N}R\right)} \tag{3.11}$$

$$g^{*}=\frac{1}{1+\beta^{*}\left(t_{L}^{*}\left(1-s_{L}\right)+t_{K}^{*}\left(1-s_{N}\right)R^{*}\right)} \tag{3.11*}$$

$$\left(1-t_{K}\right)R=\left(1-t_{K}^{*}\right)R^{*} \tag{3.12}$$

## 3.3 Industry Location and Relative Infrastructure

Public infrastructure exerts a positive effect on the profits in the manufacturing sector as we have seen in section 3.2.5. To analyze the full general equilibrium effects of a dual income tax regime, which uses the tax proceeds to provide public infrastructure, two schedules from the above characterized international equilibrium system can be derived and used in a very intuitive graph to illustrate the main findings.

A first schedule is obtained by combining (3.10), (3.10*) and (3.12). It denotes the share of industry in home for given levels of relative infrastructure. Eliminating the rate of returns and solving for the share of domestic firms, we obtain

$$s_{N}\left(\overset{+}{G}\right)=\frac{\phi-G\Lambda\left(s_{L}+\phi^{2}\left(1-s_{L}\right)\right)}{\left(G-\phi\right)\left(G\Lambda\phi-1\right)+G\left(1-\Lambda\right)\left(1-\phi^{2}\right)s_{L}}. \tag{3.13}$$

In (3.13) we switch off any influences from financing the infrastructure on the decision of capital location. Thus, the capital location decision only depends on the level of infrastructure and the tax rate on capital income. $G\equiv\frac{g^{*}}{g}=\frac{1+\beta T}{1+\beta^{*}T^{*}}$ shall be defined as a shorthand expression for the relative infrastructure levels in the two regions (taking into account the efficiency measure $\beta$ which indicates how efficiently infrastructure expenditures are transformed into services for the manufacturing sector) and $\Lambda = \frac{1-t_K}{1-t_K^*}$ is an expression for the international capital tax differential.[9]

It follows immediately from (3.13) that $\frac{ds_N}{dG} > 0$. Intuitively, the share of domestic firms rises with home's relative supply of infrastructure. This relationship is depicted as the dashed black line in figure 3.1.

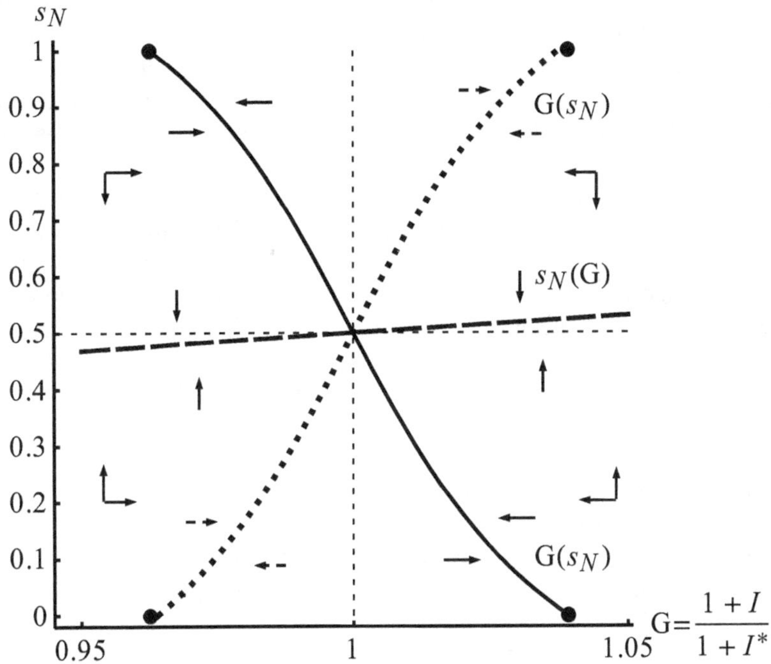


*Figure 3.1: Industry location and relative infrastructure; Figure 3.1 is based on the following assumptions:* $s_L = 0.5, \phi = 0.3, \beta = 1, \mu = 0.3, \sigma = 2, t_L = t_L^* = 0.4$ *and* $t_K = t_K^* = -0.3$ *(solid downward sloping black line),* $t_K = t_K^* = 0.3$ *(dotted upward sloping black line)*

On the dashed black line the net-return on capital invested in home is equal to the net-return invested in foreign. Above (below) the dashed black line, the net-return in home is smaller (larger) than the net-return in foreign. This induces firms to move from home $\left[s_N \downarrow\right]$ (foreign $\left[s_N \uparrow\right]$) to foreign (home) until the

9 $\Lambda > 1$ implies a tax advantage $\left(t_K < t_K^*\right)$ in home.

net-returns are equalized again (cf. the black arrows below and above the dashed black line in figure 3.1).

The comparative statics of this curve is easily derived and conveniently explained in terms of figure 3.1. First, taxes on labor $\left(t_L, t_L^*\right)$ have no effect on this schedule since these taxes do not affect the profitability of the manufacturing sector in our model.[10] Second, for any given level of relative infrastructure $G$ the domestic share of firms is increasing in $\Lambda$, i.e. the domestic share of firms is positively related to relative increases in the foreign capital tax (the dashed black line shifts up) and negatively related to relative increases to the domestic capital tax (the dashed black line shifts down). These first two results conform to the conventional wisdom. The trade and geography aspects of our analysis are contained in the next two findings. For any given level of the relative infrastructure $G$, the share of firms in the domestic economy is positively related to the share of immobile workers $s_L$ (the dashed black line shifts up). Intuitively, when firms produce under increasing returns, their profitability is positively related to the size of the market (i.e. home market effect). Finally, when trade costs are reduced (i.e. $\phi \to 1$), the dashed black line (3.13) becomes steeper which implies that the location of industry becomes more sensitive to variations in the relative infrastructure $G$. These findings can be summarized as follows:

*Result: The size of the manufacturing sector in the domestic region $\left(s_N\right)$ is positively related to home's relative supply of infrastructure $G$. For any given level of $G$, $\frac{ds_N}{dt_L}=0$, $\frac{ds_N}{dt_L*}=0$, $\frac{ds_N}{dt_K}<0$, $\frac{ds_N}{dt_K*}>0$ and, $\frac{ds_N}{ds_L}>0$ (home market effect). The share of manufacturing firms is more sensitive to variations in relative infrastructure, the higher the degree of trade freeness, i.e. $\frac{d^2 s_N}{dGd\phi}>0$.*

The second schedule is obtained by inserting (3.10) into (3.11), and (3.10$^*$) into (3.11$^*$) and eventually solving out for $g$ and $g^*$. It focuses on the aspect of financing the infrastructure expressing the relative level of infrastructure for a given share of industry in home

$$G\left(\overset{+}{\underset{-}{s_N}}\right) \equiv \frac{g^*}{g} = \frac{1+\beta\left(t_L s_L + t_K s_N R\right)}{1+\beta^*\left(t_L^*\left(1-s_L\right)+t_K^*\left(1-s_N\right)R^*\right)}. \tag{3.14}$$

In (3.14) we switch off any influences from tax rate changes on the decision of capital location. It can be verified that, for positive levels of capital taxes,

10 Again this follows from the quasi-linear preference structure.

$\frac{dG}{ds_N} > 0$ while $\frac{dG}{ds_N} < 0$ for negative capital tax rates (i.e. subsidies on capital). Hence, this curve is upward sloping (the dotted black line) for positive capital taxes (but steeper than the relationship given by (3.13)) and downward sloping (the solid black line) for negative capital taxes as depicted in figure 3.1.[11] Intuitively, a higher share of firms implies a larger tax base, higher tax revenues and a higher level of relative public infrastructure. With a subsidy on capital, a smaller share of industry in home implies less subsidies and more financial means for the provision of infrastructure. Moreover, the curve shifts from convex (for values of $G$ below 1) to concave (values of $G$ exceeding 1) for positive capital tax rates and vice versa for capital subsidies. The relationship is depicted by the dotted and solid black lines in figure 3.1.[12] On the solid black line the government budget in both regions is balanced. Above the solid black line, there is a budget deficit (surplus) in home (foreign). In order to keep the share of industry constant in home (foreign) public infrastructure in home (foreign) has to be downsized (upgraded) to reach a balanced budget in both regions.[13] Above the dotted black line there is a budget surplus (deficit) in home (foreign). To keep the share of industry constant in home (foreign), public infrastructure in home (foreign) has to be upgraded (downsized) to reach a balanced budget in both regions (cf. the black arrows to the right and left of the solid black line in figure 3.1).[14]

The comparative statics of this relationship can again be explained with the help of figure 3.1. First, the curve shifts to the right when the domestic tax on labor is increased and/ or the foreign tax on labor is reduced. Intuitively, in both cases a higher level of infrastructure can be provided in the domestic region for any given share of domestic firms, $s_N$. Second, for the very same reason, a qualitatively similar result is obtained for domestic and foreign capital taxes (subsidies). Third, for any given share of firms in the domestic economy, $s_N$, home's relative supply of infrastructure rises with its share of immobile workers, $s_L$, which is basically a tax base effect (the dotted and solid black lines shift to the right). Finally, consider a reduction in trade costs. It is easily established, that the boundaries of (3.14), marked by the large black dots in figure 3.1,

---

11 It will be shown in the following section 3.4 that a capital subsidy is optimal if identical regions engage in tax competition.

12 The solid black line applies for capital subsidies and the dotted black line applies for capital taxes in both countries.

13 Below the solid black line there is a budget surplus (deficit) in home (foreign).

14 Below the dotted black line there is a budget deficit (surplus) in home (foreign).

$$G(s_N)\Big|_{s_N=0} = \frac{\sigma(1+\beta s_L t_L)}{\sigma\left[1+\beta^*(1-s_L)t_L^*\right]+\beta^*\mu t_K^*}$$

and
$$G(s_N)\Big|_{s_N=1} = \frac{\sigma(1+\beta s_L t_L)+\beta\mu t_K}{\sigma\left[1+\beta^*(1-s_L)t_L^*\right]}$$

are independent of trade costs. However, a reduction in trade costs has the effect of 'straightening' the curves. Hence, starting from a symmetric situation, an increase (reduction) in the domestic share of firms has a stronger (smaller) effect on home's relative supply of infrastructure, the higher the degree of trade freeness. Summarizing these findings implies:

*Result: Home's relative supply of infrastructure $G$ is positively related to the size of the manufacturing sector in the domestic region $(s_N)$ if capital is taxed in both regions and negatively related if capital is subsidized in both regions. For any given level of $\frac{dG}{dt_L}>0$, $\frac{dG}{dt_L^*}<0$, $\frac{dG}{dt_K}>0$, $\frac{dG}{dt_K^*}<0$ and, $\frac{dG}{ds_L}>0$. Starting from a symmetric situation $\left(s_N=\frac{1}{2}, G=1\right)$, an increase (reduction) in $s_N$ has a stronger (smaller) positive effect on $G$ the higher the degree of trade freeness $\phi$.*

The two schedules can now be combined to obtain the share of firms in home, $s_N$, and the relative supply of infrastructure in the international equilibrium. This equilibrium is depicted by the intersection of the two curves in figure 3.1. Analytically, the equilibrium value of the domestic share of firms can be obtained by inserting (3.14) into (3.13). This produces an implicit relationship defining the domestic share of firms $s_N$ as a function of the parameters of the economy, notably on the tax rates, the efficiency of institutions, the size of the regions and the level of trade costs[15]

$$s_N = s_N\left(t_L, t_L^*, t_K, t_K^*, s_L, \beta, \beta^*, \phi, \mu, \sigma\right). \tag{3.15}$$

The general equilibrium effects of parameter variations on the location of industry in home can be obtained by implicit differentiation of (3.15) and graphically traced by bringing the previous two results together. Stability of the

15 It also depends on the preferences for manufacturing goods as well the degree of product differentiation.

symmetric equilibrium is assumed. In the case of (positive) tax rates on capital, this implies that trade integration stays within the following borders

$$0<\phi<1-\frac{2\beta\mu t_K}{\beta\mu t_K+\sqrt{\beta\mu t_K\left[2\beta\mu t_K+\sigma\left(2+\beta t_L\right)\right]}}.^{16}$$

The main findings can be summarized to the following result:

*Result: The domestic share of industry $s_N$ and home's relative supply of infrastructure, $G$, are unambiguously increasing in the domestic labor tax rate, the domestic share of immobile workers (domestic market size) and unambiguously falling in foreign's labor tax rate. Increasing (decreasing) the domestic tax (subsidy) on capital or reducing (increasing) the foreign tax (subsidy) on capital has a negative effect on the domestic share of industry, $s_N$.*

The new economic geography aspects of the dual income tax are best borne out by considering the general equilibrium effects on the domestic share of firms as a process of trade integration that takes place between the two regions. These can again be illustrated in figure 3.1. It's assumed that both regions have equal taxes on labor $\left(t_L=t_L^*\right)$ and that they are of equal size $\left(s_K=\frac{1}{2}, s_L=\frac{1}{2}\right)$. However, whilst the domestic government taxes capital and labor at an equal rate, the foreign region maintains a lower capital tax rate (i.e. $\Lambda<1$, i.e. a capital tax disadvantage in home).

Departing form a symmetric equilibrium a higher tax on capital income (lower subsidy on capital) in home shifts the dotted and solid black line to the right and the dashed black line to the lower right, indicating a lower share of industry in home. Increasing the freeness of trade $(\phi\rightarrow 1)$ the dotted and the solid black line flatten out and the dashed black line turns counter clockwise leading to a decline in the share of industry in home. The difference in capital taxation drives out capital from home to foreign, and this effect increases with trade freeness: a difference in capital taxation along with increasing trade freeness can therefore have the dramatic effect of a total loss of capital in home (i.e. the region with the tax disadvantage).

However, considering differences in the size of a region $\left(s_L>\frac{1}{2}\right)$ may well alter the above maintained results. Figure 3.1 shows that a size advantage of home works against the capital tax disadvantage. With an increase in trade freeness the share of industry in home also increases despite the tax disadvantage.

16 No additional assumptions about the variables have to be made in the case of negative capital taxes (subsidy).

The larger the market size of the home region the more capital will be attracted by a decline of trade costs. Depending on the scale of the size advantage, any tax disadvantage has no dramatic effects on the location of industry unless trade integration has proceeded far enough. The market size attenuates the loss of industry, at least for a wide range of trade costs.

Turning to the tax on labor income gives the government an additional tool to prevent the dislocation of industry. Supposing a higher tax rate on labor in home would ameliorate the domestic infrastructure. The dotted and the solid black line in figure 3.1 would thus shift to the right implying that the domestic share of industry is higher for any level of trade freeness. Such a positive infrastructure differential magnifies any market size advantage.

*Result: Consider a trade integration process between a region which taxes capital and labor at an equal rate and a trading partner region that maintains a dual income tax (i.e. taxes labor at an equal but capital at a lower rate). Even though the initial stages of trade integration have no effect on the domestic share of industry, ultimately, the domestic region experiences a dramatic reduction and even a complete loss of industry. Greater market size shelters the domestic economy from such a loss of industry. However, in order to avoid a complete loss of industry, or even to attract industry in the process of trade integration, the market size advantage has to be strong enough. The domestic region can shelter its industrial base by raising its tax rate on the immobile factor labor.*

## 3.4 Optimal Taxation

The analysis of different, exogenously chosen tax rates on labor and capital revealed the interaction of firm relocation and relative infrastructure. In the next step, we will focus on the endogenous choice of the different tax rates on labor and capital income by the government of each region.

### 3.4.1 Cooperative Choice of Tax Rates: The Solution of the Social Planner

To begin with, the optimal tax rates chosen by a social planner (i.e. optimal cooperative tax rates) will be derived. It is assumed that both regions are identical in all respects and our analysis will be based on interior equilibria only. The benevolent social planner then maximizes the sum of the indirect utility of a representative consumer in home and foreign which eliminates externalities of taxation on the location of capital. The first order condition for the optimal labor tax rate is

$$\frac{\partial v}{\partial t_L}+\frac{\partial v^*}{\partial t_L}\overset{!}{=}0,$$

leading to an optimal tax rate of labor

$$t_L=\frac{2}{\beta}\left[\frac{\mu\beta}{\sigma-1}-1\right]-\frac{\mu}{\sigma}t_K. \tag{3.16}$$

Respectively, the first order condition for the optimal tax rate on capital is

$$\frac{\partial v}{\partial t_K}+\frac{\partial v^*}{\partial t_K}\overset{!}{=}0$$

indicating an optimal tax rate on capital income of[17]

$$t_K=\frac{2}{\beta}\frac{\sigma}{\mu}\left[\frac{\mu\beta}{\sigma-1}-1\right]-\frac{\sigma}{\mu}t_L. \tag{3.17}$$

These results are identical with the optimal tax rate of labor and capital income under autarky. Inserting (3.16) into (3.17) reveals that the social planer can choose an arbitrary tax rate on either labor or capital and then gets the optimal tax rate on the other factor. Splitting up tax rates on different types of income allows the social planner to shift the tax burden of public infrastructure financing between labor and capital (e.g., increasing the tax rate on labor income decreases the tax rate on capital income and vice versa) and due to common utility maximization there is lump sum taxation of labor and capital income.

The optimal tax rate on labor income in reply to an arbitrarily chosen tax rate on capital depends on $\mu$ (i.e. the preference of consumers for the manufacturing good), $\sigma$ (i.e. elasticity of substitution between different variants of the manufacturing good) and the efficiency parameter of infrastructure provision $\beta$. A higher $\sigma$ indicates a lower tax rate on labor income (c.p.). With a higher $\sigma$

17 (3.17) can also be replicated by resolving (3.16) for $t_K$.

the tax rate on labor income declines indicating that with variants becoming more and more similar, less infrastructure is needed to support more firms and thus the number of variants available. A decline of $\mu$ also implies a lower tax rate on labor income (c.p.): with a lower preference for the industrial good, fewer infrastructure is needed and thus less variants are available. The fraction of $\mu$ and $\sigma$ determines the degree to which the tax burden can be shifted between labor and capital. Whenever consumers strongly value product differentiation (i.e. low $\sigma$ and high $\mu$), changes in the tax rate of capital induce relatively strong changes in the tax rate of labor. A high preference for the industrial good and a low elasticity of substitution between the different variants of the industrial good imply a relatively high capital tax base. Decreasing the tax rate

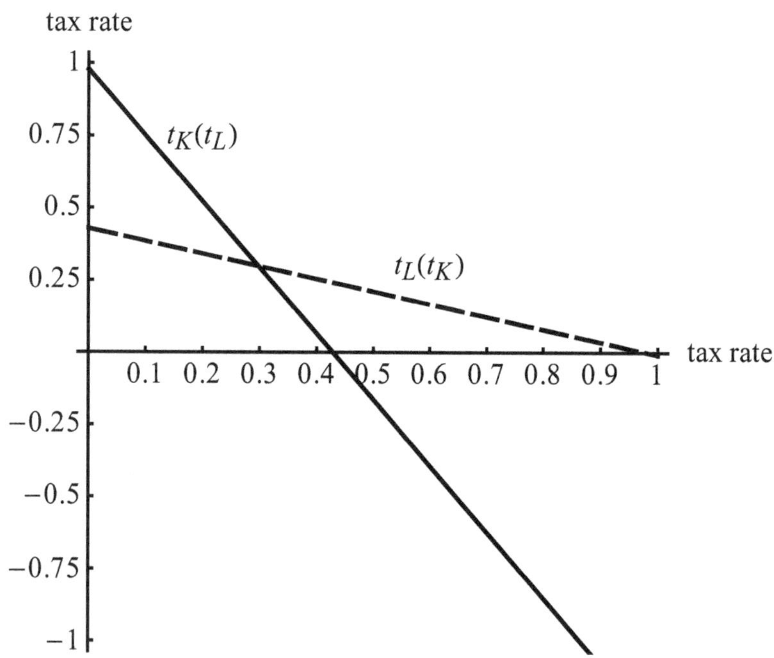


*Figure 3.2: Cooperative choice of tax rates;*
*Figure 3.2 is based on the following assumptions:* $\beta = 1.05, \mu = 0.7, \sigma = 1.6$;
*How to read the figure: the level of the first tax rate attached to the solid or dashed black line can be read from the ordinate and the corresponding tax rate in brackets can be read from the abscissa.*

on capital thus implies a relatively huge loss in tax revenues on capital income (i.e. a decline of infrastructure) which has to be compensated with a relatively large increase of the tax rate on labor income. Since the social planner treats the two regions as one entity, trade freeness $\phi$ doesn't play a role in our analysis.

The same line of arguments can be applied to analyzing the effects of tax rate changes of labor taxes on the optimal capital tax rates (3.17). Note, however, that the capital tax base changes with $\mu$ and $\sigma$ while the labor tax base remains unchanged, since the wage rate has been fixed. Therefore, it does well matter which tax rate is chosen as policy instrument by the social planner, since the capital tax rate reacts more sensitive to changes in the labor tax rate than in the opposite case, which is shown in figure 3.2

*Result: A social planner chooses a single tax rate on capital income for both regions and so changes in the tax rate on capital do not induce firms to move from one region to another. The social planner sets one tax rate exogenously while the remaining tax rate adjusts endogenously. It can be seen that the capital tax rate reacts more sensitive to changes in the labor tax rate than vice versa, reflecting that the labor tax base is constant and higher than the capital tax base.*

### 3.4.2 Non-Cooperative Taxation: A Nash Tax Game

Analyzing the location effects of separate factor taxation revealed that differentials in either tax rate (labor or capital) between the two regions induce relocation of industry. Thus, there is an externality involved with tax rate changes in one region: if home increases its capital tax rate c.p., industry will relocate to foreign (increasing the tax base in the other region). Since an increase in the tax rate in home will lower the after tax return, the market in home is less profitable, inducing industry to relocate until after-tax returns are in equilibrium again (cf. (3.12)). Therefore, the main question is whether a national tax policy will have an incentive to follow a well known beggar-my-neighbor policy: leaving capital untaxed or subsidized and thus creating an inefficient (symmetric) Nash equilibrium in comparison to the social planner solution. Acting independently, the objective of the home government would be

$$\frac{\partial v}{\partial t_L} \overset{!}{=} 0 \text{ and } \frac{\partial v}{\partial t_K} \overset{!}{=} 0, \text{ leading to}$$

$$\frac{dv}{dt_L}=\underbrace{-\frac{1}{2}}_{(a)}\underbrace{+2\frac{\mu}{\sigma-1}\frac{1-\phi}{1+\phi}\frac{ds_N}{dt_L}}_{(b)}\underbrace{-\frac{\mu}{\sigma-1}\frac{1}{1+\phi}\frac{1}{g}\left(\frac{dg}{dt_L}+\phi\frac{dg^*}{dt_L}\right)}_{(c)}\overset{!}{=}0 \quad (3.18)$$

and

$$\frac{dv}{dt_K}=\underbrace{-\frac{1}{4}\frac{\mu}{\sigma}}_{(d)}\underbrace{+2\frac{\mu}{\sigma-1}\frac{1-\phi}{1+\phi}\frac{ds_N}{dt_K}}_{(e)}\underbrace{-\frac{\mu}{\sigma-1}\frac{1}{1+\phi}\frac{1}{g}\left(\frac{dg}{dt_K}+\phi\frac{dg^*}{dt_K}\right)}_{(f)}\overset{!}{=}0 \quad (3.19)$$

assuming that both regions are identical in all respects.

Since an explicit solution for the labor and capital tax rate cannot be obtained, a twofold approach will be applied. Before presenting a graphical illustration with figure 3.3 the intuition of the effects of tax rate changes on the indirect utility will be illustrated, highlighting the different forces at work.

Referring to (3.18), the first term $(a)$ shows the income effect of a tax rate change: an increase (decrease) of the tax rate on labor income in home decreases (increases) the indirect utility. The second part $(b)$ represents the relocation effect of capital, which is larger than 0, i.e. the indirect utility in home rises (declines) with an increase (decrease) of the labor tax rate. With higher taxes on labor, there are more tax receipts that can be used to provide public infrastructure. With a higher level of public infrastructure, less capital is needed to set up a firm in home and therefore the share of industry in home rises $\frac{ds_N}{dt_L}>0$. With a higher share of industry, there are more variants of the industrial good available for consumers, increasing their utility due to the 'love of variety', implied by the utility function (cf. (3.1)). Note that the strength of the relocation effect decreases with increasing trade freeness $(\phi\rightarrow 1)$ and it positively depends on consumers' preferences for the manufacturing good (preferences for the manufacturing increase with $\mu\rightarrow 1$) as well as the market force of the manufacturing firms (the market force of manufacturing firms increase the more similar the variants on the manufacturing goods become, i.e. $\sigma\rightarrow 1$). Finally, there is a positive infrastructure effect $(c)$ at work reflecting the spill-overs from industry relocation. The relocation of industry shifts the tax base from one region to another additionally strengthening the infrastructure in one region and diminishing the infrastructure in the other region. This increases the number of available variants in home, increasing the consumers' utility in home$\left(\frac{dg}{dt_L}<0\right)$[18]. Again, the strength of this effect depends on the degree of trade integration as well as consumers' preferences and the market power of the manufacturing sector in the same way as described for the relocation effect.

Similar effects can be identified for changes of the capital tax rate (3.19). The income effect $(d)$ is again negative. The relocation effect $(e)$ however, gets negative: with a higher capital tax rate the return of invested capital in the high tax region induces firms to relocate.

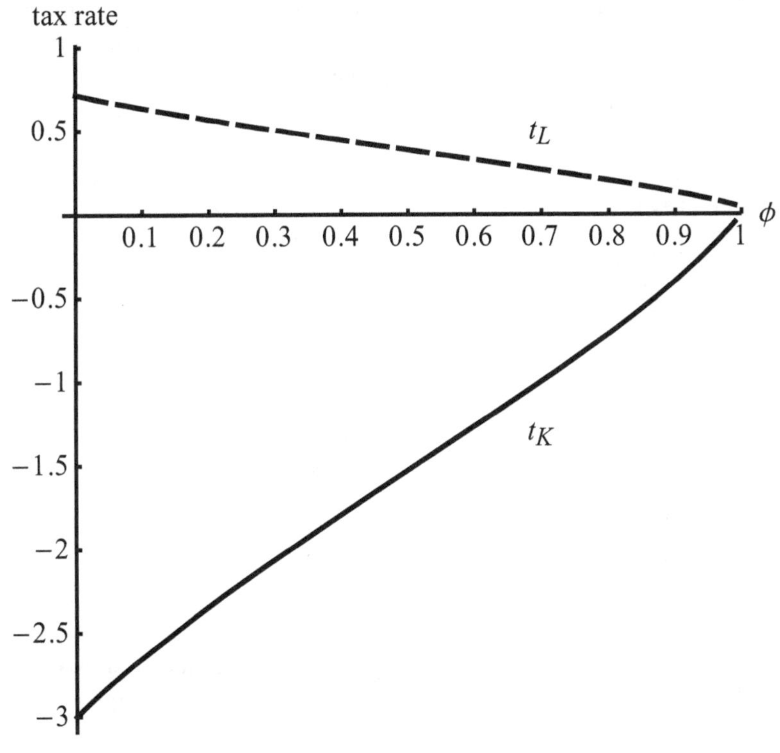


*Figure 3.3: Non-cooperative choice of tax rates; Figure 3.3 is based on the following assumptions:* $\beta = 6, \mu = 0.3, \sigma = 2$

18 Note $g \in \left]0,1\right]$ with values closer to 0 relating to a better public infrastructure, as shown in (3.6). $G = \frac{g^*}{g}$ and according to (3.11) and (3.11$^*$) $G < 1$ indicates an infrastructure disadvantage in home.

This decreases the share of firms in a region and thus the number of variants, available to consumers, decreasing the indirect utility. Finally, we can observe an infrastructure effect $(f)$ which is positive, indicating that a higher tax rate on capital leads to a higher level of infrastructure and thus to more firms in that region (i.e. more variants of the industrial good, increasing the indirect utility of consumers due to 'love of variety'). The strength of the relocation and infrastructure effects again declines with increasing trade freeness (i.e. $\phi \to 1$) and increases with greater market power of the manufacturing firms and consumer's preferences for the manufacturing good (i.e. $\sigma \to 1$ and $\mu \to 1$).

Eventually, the results obtained by numerical simulations will be illustrated. Taking the other region's tax rates as given and considering potential firm relocations, the tax rate on capital income (solid black line) and the tax rate on labor income (dashed black line) are shown in figure 3.3. With symmetric regions, the tax on capital will always be negative (i.e. capital will be subsidized). The subsidy on capital will be higher, if agglomeration forces grow stronger, i.e. if $\mu$ is larger and $\sigma$ is lower. Note that in this case the subsidy on capital income as well as the tax on labor income decrease with the degree of trade freeness $(\phi \to 1)$. This result expresses the positive welfare effect associated with trade integration: a decline in trade costs translates into a decreasing price index (3.8) which makes it less important for a region to host industry.

Therefore, the government in home does not have to compete as fiercely for capital as with higher trade costs. Unfortunately, the complexity of the results does not allow for variations in the size of the market (i.e. the share of laborers $s_L$). However, according to figure 3.1, differences in the size of a region reveal that a larger market hosts a larger number of manufacturing firms. It can thus be concluded that the market size shelters a region from loosing its industry firms (i.e. $\frac{ds_N}{ds_L} > 0$). Since the infrastructure effect of changes in the capital tax rate is positive and a larger market size of a region supports a larger share of industry, positive tax rates on capital income may possibly be maintained for low levels of trade integration, indicating that there are taxable agglomeration rents whenever industry is fully agglomerated in one region (i.e. a core-periphery equilibrium). However, with increasing trade freeness, the infrastructure effect declines and so, the pure size effects may no longer support positive tax rates. With intermediate transport costs, a region may thus subsidize capital to attract capital to keep capital in the region and increase consumers' indirect utility by a larger number of variants available in that region. With a further decline in transportations costs, consumers' proximity to industrial goods producers becomes less important, inducing governments to reduce the tax rate on capital and labor as well.

*Result: An independently acting government takes potential industry relocation into consideration in setting its tax rates. For symmetric regions, competition for mobile capital is fiercer, if the regions are less integrated (i.e. the subsidy on capital income is higher, if $\phi$ is lower). Size and degree of trade openness may finally shelter a region from (capital) tax competition.*

## 3.5 Conclusion

This chapter analyzed the relationship between public infrastructure, taxes and the location decision of firms. A simple footloose capital model, well-known from the new theories of trade and geography, has been used. Implementing separate factor taxation allowed us to refine each government's budget mix.

We have found that differentials in the capital tax rate across regions have strong location effects favoring the low (capital) tax country. This effect is strongly magnified as trade integration between two countries proceeds. If a critical level of trade integration is reached, there is full agglomeration of the manufacturing sector in the low-capital-tax country. However, a (complete) relocation of industry does not obtain when the high-capital-tax country under consideration is large enough in relation to the low-capital-tax country, concluding that the relative market size of a region offers the government some scope to set a higher tax rate on capital income than the other region.

For governments caring about their national share of industry, the analysis additionally provides the lesson that separate factor taxation, as realized with a DIT, can keep firms from moving in response to capital tax rate differentials. Increasing the tax rate on the immobile factor can raise the tax receipts used to provide public infrastructure, attracting additional firms. Consumers may well gain from the increased tax burden since an improvement of public infrastructure may attract additional firms, increasing the number of available variants in this region.

Increasing trade integration, modeled by declining transportation costs of the industrial composite good, induces firms to react more sensitive to differences between the two regions making firms' location decisions more unstable.

International tax competition revealed that identical countries will subsidize capital and only tax the immobile labor income at a positive rate. This supports the findings from the BTCM. With increasing trade integration however, tax competition weakens, saying that the subsidies on capital income will be reduced as well as the tax rates on labor income.

These results confirm the view that solely focusing on plain tax rates, as, for example, in the present capital tax harmonization efforts of the EU, is very much misleading.[19] Public infrastructure has an influence on the location decision of firms and thus, a harmonization of capital tax rates within the EU may simply open the gates for the EU member states to engage in public infrastructure competition financed via taxes on immobile factors, which is more important if the countries are less integrated.

# Appendix 3.A Analytical Annotations

Section 2.4.2 derived the non-cooperative tax rate choice of home. The objective of the government in home was to choose the tax rates on capital and labor income so that it maximizes the indirect utility of a representative household in home as indicated by (3.18) and (3.19). Since the complexity of the model did not allow to derive explicit results for the capital and labor income tax rates, appendix 3.A. should present the changes in industry share $(s_N)$ and infrastructure $(g)$ in home.

Effects of tax rate changes on the location of firms in home:

$$\frac{ds_N}{dt_L} = \frac{\beta\sigma\phi}{\beta\mu t_K\left((1-\phi)^2 - 4\phi\right) + \sigma(2+\beta t_L)(1-\phi)^2} > 0$$

$$\frac{ds_N}{dt_K} = -\frac{\beta\mu t_K(1+\phi)^2 + \sigma(2+\beta t_L)(1+\phi)^2 - 4\beta\mu\phi}{4(1-t_K)\left[\beta\mu t_K\left((1-\phi)^2 - 4\phi\right) + \sigma(2+\beta t_L)(1-\phi)^2\right]} < 0$$

$$\frac{ds_N}{dt_L^*} = -\frac{\beta\sigma\phi}{\beta\mu t_K\left((1-\phi)^2 - 4\phi\right) + \sigma(2+\beta t_L)(1-\phi)^2} < 0$$

$$\frac{ds_N}{dt_K^*} = \frac{\beta\mu t_K(1+\phi)^2 + \sigma(2+\beta t_L)(1+\phi)^2 - 4\beta\mu\phi}{4(1-t_K)\left[\beta\mu t_K\left((1-\phi)^2 - 4\phi\right) + \sigma(2+\beta t_L)(1-\phi)^2\right]} > 0$$

19 Within the European Union there are e.g. harmonization efforts for indirect taxes, for the company tax base and proposals to introduce a common consolidated tax base for multinational firms, as illustrated in Schratzenstaller (2007).

Effects of tax rate changes on the level of public infrastructure in home:

$$\frac{dg}{dt_L}=-\frac{2\beta\sigma^2\left[\beta\mu t_K\left((1-\phi)^2-2\phi\right)+\sigma(2+\beta t_L)(1-\phi)^2\right]}{\left[\beta\mu t_K+\sigma(2+\beta t_L)\right]^2\left[\beta\mu t_K\left((1-\phi)^2-4\phi\right)+\sigma(2+\beta t_L)(1-\phi)^2\right]}<0$$

$$\frac{dg}{dt_K}=\frac{2\beta\mu\sigma\left[\beta\mu t_K\left(2\phi-(1-\phi)^2(1-t_K)\right)+\sigma(2+\beta t_L)\left((1+\phi^2)t_K-(1-\phi)^2\right)\right]}{(1-t_K)\left[\beta\mu t_K+\sigma(2+\beta t_L)\right]^2\left[\beta\mu t_K\left((1-\phi)^2-4\phi\right)+\sigma(2+\beta t_L)(1-\phi)^2\right]}<0$$

$$\frac{dg}{dt_L^*}=\frac{4\beta\sigma^2\phi\,\beta\mu t_K}{\left[\beta\mu t_K+\sigma(2+\beta t_L)\right]^2\left[\beta\mu t_K\left((1-\phi)^2-4\phi\right)+\sigma(2+\beta t_L)(1-\phi)^2\right]}<0$$

$$\frac{dg}{dt_K^*}=-\frac{4\sigma\phi\,\beta\mu t_K\left(2\beta\mu t_K+\sigma(2+\beta t_L)-\beta\mu\right)}{(1-t_K)\left[\beta\mu t_K+\sigma(2+\beta t_L)\right]^2\left[\beta\mu t_K\left((1-\phi)^2-4\phi\right)+\sigma(2+\beta t_L)(1-\phi)^2\right]}>0$$

# Appendix 3.B Public Consumption Good

In the following sections the model described in the main section of this chapter will be modified by replacing ('hard') public infrastructure by a public consumption good. In the logic of the introductory part, this setup may also be seen as reflecting 'soft' public infrastructure like education, property rights or an independent legal system. Government spending is now directed to finance a public consumption good instead of public infrastructure.

## 3.B.1 The Model

Each domestic consumer has a quasi-linear utility function given by

$$u=C_A+\mu\ln C_X+\delta\ln[1+b]-\left[\mu(\ln\mu-1)\right]\text{ with }C_X=\left[\int_0^M x_i^{\frac{\sigma-1}{\sigma}}di\right]^{\frac{\sigma}{\sigma-1}}\quad(3.B.1)$$

where $\sigma > 1$, $\mu > 0$ and $\delta > 0$. $C_A$ is consumption of the outside numéraire good, $C_X$ represents the consumption of the manufacturing composite as in Dixit and Stiglitz (1977), $x_i$ is the quantity of variety $i$, $M$ is the mass of varieties produced in manufacturing and $\sigma$ is the elasticity of substitution between any two manufacturing varieties. $b$ now measures the consumption of the public good provided by the government. For an individual with net income $y$, the budget constraint is

$$C_A + \int_0^M p_i x_i di = y \tag{3.B.2}$$

where $p_i$ is the consumer price of variety $i$. Utility maximization leads to the demand functions $x_i$, $C_X$, $C_A$ and indirect utility $v$:

$$C_A = y - \mu, \qquad C_X = \frac{\mu}{P}, \qquad x_i = \frac{\mu P^{\sigma-1}}{p_i^{\sigma}} \tag{3.B.3}$$

$$v = y - \mu \ln P + \delta \ln[1 + b] \tag{3.B.4}$$

where

$$P \equiv \left[ \int_0^M p_i^{1-\sigma} di \right]^{\frac{1}{1-\sigma}} \tag{3.B.5}$$

is the perfect CES price index for the manufacturing composite. To ensure that the consumption of the outside good is positive $\mu < y$ is assumed to always hold.

The numéraire good is produced with labor as the only input under a linear technology: $X_A = N_A$, where $X_A$ is output and $N_A$ is the input of labor. Perfect competition implies that this good is priced at marginal costs. Hence, the wage equals labor's marginal product (i.e. one). Costless trade implies the equalization of the wage across regions at unity.

Each variety of manufactures is supplied by a single firm $i$. Each firm requires one unit of physical capital to be able to produce at all. One unit of each variety is then produced with $c$ units of labor. Total costs of a domestic firm $i$ are therefore given by $R + cX_i$, where $R$ denotes the compensation of a unit of capital and $X_i$ is total output. Trade costs $\tau \geq 1$ are of the iceberg type: only $\frac{1}{\tau}$ of a unit bought in the foreign region arrives for consumption. With producer prices indicated by a hat, we have $p_i = \hat{p}_i$ for domestic products. For imported varieties, $p_j = \tau \hat{p}_j$ where $j$ denotes varieties produced in foreign. Mill pricing is optimal in the Dixit-Stiglitz model of monopolistic competition. Profits of firm $i$ in the domestic region are

$$\Pi_i = [\hat{p}_i - c] X_i - R. \tag{3.B.6}$$

The provision of a public consumption good has now no effect on business activity. The maximization of profits gives the optimal producer price of each variety

$$\hat{p}_i = \hat{p} = \frac{c\sigma}{\sigma - 1}. \tag{3.B.7}$$

Again, we normalize marginal costs to $c = \frac{(\sigma-1)}{\sigma}$, which implies $\hat{p} = 1$. Hence, the consumer price index of the manufacturing composite in the domestic region is

$$P = \left[ s_N + \phi(1 - s_N) \right]^{\frac{1}{1-\sigma}} \tag{3.B.8}$$

where $s_N$ is the share of firms in the domestic region and where $0 \leq \phi \equiv \tau^{1-\sigma} \leq 1$ stands for the degree of trade freeness. Since each firm requires one unit of physical capital, the number of varieties produced in the domestic region is $s_N$.

In the framework of monopolistic competition, competition drives pure profits to zero and the reward to capital is then equal to the operating profit $\left(\frac{X_i}{\sigma}\right)$. Hence, using (3.B.6), (3.B.7) and the normalization of marginal costs, obtains the following relationship between capital's rate of return in home and the output of firm $i$

$$R = \frac{1}{\sigma} X_i. \tag{3.B.9}$$

Aggregate demand for variety $i$ from home and foreign (which includes indirect demand associated with the iceberg trade costs) can be derived from (3.B.3), (3.B.7), (3.B.8) and their foreign analogues. This yields

$$X_i = \mu\left[\frac{s_L}{s_N + \phi(1-s_N)} + \frac{\phi(1-s_L)}{\phi s_N + (1-s_N)}\right]$$

where the total endowment of labor across the two regions is normalized at unity (i.e. $L^W = 1$).[20] Substituting this market clearing condition into (3.B.9) yields

$$R = \frac{\mu}{\sigma}\left[\frac{s_L}{s_N + \phi(1-s_N)} + \frac{\phi(1-s_L)}{\phi s_N + (1-s_N)}\right]$$

The government levies a tax $t_L$ on labor income and a source tax $t_K$ on capital income. Aggregate net income of the private sector in home is then given by $y = (1-t_L)s_L + (1-t_K)s_K R$ and domestic government's tax receipts amount to $T = t_L s_L + t_K s_N R$ which is taken to finance the public consumption good, so that $b = T = t_L s_L + t_K s_N R$.

The international equilibrium in the manufacturing sector can be represented by a system of three equations which have been put together below for convenience reason. For a given allocation of firms across regions, $s_N$, the rate of return of capital in home, $R$, is determined by (3.B.10) together with (3.B.11) and the rental rate for capital invested in foreign $R^*$ (3.B.10*). Arbitrage ensures that physical capital, and hence firms, move until the after-tax rate of returns are equalized (3.B.11) in an internal location equilibrium

$$R = \frac{\mu}{\sigma}\left[\frac{s_L}{s_N + \phi(1-s_N)} + \frac{\phi(1-s_L)}{\phi s_N + (1-s_N)}\right] \quad (3.B.10)$$

$$R^* = \frac{\mu}{\sigma}\left[\frac{\phi s_L}{s_N + \phi(1-s_N)} + \frac{(1-s_L)}{\phi s_N + (1-s_N)}\right] \quad (3.B.10^*)$$

$$(1-t_K)R = (1-t_K^*)R^*. \quad (3.B.11)$$

20 The quasi-linear utility function implies that the aggregation of demand basically amounts to a head count.

## 3.B.2 Industry Location

These three equations jointly determine the three variables $s_N, R, R^*$. Solving the above illustrated system of three equations gives us the location of industry in home as the share of domestic firms

$$s_N = \frac{1}{2} - \frac{1}{2}\frac{(1+\phi)\left[1-\Lambda\phi-(1+\Lambda)(1-\phi)s_L\right]}{(1-\phi)\left[1-\Lambda\phi-(1-\Lambda)(1+\phi)s_L\right]}, \qquad (3.B.12)$$

where $\Lambda = \frac{1-t_K}{1-t_K^*}$ is an expression for the international capital tax differential with

$$\Lambda \begin{Bmatrix} >1 \\ =1 \\ <1 \end{Bmatrix} \Leftrightarrow \begin{Bmatrix} t_K < t_K^* \\ t_K = t_K^* \\ t_K > t_K^* \end{Bmatrix}.$$

Obviously, neither the domestic nor the foreign tax on labor has an impact on the domestic share of industry. This result is a reflection of the quasi-linear utility function which implies that there is no income effect for manufactured goods.

The impact of taxes and other parameters on the location of firms can best be explained by means of figure 3.B.1 which focuses on the relationship between the domestic share of firms, $s_N$, and the size of the domestic population, $s_L$ (i.e. domestic market size). To obtain interior solutions $s_N \in ]0,1[$ the share of domestic labor has to lie within the interval

$$\frac{\phi(1-\Lambda\phi)}{\Lambda(1-\phi^2)} \le s_L \le \frac{1-\Lambda\phi}{1-\phi^2}.$$

For any $s_L$ at or below (above) the threshold levels of this interval, a boundary solution $s_N = 0$ $(s_N = 1)$ obtains.[21] Moreover, since $s_L$ itself lies within the unit interval, i.e. $s_L \in [0,1]$, it must be the case that $\frac{1}{\phi} > \Lambda > \phi$ in an interior solution. From this condition, we can also conclude that

21 The first of these thresholds has been termed the 'peripherality point' because it indicates the critical market size, at which a region becomes industrialized; c.f. Baldwin et al. (2003).

$$\frac{ds_N}{ds_L}=\frac{1+\phi}{1-\phi}\frac{(\Lambda-\phi)(1-\Lambda\phi)}{\left[1-\Lambda\phi-(1-\Lambda)(1+\phi)s_L\right]^2}>0.$$

Hence, the relationship between the domestic share of firms and the domestic share of the immobile labor force in an interior equilibrium is unambiguously positive.

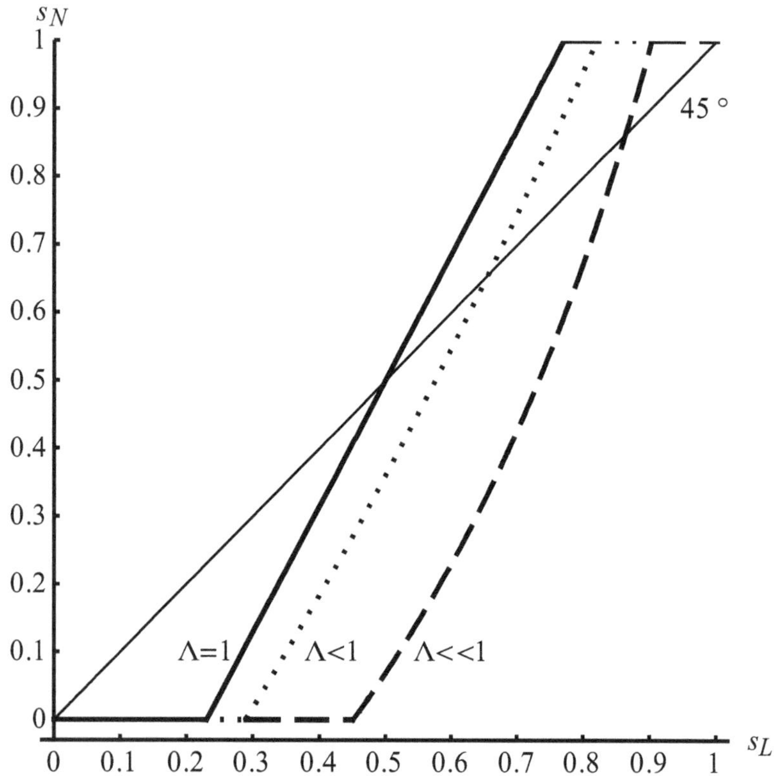


*Figure 3.B.1: Industry location;*
*Figure 3.B.1 is based on the following assumption:* $\phi \equiv \tau^{(1-\sigma)} = 0.3$

The solid black line in figure 3.B.1 depicts the situation where capital taxes are equal in the two regions (i.e. $\Lambda = 1$) and where trade freeness is at an inter-

mediate level $(\phi = 0.3)$. It is easily verified analytically, that under this assumption, $s_N = \frac{1}{2}$ is implied by $s_L = \frac{1}{2}$ for all levels of trade freeness.
Moreover,

$$\left.\frac{ds_N}{ds_L}\right|_{\Lambda=1} > 1,$$

i.e. increasing the domestic market share raises the domestic share of firms more than proportionately. This is the home market effect of Helpman and Krugman (1985). Moreover, note that the slope of this curve is flatter (steeper) the lower (larger) the level of trade freeness (for $\phi \to 1$ trade costs decline and the curve in figure 3.B.1 turns counter clockwise). Hence, any given increase in the domestic share of workers (market size) has a much stronger effect on industrial location when the level of trade freeness is higher.

The location effects of capital taxes are now easily described in terms of figure 3.B.1. If the domestic tax on capital exceeds the foreign tax on capital, i.e. if $\Lambda < 1$, the curve (3.B.12) shifts out to the right implying that the share of firms in the domestic region falls for any given level of its market size.

More generally, raising (reducing) the domestic (foreign) tax on capital shifts the curve out to the right with the effect that the domestic share of firms falls. Summarizing these effects we obtain:

*Result: In an interior equilibrium, the domestic share of industry $s_N$ increases more than proportionately in the domestic share of immobile workers (domestic market size,) $s_L$ (home market effect). Besides, $s_N$ is unaffected by the domestic and foreign tax on labor and is falling (increasing) in the domestic tax (foreign tax) on capital income. The effect of any differential in market size or capital tax rates across regions gets magnified when trade costs between the two regions are reduced.*

We can now explain the new economic geography aspects of this kind of dual income tax by considering the general equilibrium effects on the domestic share of firms as a process of trade integration unfolds between the two regions. These are depicted in figure 3.B.2 which assumes that the domestic government taxes capital and labor at an identical rate whereas the foreign region maintains a lower capital tax rate ($\Lambda < 1$, so that there is a relative tax advantage for capital income in foreign).

The dotted black line shows the case where both regions are of equal size $(s_L = \frac{1}{2})$. Due to its tax advantage, the foreign region has a (slightly) larger share of industry at high trade costs (i.e. high values for $\tau$). In the initial stages of a trade integration process, the tax differential has only a small negative effect on the location of domestic firms. However, once trade integration has proceeded far enough, there is a dramatic relocation of firms into the foreign region.

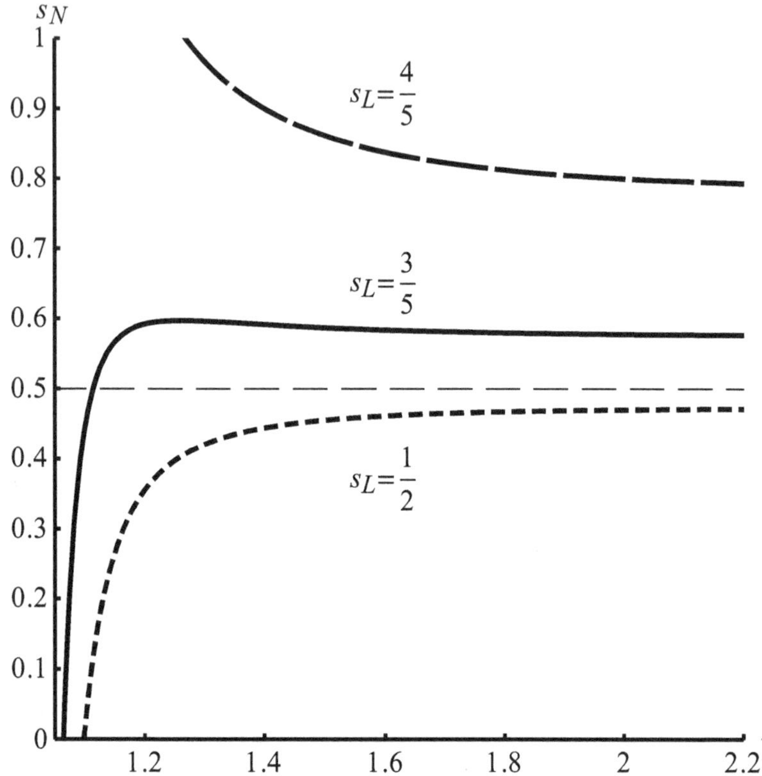


*Figure 3.B.2: Industry location, taxation and market size;*
*Figure 3.B.2 is based on the following assumptions:* $\Lambda = \frac{1-t_K}{1-t_K^*} = 0.9, \sigma = 6$

Ultimately, the domestic region loses all of its industry when trade integration proceeds far enough (i.e. $\tau \to 1$). Now consider the solid black curve which describes the case where the domestic region has a slightly larger population share than foreign $\left(s_L = \frac{3}{5}\right)$. This market size advantage outweighs the tax disadvantage of the domestic economy at early stages of trade integration and over a wider range of trade costs. Indeed, the share of industry first slightly increases with decline trade costs. However, in the end there is again a dramatic flight of industry out of the domestic and into the foreign region if trade costs are low enough. Finally, consider the dashed black line which assumes that the domestic economy is yet larger compared to foreign $\left(s_L = \frac{4}{5}\right)$. In this case, the capital tax disadvantage of home is dominated by the positive market size effect. Actually, the domestic economy gains industry in the process of trade integration.

If the domestic economy decided to follow its trading partner in maintaining a dual income tax system with identical tax rates, a process of trade integration would have no effect on the location of industries when the regions are of equal size and identical with respect to the other parameters. However, a market size advantage could have the effect, that the domestic economy would attract industry when trade integration proceeds.

*Result: Consider a trade integration process between a region which taxes capital and labor at an equal rate and a trading partner region that maintains a dual income tax (i.e. taxes labor at an equal but capital at a lower rate in comparison to home). Even though the initial stages of trade integration have little or no effect on the domestic share of industry, ultimately, the domestic region experiences a dramatic reduction and even a complete loss of industry. Greater market size could shelter the domestic economy from such a loss of industry. However, in order to avoid a complete loss of industry, or even to attract industry when trade integration gets deeper, the market size advantage has to be strong enough.*

## 3.B.3 Optimal Taxation

The previous section presented the effects of dual income taxation on the location of industry with a public good in the utility function. Allowing for differences in the size of each region, tax rates were exogenously modified to illustrate the implications on industry location.

Considering capital mobility and free trade in goods, this section addresses the endogenous choice of the different tax rates on labor and capital income by the government of each region or rather a social planner, based on the indirect utility function (3.B.4).

Before analyzing the individual tax rate setting behavior of a region (i.e. non-cooperative tax rate choice), we begin with deriving the optimal cooperative choice of tax rates, i.e. the tax rates a social planner would implement. It is assumed that both regions differ in their market sizes only (i.e. they are identical in all other respects).[22] The objective function of a benevolent social planner is to choose the capital and labor tax rates so that the indirect utility of the representative household (3.B.4) in each region will be maximized. We can derive the cooperative tax rate by maximizing the joint welfare, which is the sum of indirect utility (3.B.4) of both regions. The first order conditions are to choose the tax rates on capital and labor income such that

$$\frac{\partial v}{\partial t_K}+\frac{\partial v^*}{\partial t_K}\overset{!}{=}0 \quad \text{and} \quad \frac{\partial v}{\partial t_L}+\frac{\partial v^*}{\partial t_L}\overset{!}{=}0 .$$

Thus, the social planner controls for the externalities of taxation.[23] With a public consumption good changes in the labor tax rate do not influence the allocation of capital across the two regions. A social planner thus chooses a uniform capital tax rates for both regions. The tax rate on labor income will then be derived for both regions according to (3.B.14) and (3.B.15). Since we allow for size asymmetries, the tax rates on labor income can differ between the two regions

$$t_K = t_K^* \in [0,1] \tag{3.B.13}$$

$$t_L = \frac{\delta-1}{s_L} - \frac{\mu}{\sigma}\frac{\left[s_L - \phi(1-s_L)\right]}{s_L}\frac{t_K}{(1-\phi)} \tag{3.B.14}$$

$$t_L^* = \frac{\delta-1}{1-s_L} - \frac{\mu}{\sigma}\frac{\left[(1-s_L)-\phi s_L\right]}{(1-s_L)}\frac{t_K}{(1-\phi)}. \tag{3.B.15}$$

With dual income taxation, the social planner has three instruments at his disposal. Referring to (3.B.12) it becomes clear, that a commonly chosen tax rate on capital income does not induce any relocation of industry. Additionally, there is no interaction between the labor tax rate and industry location (i.e. $s_N$).[24] Recognizing that households earn labor and capital income, the obtained results (3.B.13), (3.B.14) and (3.B.15) become obvious: the social planner has a univariant tax rate on capital income. After the tax rate on capital income is set, the

22 Both regions are endowed with an equal share of capital.

23 Changes in the (capital) tax rate in one region affect the (capital) tax receipts in the other region, cf. Zodrow and Mieszkowski (1986).

24 With identical tax rates on capital income the share of industry in region 1 becomes $s_N = \frac{[1+\phi]s_L-\phi}{[1-\phi]}$.

labor tax rates will be adjusted accordingly to the size of each region. Note that with fully identical regions $\left(s_L = \frac{1}{2}\right)$, the tax rate on labor income is identical in both regions

$$t_L = t_L^* = 2(\delta - 1) - \frac{\mu}{\sigma} t_K .$$

As long as the preference for the public consumption good is large enough, $(\delta > 1)$ both tax rates will be non-negative (i.e. there are no subsidies to either factor of production). First of all, (3.B.14) and (3.B.15) reveal that the optimal tax rate on labor income depends on the level of trade integration.

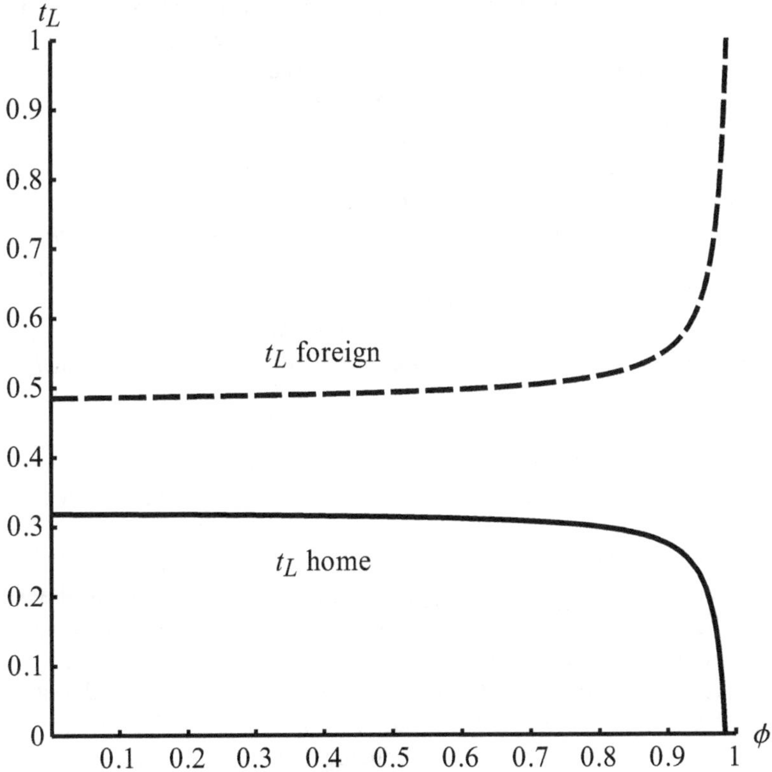


*Figure 3.B.3: Optimal tax rates: social planner;*
*Figure 3.B.3 is based on the following parameters:* $\mu = 0.3, \sigma = 4,$
$\delta = 1.2, t_K = t_K^* = 0.2, s_L = 0.6$

According to the home market effect, industry tends to agglomerate in the larger market. Thus, the larger region has a larger tax base (labor and capital) which translates into lower labor tax rates in the optimum. With decreasing trade costs $(\phi \rightarrow 1)$, additional industry will be attracted and the capital tax base will be further enlarged. As figure 3.B.3 shows, this leads to a reduction of the labor tax rate in the larger region (here: home, cf. the solid black line) and an increase of the labor tax rate in the smaller region (here: foreign, cf. the dashed black line) respectively.[25] Despite the size of the region, the tax rate on labor income depends positively on the preference for the public good and negatively on the tax rate for capital income. With agglomeration forces rising, the optimal tax rate on labor income declines in both regions. The intuition behind this observation is that with increasing agglomeration forces the Ricardian surplus of manufacturing firms increases, enlarging the (capital) tax base. It can also be seen that in this setting the tax burden can be shifted between the factors without welfare reductions in each region due to fiscal externalities.

*Result: A social planner, who aims to maximize the utility of a representative household, adopts non-negative tax rates on labor and capital income as long as the preference for the public good is large enough* $(\delta > 1)$. *Since the social planner chooses a single tax rate on capital income, any differences in the market size between the two regions, imply lower tax rates on labor income for the larger region. With increasing trade integration the optimal labor tax rate in the smaller region increases, while the counterpart in the larger region will be decreased.*

We will now turn to the case where the government of each region individually chooses its tax rates on labor and capital income. Again, the objective of the government is a capital and labor tax rate choice so that the indirect utility of a common household (3.B.4) is maximized. On of the main messages of the basic tax competition model is that under capital mobility differentials in the capital tax rate induce relocation of capital (industry). Thus, there is an externality involved with tax rate changes in one region: if home increases its capital tax rate c.p., industry will relocate to foreign (increasing the tax base in the other region).[26] Since an increase in the tax rate in home will lower the after tax return, the market in home is less profitable, inducing industry to relocate until after-tax returns are in equilibrium again (3.B.12). Therefore, the main question is whether a national tax policy will have an incentive to follow a well known beg-

25 This is shown analytically in section 3.B.5.
26 Cf. Wilson (1999) and Zodrow and Mieszkowski (1986).

gar-my-neighbor policy, leaving capital untaxed or, what is more, to subsidize it: this would lead to an inefficient Nash equilibrium. Acting independently, the objective of the home government would be

$$\frac{\partial v}{\partial t_K}\overset{!}{=}0 \quad \text{and} \quad \frac{\partial v}{\partial t_L}\overset{!}{=}0 \quad \text{respectively.}$$

Taking the other region's tax rates as given and considering potential firm relocations, the tax rate on capital and labor income will now be

$$t_K = (1-\phi)H \tag{3.B.16}$$

$$t_L = \frac{\delta - 1}{s_L} - \frac{\mu}{\sigma}\frac{\left[s_L - (1-s_L)\phi\right]}{s_L}H, \tag{3.B.17}$$

with $\quad H = \dfrac{\phi - \sigma(2+3\phi) + (3\sigma - 1)(1+\phi)s_L}{(\sigma-1)(1+\phi)\left[\phi(1-s_L)+s_L\right]}.$

The upper panel of figure 3.B.4 shows that for fully symmetric regions the tax on capital will always be negative (i.e. capital will be subsidized) which is shown analytically in section 3.B.5. The subsidy on capital will be higher, the stronger the agglomeration forces are. Note that the subsidy on capital income as well as the tax on labor income decrease with the degree of trade freeness $(\phi \to 1)$.[27]

This result expresses the positive welfare effect associated with trade integration: a decline in trade costs translates into a decreasing price index (3.B.8) which makes it less important for a region to host industry. Therefore, the government in home does not have to compete as fiercely for capital as it would have if trade costs were higher. The larger the differences in the size of the regions become, the smaller the capital subsidy provided by the larger region will be. For medium differences in size, the larger region puts a positive tax rate on capital income. With increasing trade integration this tax on capital income will be reduced and eventually turned into a subsidy (as long as the differences in size are not too large), which will again be lowered with further trade

27 This is true as long as there are no corner solutions for the tax and subsidy rate as will be the case for very high values of $\delta$.

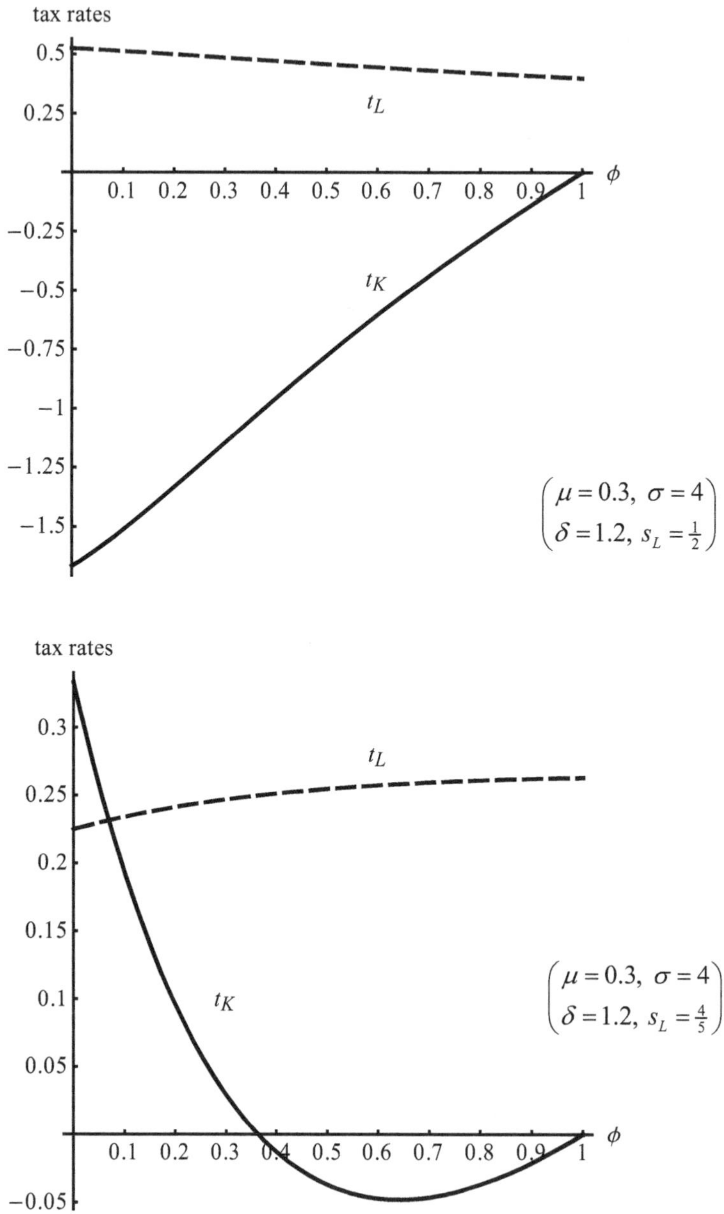


*Figure 3.B.4: Optimal tax rates: Nash solution*

integration.[28] This behavior indicates a fiercer competition for mobile capital as in the case for symmetric regions originating from the larger region (cf. lower panel of figure 3.B.4).

Two reasons can be found to explain this observation: the externality that comes along with the changes in the capital tax rates induces industry to relocate. Since there are agglomeration forces at work, the home market effect (home market magnification) indicates that these relocation effects are non-linear (cf. figure 3.B.1). Therefore, though integration comes along with welfare improvement due to a declining price index, the negative effects of maintaining an unadjusted (capital) tax differential will dominate the former.

*Result: An independently acting government takes potential industry relocation into consideration in setting its tax rates. For fully symmetric regions, competition for mobile capital is fiercer, the less integrated the regions are (i.e. the subsidy on capital income is higher, the lower $\phi$ is). From the perspective of a relatively large region, (capital) tax competition first becomes fiercer and then decreases again with a further trade integration of the two regions. Thus, size and degree of trade openness shelter the relatively large region.*

## 3.B.4 Conclusion

Comparing the results obtained in the main section of this chapter where the tax receipts were taken to finance public infrastructure, it is first necessary to note that the relocation effects of tax rate changes differ: manipulations of the labor tax rate do not alter the location decision of a firm in the case of the public consumption good, while tax rate changes of the labor tax rate do have an effect on the location decision in the case of public infrastructure.

We could see that the role of the relative market size remains unchanged: the relative larger region can impose higher tax rates on capital income, without fearing to fully lose its industrial base, indicating that the relative market size acts as shelter form the loss of the industrial base due to differentials of the tax rate on the mobile factor. This observation is similar to the results obtained by the BTCM though the reasoning is different. In the above setting the reason for industry to remain in the high tax region is the home market effect.

28 The critical level of trade integration for which the subsidy becomes a tax as well as the level of trade integration for which the subsidy will be decreased is analytically illustrated in section 3.B.5.

Strong industry location effects due to differentials in the capital tax rate favoring the low (capital) tax country can be obtained when the regions are fully symmetric. These location effects could also be seen in the main section of this chapter and they point to the same direction as the BTCM.

The analysis of tax competition with a public consumption good also delivered qualitatively the same results compared to the main section. With identical regions in all respects, both countries subsidize the mobile factor while the immobile factor is taxed at a positive rate. Note, however, that trade integration eases tax competition, since a decline of transportations costs leads to lower subsidies as well as lower labor tax rates.

An additional insight of this appendix contributes to the analysis of tax competition between regions that differ in their market size.[29] Differences in the size of one region alter the above results: the relatively larger region now sets a positive tax rate on capital and labor income. Thus, depending on the relative size differential, the tax rate on the mobile factor can well be transferred into a subsidy on capital and vice versa. With declining trade integration, the tax rate on capital will be lowered and to compensate for the loss of revenues, the tax rate of labor income will be raised. According to figure 3.B.4, economic integration first increases tax competition (the capital tax rate will be lowered and even turns into a subsidy) and then lowers the degree of tax competition (capital subsidies will be reduced). Figure 3.B.4 also reveals that the subsidies are the largest under an intermediate level of trade integration which is when agglomeration forces are the largest.

Therefore, it seems that the main conclusions are robust as to whether government spending is directed towards a public consumption good or towards the provision of public infrastructure.

## 3.B.5 Analytical Annotations

The analytical presentation of the effects of trade integration on the labor tax rate

in home $$\frac{\partial t_L}{\partial \phi} = \frac{\mu}{\sigma} \frac{(1-2s_L)}{(1-\phi)^2} \frac{t_K}{s_L} < 0 \quad \text{for} \quad s_L > \frac{1}{2}$$

29 Due to complexity of the equations this analysis could not have been performed in the main section.

and in foreign $\frac{\partial t_L^*}{\partial \phi} = -\frac{\mu}{\sigma}\frac{(1-2s_L)}{(1-\phi)^2}\frac{t_K}{(1-s_L)} > 0 \quad$ for $\quad s_L > \frac{1}{2}$

shows that, with increasing trade freeness, the tax rate on labor income will be reduced in the larger region and increased in the smaller region.

With fully symmetric regions the optimal Nash-tax rates on capital and labor income are

$$t_K = -F \qquad \text{and} \qquad t_L = 2(\delta - 1) + \frac{\mu}{\sigma}F$$

with $\quad F = \frac{(1-\phi)[1+\sigma+\phi(3\sigma-1)]}{(\sigma-1)(1+\phi)^2} > 0,$

indicating that in this setup capital will always be subsidized. With (sufficient) differences in the market size of the regions,

$$\phi = \frac{\sigma - 1}{(3\sigma-1)(1-s_L)} - 1$$

indicates the level of trade integration at which the tax on capital income turns into a subsidy. At

$$\phi = -\frac{\sigma}{2\sigma-1} + \frac{\sqrt{(\sigma-1)(1-s_L)[s_L(3\sigma-1)-\sigma]}}{(2\sigma-1)(1-s_L)}$$

a further decline of trade costs will lead to a reduction of the subsidy until it turns 0 at $\phi = 1$.

# 4 Economic Integration and the Taxation of Multinationals: Separate Accounting vs. Formula Apportionment

Multinational Enterprises (MNE) are a distinctive characteristic of the globalized economy. Though not all, many multinational firms are big corporations being able to exercise substantial market power. Since they are spread over a range of different countries, they can circumvent national policies and regulations by shifting activities between their subsidiaries. This footloose character of multinational firms creates the fear that fiscal autonomy of countries can be undermined by shifting profits from high- to low-tax jurisdictions, using transfer pricing. Thus, for the European Union, a major reform of taxing multinational firms will be introduced: the present system of separate taxation (SA), in which profits are taxed in the region where the subsidiary is located, will be replaced by a system of formula apportionment (FA), in which all profits of a multinational firm will be lumped together and taxed with an average tax rate that is made of several apportionment factors reflecting the economic activity of the MNE in various regions. The present chapter analyzes the effects of economic integration on the use of transfer pricing under the two different taxation schemes of SA and FA, using a model of oligopolistic competition in a market with spatial product differentiation. In lowering the traveling costs a consumer would have to pay in order to reach the seller (i.e. modeling a closer integration of the economy), we will find that in a more integrated economy the transfer price reacts more sensitively to relative tax rate variations in a FA setting than in the SA scenario.[♦]

---

♦ This chapter has partially been presented at the 9th Conference of the "Association for Public Economic Theory", July 2008, Seoul, Korea, at the 64th Conference of the "International Institute of Public Finance", August 2008, Maastricht, The Netherlands and at the 101st Annual Conference on Taxation of the "National Tax Association", November 2008, Philadelphia, PA, USA. Financial support from the German Federal Reserve Bank (Deutsche Bundesbank) (Vortragsprämie 2008-766) and the German Research Foundation (DFG) (KON 1107/2008 MU 2882/2-1) is gratefully acknowledged.

## 4.1 Introduction

There is an ongoing discussion in the European Union (EU) about a harmonization or co-ordination of taxes on corporate income.[1] Meanwhile, the European Commission (COM) decided to implement a system of formula apportionment to tax corporate income of multinational enterprises (MNE).[2]

MNE have become a fundamental part of the world economy in the last decade. The process of an increased cross-boarder integration of markets for goods, services and capital spurred the slicing up of value chains increasing the dominance of Multinational Enterprises in world production.[3] This can be inferred by data illustrated in OECD (2007a), showing that foreign direct investments (FDI) have been the fastest growing segment of international transactions within the last decade. Since FDI are necessary to set up affiliated companies which make up a MNE many authors use these both terms interchangeably[4].

While the notion 'multinational' supports the idea of companies with a vast geographical dispersion around the globe through different affiliated branches, UNCTAD (2007) shows that geographical proximity becomes a more crucial aspect of recent bilateral FDI relations. Hence, the FDI data investigated in UNCTAD (2007) reveal that European countries share a more-than-average FDI intensity with each other than with countries outside the EU.[5]

In comparison to purely national firms, MNE stand out for being relatively large and having competitive market power. Within a MNE the different entities exchange goods and services as well as intangible assets (e.g. property rights, patents, technology transfer, etc.) or transfer funds to run the business. To settle this kind of primary input exchange across the different companies belonging to a MNE use transfer prices.[6] Due to their global presence, they can circumvent national policies and regulations much more easily than their national business rivals. These specific characteristics of multinational firms as well as the recent developments in transnational activity of firms have stimulated the public debate about the tax treatment of MNE. Since a more detailed illustration of stylized

---

1 Devereux (2004) offers a draft historical overview, showing the proposals for corporate tax co-ordination; also cf. Schratzenstaller (2007).

2 In COM (2005, 2007c) legislative measures for implementing a "common consolidated corporate tax base" (CCCTB) are proposed.

3 See e.g. OECD (2007b).

4 Cf. Navaretti and Venables (2004).

5 This is also true for the USA and Canada as well as for Japan and other Asian Countries.

6 Cf. OECD (2005).

facts about FDI/ MNE would be too extensive at this point, appendix 4.C delivers some data on the development of FDI.

The EU consists of numerous nation states with different national tax systems. Currently, a multinational enterprise with affiliates in several member states of the EU is not treated as a single tax unit. Rather, each foreign subsidiary is a separate entity and thus subject to the corporate tax code of the state where the subsidiary is located. Referring to the fiscal accounts of MNE entities, national tax authorities only tax the share of MNE overall profits accruing to MNE affiliates within the jurisdictional territory. This system of separate accounting (SA) is subject to controversial debates, since it offers multinational firms the possibility of a strategic interaction of the location of investment, production and profits. Due to an extended network of affiliated companies, a multinational firm could easily shift profits from high-tax to low-tax jurisdictions or countries. With an increasing integration of production procedures through exchanging services and primary inputs, MNE can artificially increase costs of production in regions with high tax rates in choosing a high transfer price for these intermediate goods or services. Thus, corporate profits can be transferred to other entities of the MNE, which are located in regions with lower tax rates on profits. Swenson (2001), Clausing (2003) as well as Bernard et al. (2006) deliver empirical evidence that MNE use indeed transfer pricing to shift profits in order to avoid taxation.[7]

In the present tax system of SA, costly control systems have been installed by governments to estimate the 'true' value of services and intermediate products exchanged by MNE entities across national borders and to monitor closely the transfer prices used. Such measures aim to prevent MNE from an excessive use of transfer pricing and to force MNE to apply the arm's length principle also for intra-firm transactions.[8]

Following the example of Canada[9]/ USA on taxing its domestic firms operating in several provinces/ states, the European Commission aims to replace the contemporary way of taxing MNE profits with a formula apportionment (FA)

---

7 However, Grubert (2003) shows that transfer pricing is not the only tool applied by MNE to relocate profits. Mintz and Weichenrieder (2005) or Hines (2005) carry out empirical studies, illustrating that MNE also use various kinds of direct financial transactions (e.g., intra-firm loans) to shift profits. Clausing (2009) tries to disentangle the tax revenues losses for the U.S. government due to real and financial responses to tax policies.

8 According to OECD (2009) the arm's length principle should also be applied to intra-firm transactions, i.e. intra-firm transactions should carry the same price tag than market transactions.

9 See e.g. Wildasin (2000) and Nielsen et al. (2003).

profit tax scheme.[10] This system takes the overall profits of the whole multinational firm and allocates the tax base to the jurisdictions, in which the MNE operates affiliated entities, according to the business activity of each affiliate. Taking the MNE as a single business unit, certain corporate key variables which should serve as proxies for the entrepreneurial activity in each jurisdiction (e.g., assets, turnover and/ or payroll) are employed to calculate formulas to divide the overall tax base between the jurisdictions. Since this system takes the overall profits of the whole multinational firm and allocates the tax base to the jurisdictions, in which the MNE operates affiliated entities, this system is praised for not offering any scope for profit shifting.

According to the European Commission, implementing a common consolidated corporate tax base (CCCTB) for European multinational companies would end the strategic flow of profits and thus remedy distortions in firm's location decisions and cross-boarder investments. This would decrease compliance costs, foster international tax planning and enhance the efficiency of corporate taxation. Finally, corporate investment would be stimulated spurring growth in Europe.[11]

The model presented in this chapter investigates the impact of economic integration on the transfer pricing behavior of a multinational corporation for services provided by the main office for affiliated companies. It aims to analyze which of the both tax systems induces multinational firms to engage more intensely in transfer pricing under economic integration for a given difference in tax rates. We do not focus on a conceptual comparison between these two taxing systems. The role of double tax relief agreements will also not be addressed here. Besides, there is no discussion about the possible technical problems that come along with a shift from separate accounting to formula apportionment. However, there will be a short discussion about the role of apportionment factors on the obtained results.

To keep things as simple as possible, a stylized approach is applied. We envision a world consisting of two regions and two enterprises, one MNE (consisting of a main office and an affiliate) and one single firm. An oligopolistic Bertrand competition model of spatial product differentiation à la Hotelling (1929) is then used to highlight the transfer pricing behavior in a partial equilibrium setting. Two firms, the affiliate of the MNE main office and a competitor, are each located at the end of a straight line (region B), each producing and selling a

10 Cf. Devereux (2004) and COM (2005, 2007c). The progress of the Working Group "Common Consolidated Corporate Tax Base (CCCTB)" which has been installed by the EU Commission can be tracked online under http://ec.europa.eu/taxation_customs/taxation/company_tax/common_tax_base/index_en.htm

11 See Wellisch (2004) and COM (2005, 2007c).

homogeneous good. By choosing the price of the final consumption good, both firms are competing for customers who incur traveling expenses to purchase the good from one of the two firms. To account for the fact that the administrative center of the MNE (region A) and the affiliate can engage in profit shifting, we assume that the main office delivers business services, which the affiliate has to pay for. This transfer will be modeled in a broader way, so that it can also be interpreted in terms of a loan or the direct shift of financial funds.[12] While the affiliate is allowed to maximize its profits by choosing autonomously the optimal price in its market (region B), the holding company selects the optimal transfer price to maximize the overall profits of the MNE. This offers the scope for strategic interaction of market power and competition in the region B market.

The structure of the model can easily be applied to a whole range of different industries within the EU. Companies operating on markets for homogeneous products can be found on all stages of production.[13] As an example for the commodities processing industries, we would propose the market for newsprint and magazine paper[14,15], the market for rustless steel[14,15] and discarded copper[14]. Further examples for industrial goods can be found on the market for standardized plant and machinery equipment, e.g. supersonic testing facilities[14] or heavy steam raising units[14] as well as machine tools. Parts for automobiles[15] as well as construction material[16] can further be added. Finally, considering consumer goods, pharmaceutical products could be proposed[17].

The model carries the following results. First, no matter which taxation scheme is applied, the MNE has always an incentive to engage in profit shifting to counteract adverse tax rate changes. In both taxing regimes transfer pricing is used to lift the affiliate in the position of a Stackelberg leader (strategic effect). Besides, taxes also deliver an incentive to use transfer pricing (tax effect). In both tax scenarios, transfer pricing is used to shift taxes from the high-tax to the low-tax jurisdiction. Under SA the mechanism is straight forward: a higher (lower) transfer price for services extracts (transfers) profits from (to) the affiliate which decreases (increases) its tax liabilities. Depending on the tax differen-

12 Examples for different ways of intra-firm resource allocation mentioned in the business literature can be found in Mahoney (1992) (e.g., loans) or in Rajan and Reichelstein (2004) (e.g., capital budgeting, delegated contracting).

13 Information about the degree of product homogeneity has been taken from the main reports of the German Monopolies Commission (Monopolkommission).

14 Cf. Monopolkommission (2000).

15 Cf. Monopolkommission (2002).

16 Cf. Monopolkommission (2004).

17 Cf. Monopolkommission (1998).

tial between the main office and the affiliate, the overall tax liabilities of the MNE are depressed. Under FA the mechanism is more complex. Tax liabilities are not shifted directly, but indirectly by changing the scale of production. Since the tax formula depends on the output of the affiliate, a shift in the tax liabilities can only work through this channel. This is a crucial aspect of the analysis which will be highlighted later on.

Secondly, with decreasing traveling costs, i.e. a further integration of the economy, the incentive for profit shifting, in reply for increasing tax differentials, declines under SA. With a decline in traveling costs, markets become more competitive and this reduces the strategic effect. Therefore, market integration limits the scope for transfer pricing to shift profits. Things look different for formula apportionment. Tax liability depends on the return. To limit tax payments in the region with the higher tax rates induces the enterprise to lower the output. According to the prevalent tax differential the whole production will be changed and optimally adjusted.

This indicates that with further integration a change of the current system of MNE profit taxation (i.e. SA) to FA may not lead to the expected results, namely, to discourage MNE to use transfer pricing for profit shifting.

Models of oligopolistic competition and strategic interaction have been used in international economics (cf. Brander and Spencer (1985) and Eaton and Grossman (1986))[18] and also in the setting of MNE behavior. Focusing on separate accounting only, Schjelderup and Sørgard (1997) compare the incentives for MNE to engage in transfer pricing under Cournot and Bertrand competition, using imperfect substitutes in the later case. They conclude that the optimal transfer price depends on the underlying market structure. In a numerical example they show that the transfer pricing incentives can be very strong due to an interaction of a strategic and a taxation motive. Nielsen et al. (2003) compare the different incentives for transfer pricing under SA and FA. Their Cournot competition model with perfects substitutes does not feature economic integration. They show that firms still have an incentive to use transfer pricing to shift profits under FA and conclude that a shift from SA to FA may even strengthen profit shifting behavior, due to strategic considerations of market power.

Taking spatial aspects of competition and taxation into consideration, the following model shows that an increase in consumer's mobility (i.e. an increase in economic integration) actually encourages multinational firms to use transfer pricing more intensely under FA than under SA. It thus highlights an important issue that should be taken into consideration in the debate of the European Commission's reform plans of corporate taxation.

---

18 A survey of this topic can also be found in Helpman and Krugman (1989).

Corporate Taxation in the context of a consolidated tax base is a widely debated issue in literature. The aspects and problems of FA are closely reported in Wellisch (2003a,b) and Wellisch (2004). McLure and Weiner (2000) and Hellerstein and McLure (2004) provide a more general analysis of introducing formula apportionment of corporate income in the EU referring to the problems that arose in the USA. Further articles concerning efforts of corporate tax harmonization in a broader setting, are provided by Mintz (2004), Sørensen (2004) and most recently by Nicodème (2009).

This chapter is set up as follows. The basic model will be presented in the next section. Section 4.3 then studies the optimal choice of transfer pricing under separate accounting and formula apportionment while section 4.4 performs the analysis under the assumption of economic integration before section 4.5 concludes.

# 4.2 The Model

## 4.2.1 Basic Structure

Since the objective of the model is to shed light on the optimal choice of transfer pricing within a multinational firm (MNE), we abstract from the basic decision concerning the optimal location choice for all kinds of production and distribution facilities used for serving customers in different market places.[19] A further simplification applies by assuming that the MNE does not maintain two different systems of bookkeeping (one for the tax authorities and one for internal controlling purpose)[20] since this would incur high transactions costs.[21]

Figure 4.1 shows that the MNE consists of a main office, located in region A and an affiliate, located in region B. The main office produces a final consumption good, which is solely sold in region A, so that the central office acts as a monopolist in this market. The affiliate produces and sells a final consumption good in region B. Within the holding company funds can be transferred between the main office and the affiliate. These transfers are related to the output pro-

19 Grosse (1985) develops a model explaining major MNE decisions in an imperfect competition setting.

20 Cf. Choi and Day (1998). However, a survey conducted by Ernst & Young (2007b) reveals that transfer pricing is mainly a taxation issue.

21 The purpose of two different bookkeeping systems is illustrated in Knirsch (2007).

duced by the affiliate, so that they can be thought of as kinds of administrative services that the affiliate has to pay for.

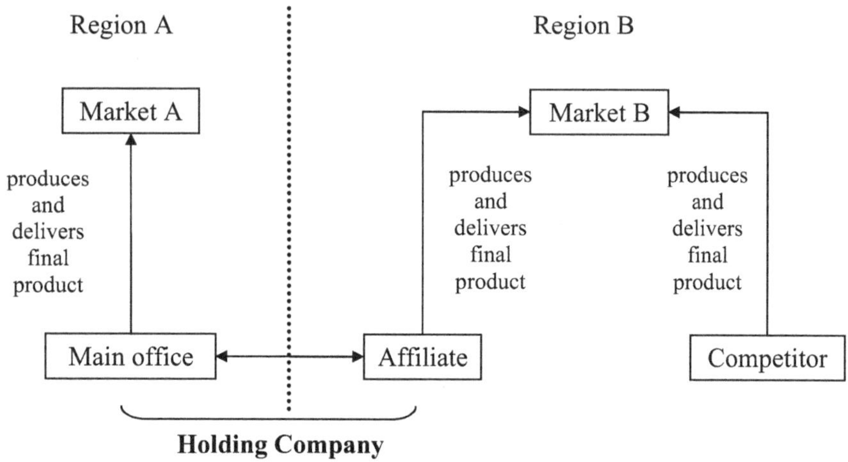


*Figure 4.1: Illustration of the basic model*

However, they can also be seen as loans or other funds transferred from one party to another, depending on the economic activity of the affiliate. There is an additional business rival operating in region B. The structure of this market builds on a simple version of an oligopolistic competition model with spatial product differentiation, as introduced by Hotelling (1929).[22] The two competing firms $i$ $(i=1,2)$ are each offering a homogeneous good at a positive price $p_i$ on the market in region B. This market place will be illustrated by a horizontal line, on which the consumers of this good are equally distributed; the number of consumers is normalized at 1. Each firm is immobile and located at the very end of this line, and produces a homogeneous good at constant marginal cost $c_i > 0$. In order to buy a unit of the good, each consumer has to travel to one of the two firms, incurring linear travel expenses $(\tau > 0)$ thereby.[23] In the following we will therefore take $\tau$ as a measure for the degree of spatial product differentiation in region B. In order to minimize expenses, a consumer will always buy the good from the cheapest producer (in terms of distance and price). Both firms

22 The description in this part draws on Bester (1992).
23 These travel expenses can be measured in real or money terms.

have similar costs of production, and we assume that they are always operating in equilibrium. The firm specific demand functions in region B are

$$x_1(p_1, p_2) = \frac{\tau + p_2 - p_1}{2\tau} \tag{4.1a}$$

for the affiliate (index 1) and

$$x_2(p_1, p_2) = \frac{\tau + p_1 - p_2}{2\tau} \tag{4.1b}$$

for the business rival (index 2), with $x_i$ denoting firm-specific consumer demand of the homogeneous good from the affiliate and the competitor, and with $p_i$ expressing the corresponding sales price.[24] To keep things simple, we assume a linear demand function for the final good sold by the main office (index 3) in region A

$$x_3 = a - p_3, \tag{4.1c}$$

with $x_3$ indicating the demand, $p_3$ showing the sales price of the monopolist good and the demand parameter $a > 0$. The profits of the main office $(\pi_3)$, the affiliate $(\pi_1)$, the competitor $(\pi_2)$ as well as the holding company $(\pi_{MNE})$ can then be derived

$$\pi_3 = [p_3 - c_3]x_3 + \theta x_1 \tag{4.2a}$$

$$\pi_1 = [p_1 - c_1]x_1 - \theta x_1 \tag{4.2b}$$

$$\pi_2 = [p_2 - c_2]x_2 \tag{4.2c}$$

$$\pi_{MNE} = \pi_3 + \pi_1. \tag{4.2d}$$

The transfer price between the main office and the affiliate is denoted by $\theta$. The sales price is $p_i$, $c_i$ expresses constant marginal costs of production and $x_i$ states the quantities of production $(i = 1,2,3)$. Note that the transfers between the main office and the affiliate depend on the output of the affiliate, indicating that a higher output also requires more services or intermediate products. Firms aim

24 The two demand functions are derived in appendix 4.B.

to maximize their profits, using the price as the strategic variable. Note that the term transfer price generally describes the chosen price for these MNE internal transactions. The term is not bound to taxation issues linked to MNE activity according to OECD (2009).

## 4.2.2 The Strategic Effect of Transfer Pricing

In the following, we assume a two stage game: first, the central office of the MNE would set and announce its transfer price $\theta$. Subsequently, the affiliate and its business rival maximize their profits by setting their sales prices independently, taking the transfer price as given. Solving this problem via backward induction, the first order conditions of the affiliate and the business rival in region B can be derived by differentiating each firm's profits with respect to its own price

$$\frac{\partial \pi_1}{\partial p_1} = \frac{\tau + \theta + c_1 - 2p_1 + p_2}{2\tau} \overset{!}{=} 0 \tag{4.3a}$$

$$\frac{\partial \pi_2}{\partial p_2} = \frac{\tau + c_2 - 2p_2 + p_1}{2\tau} \overset{!}{=} 0 . \tag{4.3b}$$

These two equations can then be resolved to get the following reaction functions

$$p_1 = \frac{\tau + c_1 + \theta + p_2}{2} \tag{4.4a}$$

$$p_2 = \frac{\tau + c_2 + p_1}{2} , \tag{4.4b}$$

illustrated by the solid black lines in figure 4.2, labeled $R_1(p_2)$ and $R_2(p_1)$ respectively.

Solving (4.4a) and (4.4b) then indicates the pair of optimal prices

$$p_1^* = \frac{3\tau + 2(c_1 + \theta) + c_2}{3} \tag{4.5a}$$

$$p_2^* = \frac{3\tau + 2c_2 + (c_1 + \theta)}{3}, \tag{4.5b}$$

as well as the pair of optimal quantities demanded

$$x_1^* = \frac{3\tau - c_1 + c_2 - \theta}{6\tau} \tag{4.6a}$$

$$x_2^* = \frac{3\tau + c_1 - c_2 + \theta}{6\tau}, \tag{4.6b}$$

which both depend on the transfer price, chosen by the main office of the MNE. Then the main office maximizes its monopoly profit, choosing the optimal price in region A, in which it is the only vendor of the good $x_3$. The first order condition of the main office in region A will be

$$\frac{\partial \pi_3}{\partial p_3} = a + c_3 - 2p_3 \overset{!}{=} 0$$

indicating the optimal price $p_3^*$ and optimal quantity $x_3^*$ the main office charges in its monopoly market (region A)

$$p_3^* = \frac{a + c_3}{2} \quad \text{and} \quad x_3^* = \frac{a - c_3}{2}.$$

Finally, taking the reaction functions (4.4a) and (4.4b) into consideration, the first order condition of the MNE is the differentiation of its overall profits (4.2d) with respect to the transfer price

$$\frac{\partial \pi_{MNE}}{\partial \theta} = \frac{3\tau - 4\theta - c_1 + c_2}{18\tau} \overset{!}{=} 0$$

leading to an optimal transfer price of

$$\theta^* = \frac{3\tau - c_1 + c_2}{4}. \tag{4.7}$$

Substituting (4.7) into (4.5a) and (4.5b) then gives the optimal prices chosen by the affiliate and the competitor

$$p_1^* = \frac{3\tau + c_1 + c_2}{2} \tag{4.8}$$

$$p_2^* = \frac{5\tau + c_1 + 2c_2}{4} \tag{4.9}$$

in region B.

The idea of the strategic effect of the transfer price is illustrated in figure 4.2. If the MNE main office chooses a transfer price $\theta = 0$, the intersection of the reaction functions $R_1(p_2)$ and $R_2(p_1)$ shows the unique Nash equilibrium of the Bertrand competition game in region B, labeled N in figure 4.2. Furthermore, the two sets of u-shaped lines labeled $\pi_1$ (solid black lines) and $\pi_2$ (dashed black lines) indicate the level of profits of the subsidiary and the competitor respectively, with lines further up/ to the right representing higher profit levels.

Since the consumption goods are perfect substitutes, the demand for a good depends positively on the price charged by the competitor. Thus, the reaction functions have a positive slope indicating that the firms' strategies are strategic complements.[25] The reaction function of the affiliate (4.4a) directly depends on the transfer price. An increase of $\theta$ would induce the subsidiary to raise the price of its final good as can be seen in (4.5a). This would shift the subsidiary's reaction function to the right, shown by the dotted black line in figure 4.2. Note that this shift of the reaction function would increase the profits of the subsidiary, as long as the increase is not too large (i.e. to the left of point S in figure 4.2).

Therefore, by choosing an appropriate transfer price the main office can trigger a favorable reaction of the competitor and thus lift the affiliate in the position of a Stackelberg leader, increasing its profit.[26] The last iso-profit line that is just tangent to the reaction function of the competitor indicates the maximum profit and thus gives the main office the optimum transfer price, respectively.

25 It's optimal for one company to charge a higher price, the higher the price of the competitor is.

26 This will also increase the profit of the competitor (Bertrand setting).

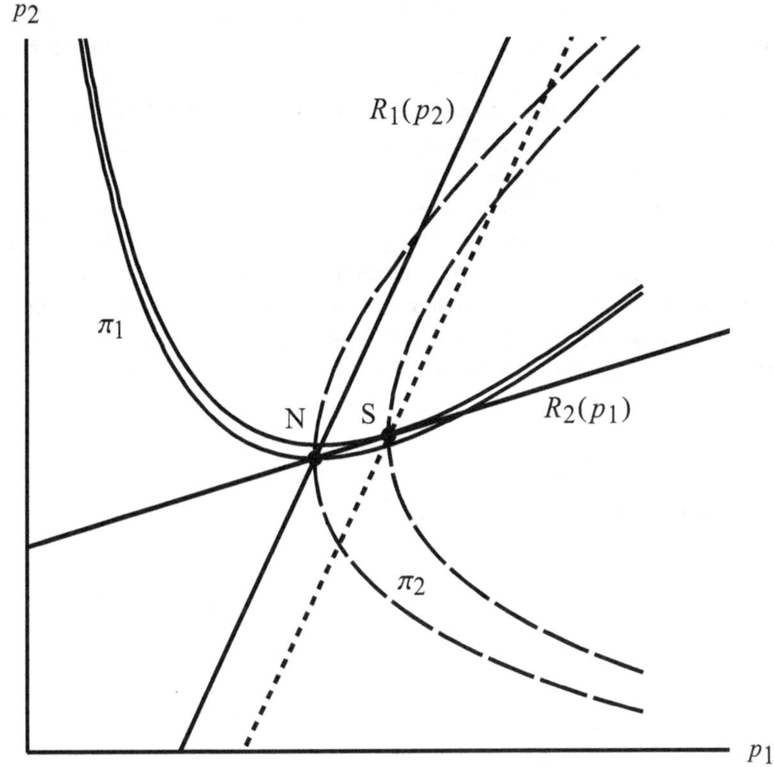


*Figure 4.2: Illustration of the strategic effect*

Equation (4.7) reveals that in this scenario the transfer price will be larger than 0, as long as $\tau > \frac{c_1 - c_2}{3}$ holds. Since $\tau$ is an index of the degree of spatial product differentiation and $(c_1 - c_2)$ reflects the differences in production costs between the affiliate and the competitor, the transfer price exceeds 0 as long as market power (due to spatial market separation $\tau$) is persistent enough to dominate certain differences in the cost pattern of production.

## 4.3 Transfer Pricing under Taxation

The proceeding section illustrated the benefits for a holding company to give an affiliate autonomy in its own pricing decision and set a transfer price at the central level, taking the affiliate's decision into consideration. Thus, even without taxation the MNE has an incentive to engage in transfer pricing, since there is a strategic effect due to market power.

Since MNE are spread over several countries, this offers MNE the chance to shift income from high-tax jurisdictions to low-tax jurisdictions just by choosing transfer prices that increase the production costs in regions with high taxes and lower the production costs in regions with relatively low tax rates.[27] This suggests that MNE would choose transfer prices that are either the highest or the lowest possible (depending on the tax differential between two or more regions), which would result in a binary system of maximum or minimum transfer price within certain (e.g., statutory) limits. The following sections analyze the taxation behavior of the MNE in the previously illustrated two region setting.

### 4.3.1 Transfer Pricing under Separate Accounting (SA)

To illustrate the implications of taxation on transfer pricing (i.e. taxation effect) we analyze a situation in which the government of each region levies a non-negative source tax on profits.[28] Consequently, there is separate (tax) accounting within each region, indicating that we abstract from the existence of tax credit rules between regions to address the issue of double taxation.

Again, the main office first sets and announces its transfer price and eventually the affiliate and the competitor decide over their optimal sales prices. With taxes, the total profits of the MNE now amount to

$$\pi_{MNE}^{SA} = \pi_3 \left(1 - t_A\right) + \pi_1 \left(1 - t_B\right), \tag{4.10}$$

with $t_A$ and $t_B$ denoting the tax rates of region A and region B respectively. Further, the first order condition reads

$$\frac{\partial \pi_{MNE}^{SA}}{\partial \theta} = \frac{3\tau - 4\theta + \left(6\theta - 9\tau\right)t_A - \left(2\theta - 6\tau\right)t_B + \left(c_1 - c_2\right)\left(3t_A - 2t_B - 1\right)}{18\tau} \overset{!}{=} 0,$$

27 Cf. Nielsen et al. (2003) and Wellisch (2004).

28 Since this is a partial equilibrium model, government spending of tax receipts will not be addressed explicitly.

which finally gives the optimal transfer price under taxation

$$\theta^{SA} = \left(\frac{3\tau - c_1 + c_2}{4}\right)\left(\frac{6t_A - 4t_B - 2}{3t_A - t_B - 2}\right). \tag{4.11}$$

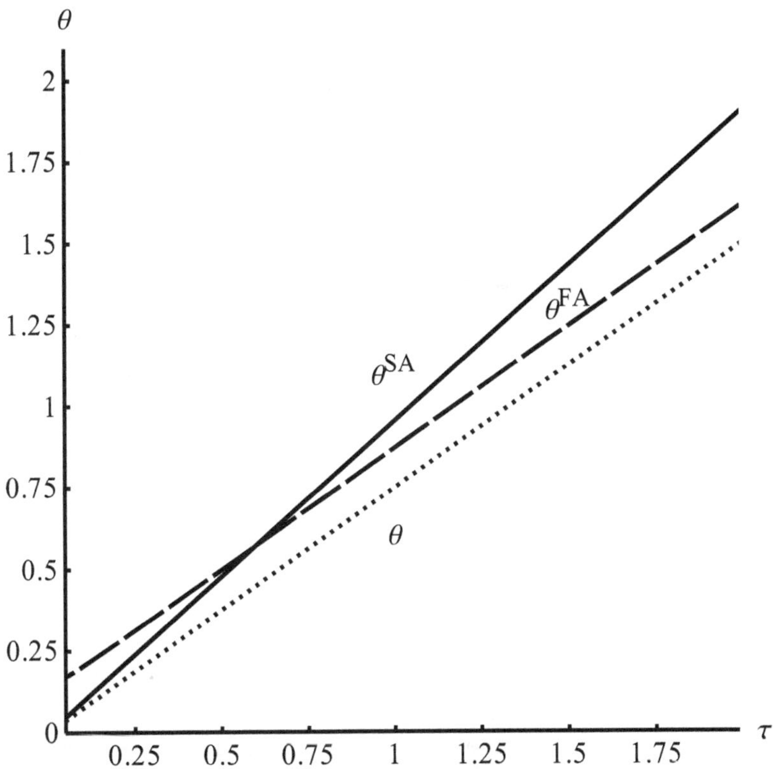


*Figure 4.3: Transfer prices for variations in the degree of spatial product differentiation; Figure 4.3 is based on the following assumptions:* $a = 7, c_1 = c_2 = c_3 = 1,$ $t_B = 0.2, t_A = 0$

Now, the optimal transfer price consists of two components. The first term in brackets reflects the strategic effect of transfer pricing as already indicated by (4.7): the higher the spatial product differentiation, the higher the transfer price chosen by the MNE. This effect is illustrated in figure 4.3. The dotted black line labeled $\theta$ has a positive slope, indicating that the transfer price rises with the degree of spatial product differentiation $(\tau \uparrow)$.

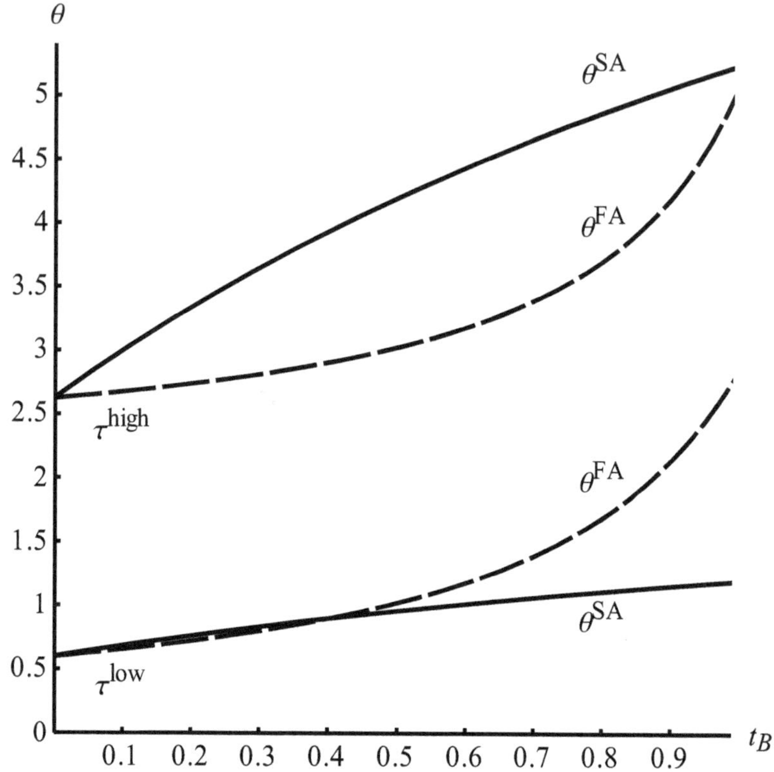


*Figure 4.4: Variations in the transfer price for tax rate differentials;*
*Figure 4.4 is based on the following assumptions:* $a = 7, c_1 = c_2 = c_3 = 1$, $\tau^{high} = 3.5, \tau^{low} = 0.8, t_A = 0$; *since* $\theta^{FA} = \theta^{SA}$ *for* $t_A = t_B$ *the graphical analysis concentrates on tax rate differentials, setting* $t_A = 0$

This effect is now augmented by a tax effect, which is always positive for $t_A < t_B$. We will keep this assumption (i.e. a tax advantage of region A over region B) for simplicity reasons throughout the rest of the analysis.[29] As long as

29 For $t_A > t_B$ analogous results can be obtained. However, for large tax rate differentials the obtained results are non-monotonic.

region A offers a tax advantage over region B (i.e. $t_A < t_B$) the strategic effect of transfer pricing will be augmented by the positive tax effect of profit shifting, indicating that $\theta^{SA} > \theta$.

The relative higher tax burden in region B prompts the main office to shift profits from the high-tax to the low-tax region, using transfer pricing. It can be seen in figure 4.3 that for increasing spatial product differentiation $(\tau \uparrow)$ the transfer price under SA labeled $\theta^{SA}$ (the solid black line) is always larger than $\theta$ (i.e. transfer price without taxation).

The pure strategic effect is independent from the degree of tax rate differentials, while the pure tax effect only depends on the tax rate differentials. Consequently, a relative increase of the tax rate in region B will induce the main office to shift profits to the relative low-tax region (region A), through an increase of the transfer price, no matter how large spatial product differentiation will be. This can be seen in figure 4.4 (both solid black lines are positively sloped for an increase in the tax rate differential). Returning to the part of spatial product differentiation, (4.11) also shows that for each given tax rate differential $t_A < t_B$, the higher $\tau$, the higher the transfer price will be chosen by the MNE, since the strategic effect increases with $\tau$.

With an increase in $\tau$, market power rises and thus firms engage more intensively in transfer pricing at a given tax rate differential, shown by the dotted black line (labeled $\theta$) in comparison to the solid black line (labeled $\theta^{SA}$) in figure 4.3.

*Result: Under taxation according to a separate accounting scheme, the strategic incentive of transfer pricing is augmented by a tax incentive for transfer pricing. This increases the overall incentive for transfer pricing. Thus, the transfer price under taxation increases more rapidly with the degree of spatial product differentiation than the transfer price without taxation. Additionally, it is always increasing with an increasing tax gap* $([t_A < t_B] \uparrow)$.

### 4.3.2 Transfer Pricing under Formula Apportionment (FA)

The outcome of the preceding section revealed that beside the strategic role of the transfer price in terms of market power, taxation implies an additional incentive for transfer pricing: depending on the tax rate differential, the transfer price can be used to shift profits from the high-tax jurisdiction to the low-tax jurisdiction. To limit the scope to which MNE can shift profits, various countries proposed and implemented the formula apportionment method of taxing firms with subsidiaries in various regions.[30] Under such a taxation scheme global profits of a MNE are apportioned to each region according to the activities of the MNE in the respective region, proportional to the world wide activities of the MNE. A general formula apportionment system allocates parts of the total tax base of the MNE to a region for instance, according to the relative capital invested, the relative payroll paid and the relative revenue received by the MNE in this region. Each factor is weighted by a specific factor.[31] Since these apportionment factors are tied to the real economic activities of MNE affiliates, shifting profits between different MNE entities remains a sole virtual exercise, according to the proponents of FA. Then, each regional government can independently choose its own rate at which it taxes the MNE activities (i.e. the MNE tax base) assigned to its jurisdiction. Two further simplifying assumptions are applied in our analysis: revenues are taken as the only apportionment factor and taxable profits do not deviate from true profits, since there are no tax exemptions.[32] Thus, the after-tax profits of the MNE under FA become

$$\pi_{MNE}^{FA} = (\pi_3 + \pi_1) - t_A\left(\frac{r_3}{r}\right)(\pi_3 + \pi_1) - t_B\left(\frac{r_1}{r}\right)(\pi_3 + \pi_1)$$

$$\Leftrightarrow \quad \pi_{MNE}^{FA} = (\pi_3 + \pi_1)\left(\frac{r_3(1-t_A) + r_1(1-t_B)}{r}\right), \tag{4.12}$$

with $r = r_3 + r_1$, denoting the sum of the return generated by the main office and the affiliate and the fraction in the second bracket indicating the average tax burden of the MNE. The first order condition of the MNE becomes

$$\frac{\partial \pi_{MNE}}{\partial \theta} = \frac{ABC(1-t_B) - D\big(AC - B(3\tau - c_1 + c_2 - 4\theta)\big)}{18\tau B^2} \overset{!}{=} 0, \tag{4.13}$$

with

$$A = (3\tau - 4c_1 + c_2 - 4\theta)$$

30 Cf. Wellisch (2003a,b) and Nielsen et al. (2003).

31 See Nielsen et al. (2003) for a more detailed description.

32 The choice of apportionment factors is crucial to the outcome of the analysis. Whenever there are apportionment factors that are not in control of the company, shifting taxes becomes impossible. See Wellisch (2004) for further analysis.

$$B = 6\theta\tau - 4\left(\theta^2 + c_1^2\right) + 9\tau\left(a^2 + 2\tau - c_3^2\right) - 2\left(c_1\left(4\theta - 3\tau - c_2\right) - c_2\left(\theta + 6\tau + c_2\right)\right)$$

$$C = 6\theta\tau - 4\theta^2 + 9\tau\left(a^2 + 2\tau\right) - 2\left(c_1 - c_2\right)\left(6\tau - c_1 + c_2 + \theta\right) - 9\tau c_3\left(18a - c_3\right)$$

$$D = -6\theta\tau + 4\theta^2 - 9\tau\left(a^2 + 2\tau\right) + 9\tau\left(c_3^2\left(1 - t_1\right) + a^2 t_A\right) +$$
$$2\left(1 - t_B\right)\left(\left(2c_1^2 - c_2^2\right) + \left(c_1\left(4\theta - 3\tau - c_2\right) - c_2\left(\theta + 6\tau\right)\right)\right) - 2t_B\left(\theta - 3\tau\right)\left(2\theta + 3\tau\right).$$

Since it is not possible to solve (4.13) explicitly for the optimal transfer price under the FA tax schedule, we have to rely on numerical simulations to illustrate the optimal response of the MNE to tax rate changes in the region where the affiliate is located. Referring to figure 4.4, it can be seen that under the FA tax scheme, there is also an incentive for the MNE to use transfer pricing to shift profits away from the high-tax region to the low-tax region. This incentive increases with the tax rate differential $\left(\left[t_A < t_B\right]\uparrow\right)$ between the two regions (dashed black lines labeled $\theta^{FA}$), independently from the degree of spatial product differentiation.

Again, the strategic effect is working in the same way as illustrated before. The MNE can lift the affiliate in the position of the Stackelberg leader: increasing the transfer price increases the profits of the MNE. This has been illustrated in figure 4.2 and explained for the case without taxes.

The tax effect of FA now works through a change of the average tax rate of the MNE: increasing the transfer price changes the output of the affiliate and thus the average tax rate facing the MNE. Let's assume that the tax rate in region B is higher than in region A. Hence, the main office now increases the transfer price. Revenues in region B decline and so does the weight attached to $t_B$ in the formula of the average tax rate. This can be seen referring to figure 4.2. The point N and S will not be altered due to taxes. Due to the strategic effect the main office chooses a transfer price so that S is reached. An increase in the tax rate of region B induces the MNE to increase the transfer price shifting the affiliate's reaction function further to the right, beyond point S. This lowers revenues in region B. However, this decline will be offset by lowering the weight of $t_B$ for the average tax rate. A manipulation of the transfer price leads to changes in the weights of the formula applied to determine the tax burden of the MNE.

Referring to figure 4.3 it can be seen, that the incentive to engage in transfer pricing remains with increasing spatial product differentiation $\left(\tau\uparrow\right)$, illustrated by the dashed black line labeled $\theta^{FA}$.

*Result: Under taxation according to the formula apportionment scheme the MNE increases its optimal transfer price with an increasing tax rate differential for* $t_A < t_B$. *However, the MNE engages less exhaustively in transfer pricing for relatively low-tax rate differentials between the two regions, than for relatively high-tax rate differentials for* $t_A < t_B$. *Changes in the spatial market separation keep an incentive for the MNE to do transfer pricing with the aim to reduce the overall tax.*

Finally, a comparison of the general incentives for transfer pricing under the two different taxation schemes leads to the following:

*Result: In both taxation schemes with* $t_A < t_B$, *the MNE has an incentive to use transfer pricing to shift profits form the high-tax region to the low-tax region. Switching from a tax system of SA to a tax system of FA does not prevent the MNE from the use of transfer pricing to lower its overall tax burden.*

## 4.4 Economic Integration and Transfer Pricing under Taxation

As explained in the introductory part, the main objectives of the COM for introducing a common consolidated tax base are enhancing the efficiency of corporate taxation.[33] Therefore, the aim of this section is to compare the incentives for transfer pricing (i.e. comparing the level of transfer prices) between the two different taxation schemes.

Eventually, the optimal behavior of the MNE will be analyzed on the background of increasing integration $(\tau \downarrow)$.

As explained earlier, the linear travel costs $\tau$, incurred by every consumer to reach either of the two producers of the homogeneous good in region B, can be interpreted as an indicator of economic integration (spatial market separation). Note that integration takes place within region B only. We can think of this kind of integration due to an enhanced infrastructure in this region. Referring to the examples of product markets illustrated in the introduction, the appropriate example for enhanced infrastructure would be better roads or railways. Thus, we abstract from the situation of economic integration between the two regions to

33 See Wellisch (2004) and COM (2005, 2007c).

emphasize that the EU invests large parts of the overall budget to build up the infrastructure of the new member states (cf. Ireland or Spain).

While decreasing these costs, competition between the affiliate and the competitor increases and letting the travel costs approaching zero $(\tau \rightarrow 0)$, we will get the well known Bertrand paradox, where one firm will serve the entire market as soon as the other firm would raise its price over the price of the competitor. This already implies that the strategic effect of the transfer price, as a mean to exhaust market power in region B, declines with a decline of $\tau$, no matter which rule of profit taxation applies.

For zero tax rates in both regions, i.e. referring to (4.7) which illustrates the plain strategic effect, a lower $\tau$ comes with a lower optimal transfer price without taxation. This can be seen by moving along the vertical axis in figure 4.4.

Increasing the tax rate on profits in region B (leaving the tax rate in region A unchanged) now shows that the MNE has an incentive to shift its profits from the affiliate to the main office, i.e. from the high-tax to the low-tax jurisdiction: in both tax schemes the transfer price increases. However, it is apparent that for a lower value of $\tau$ (i.e. lower spatial market separation) the MNE is less active in transfer pricing with an increasing tax rate differential under the separate accounting tax scheme, than it is with a higher degree of spatial market separation. As explained earlier, there are two effects at work: the strategic effect and the taxation effect, which both pull in the same direction.

With lower spatial market separation the sole strategic effect (i.e. assuming that $t_A = t_B = 0$) of the transfer price, which is the same for both taxation schemes, declines. With lower travel costs, the market power of each firm in region B declines, which makes it more difficult to increase the price of the affiliate. This can be seen by looking at the optimal prices without taxation (4.8) and (4.9), which positively depend on the spatial market separation $\tau$.

*Result: For a given tax rate differential with $t_A < t_B$, the degree to which the MNE uses transfer pricing to shift profits from the high-tax region to the low-tax region declines with the degree of spatial product differentiation in both taxation schemes.*

Referring to (4.15) in table 4.1, isolating the taxation effect (i.e. assuming that $\rho^S_{p_2,p_1} = 0$) under SA taxation reveals that the ability to shift profits, in response to tax rate differentials, will also be curbed by a declining $\tau$. The taxation effect depends on the price elasticity of demand (which increases with a decline in $\tau$), making it more difficult to shift profits via transfer pricing.

The proceeding section showed, that under the FA tax scheme, the MNE also has an incentive to shift profits in setting transfer prices. However, in opposite to the case of taxation according to SA, figure 4.4 showed that the incentive to engage in transfer pricing for an increasing tax differential only slightly declined, along with a decline in spatial product differentiation $(\tau \downarrow)$. Analyzing the tax effect of FA (4.16) in table 4.1 reveals the reason for this observation. Price increases (due to an increased transfer price) evoke reactions in the quantities demanded (cf. (4.6b)), which are larger for a low degree of spatial product separation (low values of $\tau$).[34] Thus, with a low level of $\tau$, even small manipulations of the transfer price are sufficient to get the desired result for $t_A < t_B$: a decline in $r_1$ and $\pi_1$, necessary to shift profits from the affiliate to the main office by lowering the average tax burden.[35] This can be interpreted as an indirect way of shifting profits, since the transfer price does not have to directly work through the goods market, as under the SA taxation scheme, but takes place within the bookkeeping system of the MNE.

*Result: With declining spatial market separation the ability of the MNE to engage in transfer pricing to shift profits from the high-tax to the low-tax region fades under SA but remains under FA.*

34 The price elasticity of demand increases with a decline in $\tau$.

35 Remember that $r_1$ denotes the return of the affiliate.

*Table 4.1: Comparison of transfer prices*

| | optimal transfer price | | strategic effect of transfer price $(t_1 = t_2 = 0)$ | taxation effect of transfer price $\left(\rho^s_{p_2,p_1} = 0\right)$ |
|---|---|---|---|---|
| without taxation | $\theta = \left( c_1 \frac{\varepsilon^d_{x_1,p_2}}{\varepsilon^d_{x_1,p_1}} - p_1 \frac{\eta^r_{r_1,p_2}}{\varepsilon^d_{x_1,p_1}} \right) \rho^s_{p_2,p_1}$ | (4.14) | $\left( c_1 \frac{\varepsilon^d_{x_1,p_2}}{\varepsilon^d_{x_1,p_1}} - p_1 \frac{\eta^r_{r_1,p_2}}{\varepsilon^d_{x_1,p_1}} \right) \rho^s_{p_2,p_1}$ | --------------- |
| separate accounting | $\theta^{SA} = \dfrac{\left( c_1 \frac{\varepsilon^d_{x_1,p_2}}{\varepsilon^d_{x_1,p_1}} - p_1 \frac{\eta^r_{r_1,p_2}}{\varepsilon^d_{x_1,p_1}} \right) \rho^s_{p_2,p_1} + (1-\Lambda) \frac{p_1}{\varepsilon^d_{x_1,p_1}}}{\Lambda - \frac{\varepsilon^d_{x_1,p_2}}{\varepsilon^d_{x_1,p_1}} (1-\Lambda) \rho^s_{p_2,p_1}}$ | (4.15) | $\left( c_1 \frac{\varepsilon^d_{x_1,p_2}}{\varepsilon^d_{x_1,p_1}} - p_1 \frac{\eta^r_{r_1,p_2}}{\varepsilon^d_{x_1,p_1}} \right) \rho^s_{p_2,p_1}$ | $\frac{(1-\Lambda)}{\Lambda} \frac{p_1}{\varepsilon^d_{x_1,p_1}}$ |
| formula apportion-ment | $\theta^{FA} = \dfrac{\psi \left( c_1 \frac{\varepsilon^d_{x_1,p_2}}{\varepsilon^d_{x_1,p_1}} - p_1 \frac{\eta^r_{r_1,p_2}}{\varepsilon^d_{x_1,p_1}} \right) \rho^s_{p_2,p_1} - \gamma c_1}{\gamma + \psi}$ | (4.16) | $\left( c_1 \frac{\varepsilon^d_{x_1,p_2}}{\varepsilon^d_{x_1,p_1}} - p_1 \frac{\eta^r_{r_1,p_2}}{\varepsilon^d_{x_1,p_1}} \right) \rho^s_{p_2,p_1}$ | $\frac{\gamma}{\gamma + \psi}(-c_1)$ |

Annotations to table 4.1

$\Lambda = \dfrac{1-t_A}{1-t_B}$ relative tax differential between region A and region B

$$\gamma = (\pi_3 + \pi_1)\frac{(t_A - t_B)r_3}{(r_1 + r_3)^2}$$

$\psi = (1-t^a) = \dfrac{r_3(1-t_A) + r_1(1-t_B)}{r_1 + r_3}$ ($t^a \equiv$ average tax rate of the MNE)

$\varepsilon^d_{x_1,p_1} = \dfrac{\partial x_1}{\partial p_1}\dfrac{p_1}{x_1}$ price elasticity of demand for good 1

$\varepsilon^d_{x_1,p_2} = \dfrac{\partial x_1}{\partial p_2}\dfrac{p_2}{x_1}$ cross-price elasticity of demand for good 1

$\eta^r_{r_1,p_1} = \dfrac{\partial r_1}{\partial p_2}\dfrac{p_2}{r_1}$ cross-price elasticity of return for the affiliate

(≡ influence of changes of the competitor price on the return of the affiliate in region B)

$\rho^s_{p_2,p_1} = \dfrac{\partial p_2}{\partial p_1}\dfrac{p_1}{p_2}$ price change elasticity

(≡ strategic effect explaining the price reaction of the affiliate for a price change of the business rival)

## 4.5 Conclusion

This chapter analyzed the implications on optimal transfer pricing under two different ways of profit taxation of MNE. We have found that the results in Nielsen et al. (2003) about the strategic impact on transfer pricing under the different tax regimes are robust, even when the two companies are engaged in Betrand competition with perfect substitutes. In particular, MNE have strong incentives to use transfer pricing for profit shifting, no matter if they were taxed according to SA or FA.

However, the analytical model used in this chapter revealed a crucial insight concerning the effects of economic integration (reflected in declining spatial market separation) on the way the MNE conducts transfer pricing: with enhanced economic integration, the market power of the MNE in region B declines and thus, the strategic effect of the transfer price also declines. Therefore, the lower the travel costs of consumers in region B are, the lower the transfer price implemented by the MNE. Furthermore, it could be seen that the taxation effect on the transfer price only declines in the SA taxation scheme, while it remains almost stable in the FA taxation scheme. Hence, with market integration, MNE engage more actively in transfer pricing under the FA scheme than they do under the SA scheme, whenever the tax differential between the two regions increases.

Governments, which are afraid of loosing their profit tax base because of enhanced profit shifting due to transfer pricing, should be very careful about relying on FA as the right instrument to retain MNE from using transfer pricing. Beside shifting profits from one jurisdiction to another, firms use transfer pricing also to exert the market power of their affiliates. This strategic device should be carefully taken into consideration, while talking about an optimal way of taxing profits of MNE.

# Appendix 4.A Separate Accounting vs. Formula Apportionment: Tax Receipts

The line of argument in the main section was developed around the question whether formula apportionment was an appropriate tool to prevent multinational firms from excessive transfer pricing. Thus, the analysis focused solely on the level of the transfer price under formula apportionment (FA) in comparison to separate accounting (SA). It showed that due to strategic considerations of MNE a system of formula apportionment would not keep firms from using transfer pricing to shift profits with the aim of 'optimizing' their tax bill. In contrast to common belief, the analysis illustrated that a system of formula apportionment still keeps up the incentives for profit shifting through transfer pricing. The analysis did not address the question of tax receipts collected from MNE activities. Therefore, the aim of this appendix is to briefly illustrate and compare the development of the total tax receipts of MNE activity under SA and FA. Since a closed form solution for the optimal transfer price under FA could not be derived in the main part, the conclusions of this part mainly rely on graphical illustrations generated from numerical simulations.

In accordance with (4.10), total tax receipts of MNE activity under separate accounting are

$$T^{SA} = \pi_3 t_A + \pi_1 t_B \tag{4.A.1}$$

and total tax receipts of MNE activity under formula apportionment are

$$T^{FA} = \left(\pi_3 + \pi_1\right)\left[\left(\frac{r_3}{r}\right)t_A + \left(\frac{r_1}{r}\right)t_B\right] \tag{4.A.2}$$

according to (4.12).

Figure 4.A.1 illustrates the level of tax receipts under the different tax regimes for changes in the tax rate of region $B$. It uses the results from the main part of this chapter concerning the optimal transfer prices under SA (4.11) and FA (4.13) as well as the corresponding output and price decisions of the MNE main office (located in region $A$) and the MNE affiliate (located in region $B$). In accordance with the analysis of the main part we focus on a situation where $t_A < t_B$ holds. For a high degree of spatial product differentiation $\left(\tau^{high} = 3.0\right)$, figure 4.A.2 reveals that for tax rate differentials between the two regions, the total tax receipts under FA are higher than tax receipts from MNE activity under SA. Recall the analysis in the main section: it showed that with an increasing tax rate in region $B$ the MNE shifts profits form the high tax region $(B)$ to the low tax region $(A)$ by increasing the transfer price in both tax regimes. However the transfer price under separate accounting was higher than the transfer price of formula apportionment. We could also see that the gap between the optimal transfer prices under SA and FA first increased and then declined with an increasing tax gap between region $A$ and region $B$. The development of tax receipts in figure 4.A.1 is in line with these observations. With an increasing tax rate in region $B$ (i.e. increasing tax gap between the two regions), fiscal authorities can collect more taxes under FA then under SA in a situation with a high degree of spatial product differentiation.

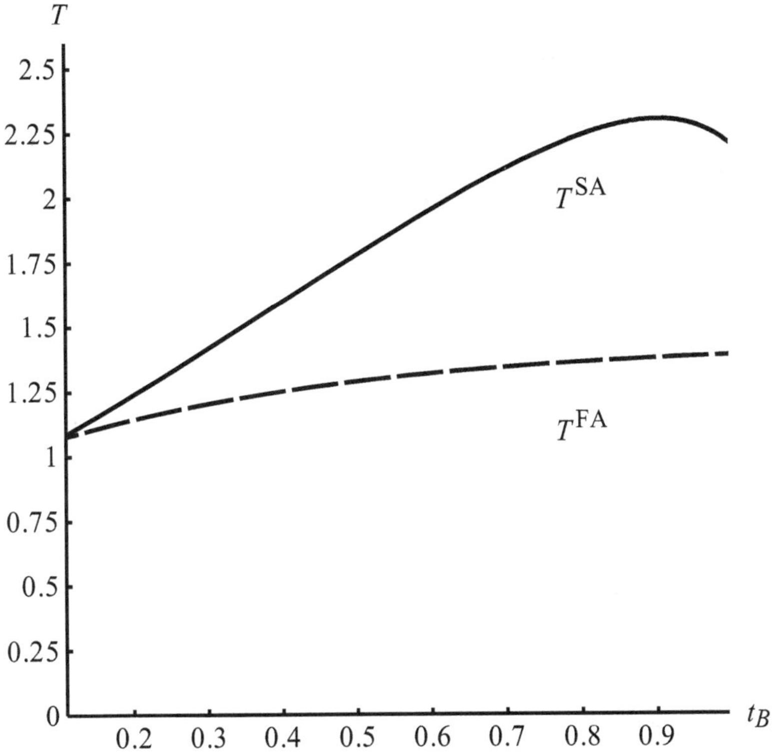


*Figure 4.A.1: Tax receipts for a high degree of spatial product differentiation; Figure 4.A.1 is based on the following assumptions:* $a = 7, \tau^{high} = 3$, $c_1 = c_2 = c_3 = 0, t_A = 0.1$; *total tax receipts of MNE activity for* $t_A < t_B$ *(i.e. the abscissa intersects with the ordinate at* $(0.1, 0)$*)*

Under high spatial market separation the strategic effect of transfer pricing profits of firms are relatively high. With formula apportionment tax receipts from MNE activity are higher indicating that total MNE after tax profits under FA are smaller than they are under SA. Since the share of overall MNE activity in each region is subject to taxation under FA it becomes more difficult to shift taxes using transfer pricing.

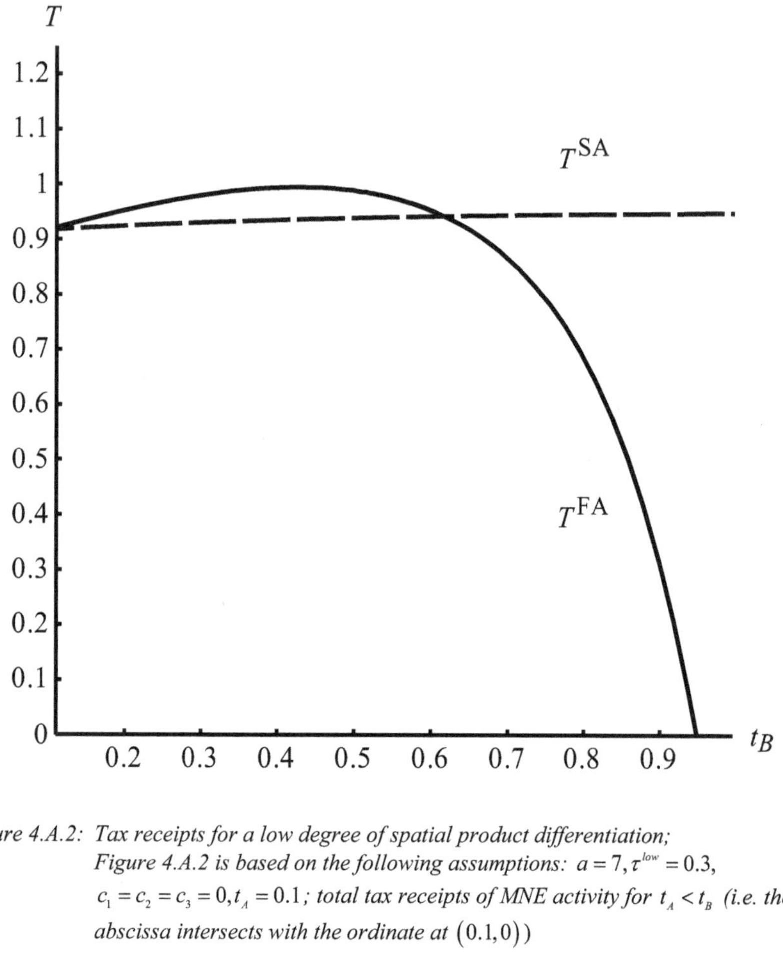


*Figure 4.A.2: Tax receipts for a low degree of spatial product differentiation; Figure 4.A.2 is based on the following assumptions:* $a = 7, \tau^{low} = 0.3$, $c_1 = c_2 = c_3 = 0, t_A = 0.1$; *total tax receipts of MNE activity for* $t_A < t_B$ *(i.e. the abscissa intersects with the ordinate at* $(0.1, 0)$*)*

Decreasing the spatial product differentiation $(\tau \downarrow)$ depresses total tax receipts in both SA and FA as illustrated in figure 4.A.2. However, with closer goods market integration in region $B$, total tax receipts under SA may be higher than total tax receipts under FA. An increasing tax gap between the two regions also slightly increases tax receipts under SA.

Under FA the tax receipts first increase for smaller tax gaps and then decline for larger tax gaps so that total tax receipts under FA may be smaller than tax receipts under SA. The use of transfer pricing under FA allows the MNE to manipulate the average tax burden so that after tax profits of MNE activity rise which ca be observed in figure 4.A.2. With low product differentiation the strategic effect of transfer pricing becomes less dominant but the tax effect is more important for the decision of the transfer price. The manipulation of the average tax burden under FA has a more pronounced effect on the level of tax receipts since it directly influences the weights that are attached to the tax base and additionally the tax base (i.e. profits) itself.

# Appendix 4.B Derivation of the Demand Functions

As mentioned in the main section, the model consists of a continuum of consumers, which are equally distributed on a straight line over the interval $[0,1]$. There are two firms $i$ $(i=1,2)$ each located at the opposite end of the interval each offering a homogeneous product to consumers. The firms face constant marginal costs $(c_i > 0)$ and compete for consumers by setting prices $(p_i > 0)$. Each consumer needs and demands a unit of the homogeneous good from either firm.[36] In order to buy a unit of the homogeneous good, each consumer has to go to one of the two firms, incurring linear travel costs of $\tau > 0$.

A consumer located at some point $\omega$ of the interval incurs total costs of $p_1 + \tau|0-\omega|$ if she buys from firm 1 and $p_2 + \tau|1-\omega|$ if she buys from firm 2. Therefore, all consumers for which $p_1 + \tau\omega < p_2 + \tau(1-\omega)$ holds, will buy from firm 1 indicating that there will be a consumer $\tilde{\omega}$ which is indifferent between buying from firm 1 and firm 2. This gives us the demand for firm 1, namely $x_1(p_1, p_2) = \tilde{\omega}$ and for firm 2, which is $x_2(p_1, p_2) = 1 - \tilde{\omega}$, respectively. Solving $p_1 + \tau\tilde{\omega} = p_2 + \tau(1-\tilde{\omega})$ for $\tilde{\omega}$ gives us the position of indifferent consumer on the line and thus the firm-specific demand functions for the two homogeneous goods

$$x_1(p_1, p_2) = \frac{\tau + p_2 - p_1}{2\tau} \tag{4.B.1a}$$

$$x_2(p_1, p_2) = \frac{\tau + p_1 - p_2}{2\tau}. \tag{4.B.1b}$$

We also assume that both firms will always be active. Note that consumers are equally divided across the two firms, when $p_1 = p_2$ holds. The demand of a firm declines in its own price and rises in the other firm's price. Spatial product

36 Each consumer's utility and budget are modeled in such a way that in equilibrium the homogenous good will always be demanded by each consumer.

differentiation ensures that demand changes with the degree of price differentiation.

# Appendix 4.C Background Information on Foreign Direct Investments

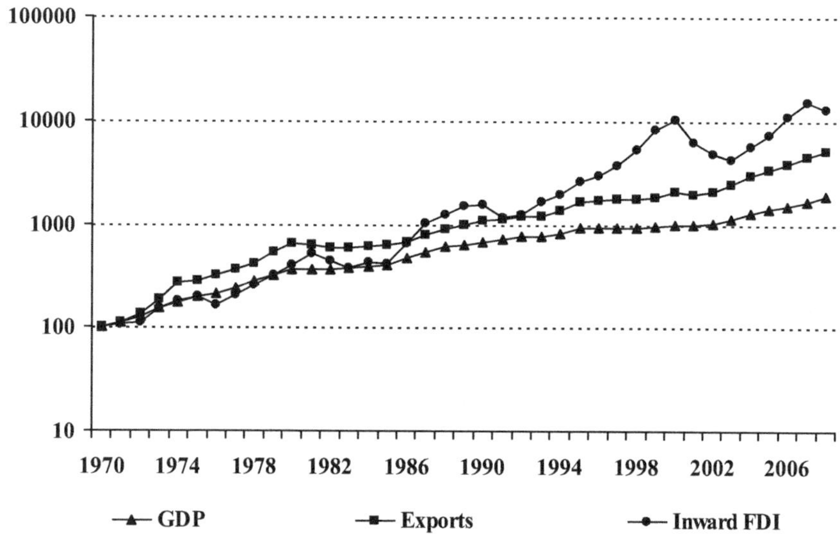


*Figure 4.C.1: Trends of World GDP, World Exports and World Inward FDI; World GDP, World Exports and World Inward FDI are measured in US $ at current prices and current exchange rates, 1970=100, logarithmic scale; country groups are taken from UNCTAD, cf. FN 37; Source: UNCTAD Handbook of Statistics Online and cf. Navaretti and Venables (2004)*

The introduction of the main section cited some facts about MNE and FDI. This appendix should deliver some further background information on foreign direct investments with data taken from the UNCTAD Handbook of Statistics Online.[37]

Though it does not present an extensive overview it sums up major developments in foreign direct investments. A more detailed illustration of stylized

37 http://stats.unctad.org/Handbook/ReportFolders/reportFolders.aspx

facts on foreign direct investments/ multinational enterprises can be found in Navaretti and Venables (2004) or Markusen (2004). Figure 4.C.1 shows the trends for world GDP, merchandise exports and inward FDI. It supports the notion of the introduction to this chapter that FDI have been a very fast growing segment in international transactions since the 1990s. It is important to recognize that in absolute terms world merchandise exports/ imports are much larger than world inward/ outward FDI flows, illustrated below in table 4.C.1.

*Table 4.C.1: FDI-flows and merchandise trade in absolute terms;*
*Figures in billions of US $ at current prices and current exchange rates;*
*Source: UNCTAD Handbook of Statistics Online*

| | **1980** | **1985** | **1990** | **1995** | **2000** | **2005** |
|---|---|---|---|---|---|---|
| **Exports** | 2035.06 | 1972.13 | 3483.38 | 5178.45 | 6448.92 | 10487.58 |
| **Imports** | 2076.86 | 2034.80 | 3595.43 | 5239.24 | 6662.89 | 10794.18 |
| **FDI In** | 54.08 | 55.89 | 207.27 | 341.14 | 1381.68 | 973.33 |
| **FDI Out** | 51.55 | 61.97 | 239.11 | 361.68 | 1213.79 | 878.99 |

The following two figures further illustrate the growing importance of FDI. Over the last 29 years there has been a growth in outward and inward FDI flows as share of the GDP. The graphical illustration of the development of outbound FDI (i.e. the sources of FDI) as percent of source country GDP supports a growing trend in FDI. For all country groups mapped in figure 4.C.2 the share of FDI increased over the last 30 years.

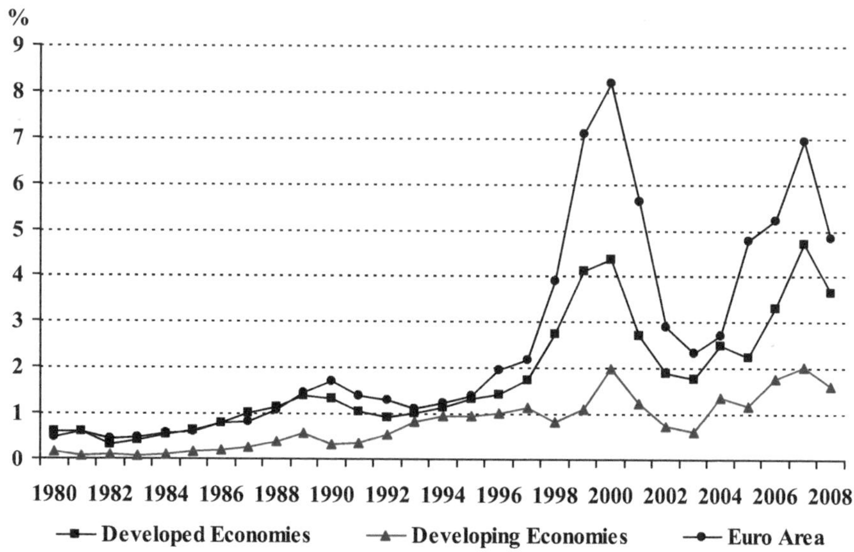


*Figure 4.C.2: Foreign direct investments (outward) as % of GDP; For country groups cf. figure 4.C.1;*

*Source: UNCTAD Handbook of Statistics Online*

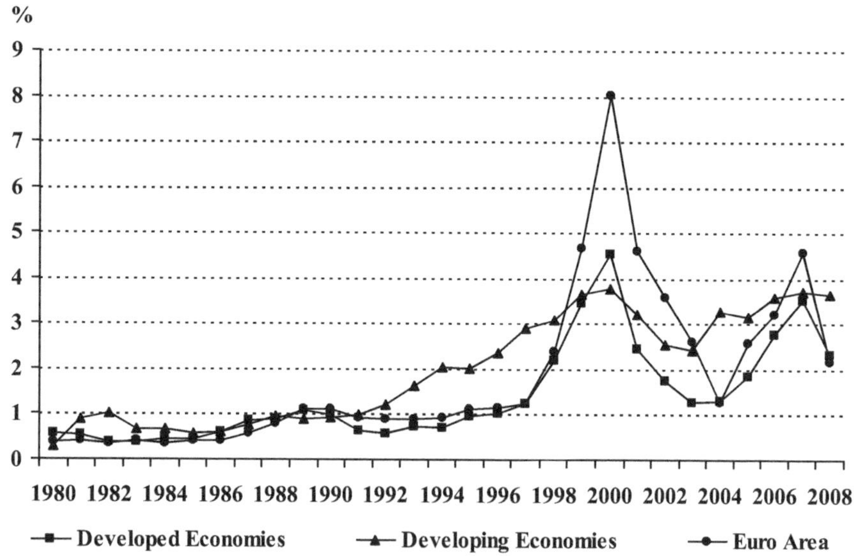


*Figure 4.C.3: Foreign direct investments (inward) as % of GDP; For country groups cf. figure 4.C.1; Source: UNCTAD Handbook of Statistics Online*

Developed countries are an important source of FDI, while FDI outflows for countries belonging to the Euro Area are the largest. According to Navaretti and Vanebles (2004) this contributes to the fact that these figures are mainly driven by intra-Euro Area investments. Figure 4.C.3 shows the development of inward FDI over time. A first glance may deliver the idea that developing countries are the major hosts for FDI. But despite the growing role of FDI in developing countries over the time period of observation, developed countries are still the major origin and destination countries of FDI.

As illustrated in figure 4.C.4 the developed countries' share of outward FDI to total FDI dominates the FDI flows in the world. On average 89% percent of world FDI outflows originated from developing countries during the above illustrated period of time. Note that the Euro Area on average accounts for a third of total FDI outflows.

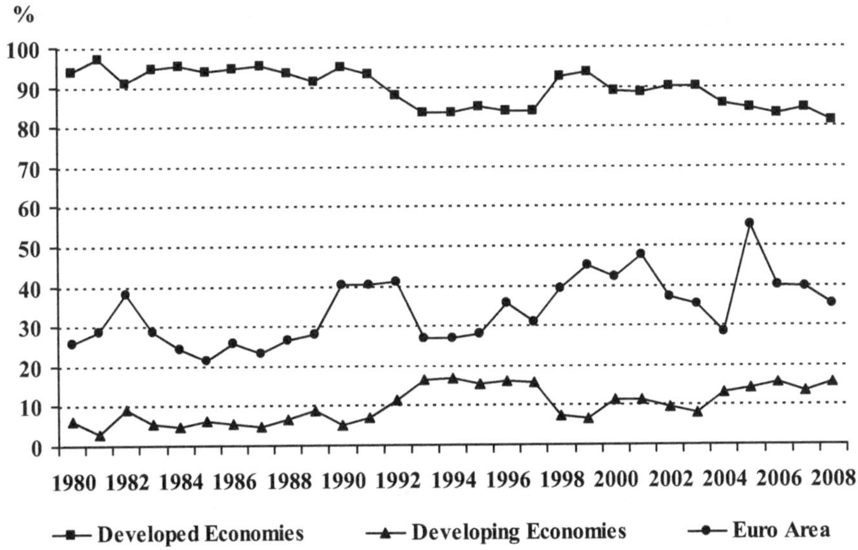


*Figure 4.C.4: Foreign direct investment (outward) as % of World FDI (outward); For country groups cf. figure 4.C.1; Source: UNCTAD Handbook of Statistics Online*

Figure 4.C.5 illustrates the role of FDI host countries. On average, almost 70% of world FDI inflows are directed into developed countries while approximately a quarter is directed into the Euro Area. The average share of inward FDI into developing countries was about 30%.

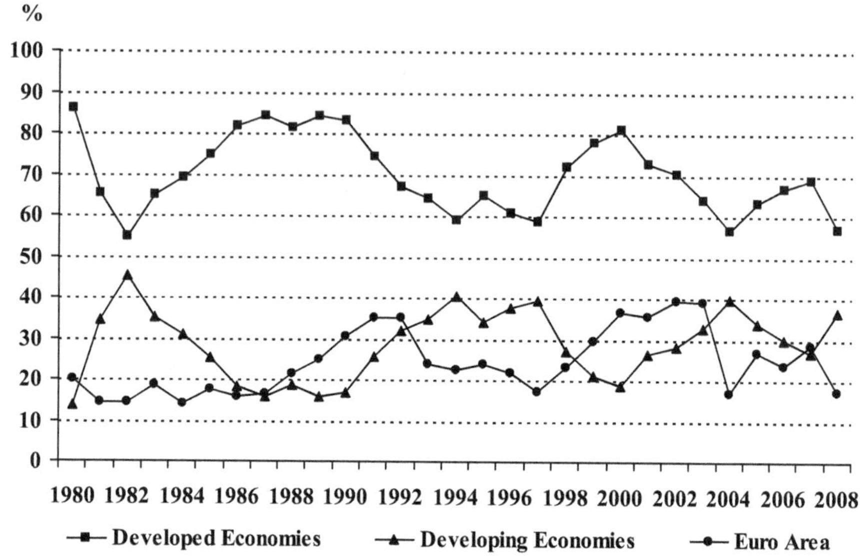


*Figure 4.C.5: Foreign direct investments (inward) as % of World FDI (inward); For country groups cf. figure 4.C.1; Source: UNCTAD Handbook of Statistics Online*

# 5 Capital Tax Competition in the Light of Agglomeration Economies: A Survey

Tax competition is a very broad research area and is still attracting many researchers, though its most prominent roots date back to the mid 1950s. The rapid pace of globalization (i.e. trade in goods and services as well as factor mobility, esp. the mobility of financial assets) within the last two decades has spurred the community to set its focus on the implications of economic integration on the fiscal policy of independent nation states, emphasizing the issue of horizontal tax competition. The present chapter provides a survey of the most recent literature that empirically investigates the interaction of economic integration and capital tax competition, with a special focus on tax competition in the presence of agglomeration economies. It briefly explains the theoretical background by illustrating the implications of the basic tax competition model and contrasting them with the findings of economic geography models with fiscal applications. After that, the empirical results of a meta-sample on the interaction of capital taxation and firm location are reported and empirical studies that address the effect of agglomeration forces on capital tax competition are summarized. We will learn that the results of tax competition models are very sensitive to the underlying assumptions and the theoretical background so that it is crucial to take the specific context in which jurisdictions 'compete' for mobile factors of production into consideration.

## 5.1 Introduction

Analyzing the fiscal implications of economic integration among independent countries occupies a large number of researchers today. The primary drive of this activity is the rapid pace at which globalization has taken place within the last decades. Two factors have mainly been responsible for this development: (1) technological progress reducing the spatial distance between countries, for example, declining costs of transportation and enhanced communication/ data transmission technology, and (2) political actions such as free trade agreements (e.g. the WTO, originating from the GATT) or economic unions (e.g. the European Union)[1]. This process of an increased cross-boarder integration of markets for goods, services and capital eventually spurred the slicing up of value chains fostering the creation of Multinational Enterprises (MNE).[2]

Governments are aware that free trade in goods and services and the increased mobility of factors – in particular the mobility of investment capital, profits and portfolio capital – interact with their national public policy. Though labor seems far less mobile, the spread of multinational firms supports the notion that jobs become increasingly mobile, too, so that the footloose character of investment and portfolio capital also influences labor markets. This may affect the structure of a government's budget with factor mobility constraining the ability of raising tax revenues and in turn limiting the expenditures for public services.[3] Finally, governments of independent countries may find themselves in competition for mobile factors of production.

There is a broad consensus among economists that increased competition between companies triggered by globalization is beneficial – while efficiency enhancing – for the whole economy. However, the issue of possible merits of fiscal competition (i.e. the "fight" of independent governments for mobile production factors = mobile tax bases) is heatedly debated as the extensive literature on fiscal competition shows.

The critics of fiscal competition caused by economic integration refer to the public finance and political economy literature that mentions possible adverse effects of globalization due to changes in government activities in response to it.

---

1 Cf. Andersen (2003).

2 According to OECD (2007a) foreign direct investments (FDI) have been the fastest growing segment of international transactions within the last decade. Cf. also appendix 4.C.

3 These effects of globalization on income distribution have to be distinguished from (direct) effects of income distribution caused by trade due to relative factor scarcity as illustrated in the Heckscher-Ohlin-Model.

This contemporary research on open-economy public finance is mainly based on analyzing the effects of factor mobility among independent countries on government behavior. Especially the topic of capital mobility has attracted considerable attention in literature and has established the wide research area of so called capital tax competition.[4] In an open-economy setting capital becomes a very mobile factor of production across borders and national governments find themselves in strategic interaction with other governments in setting up their national taxation rules for capital income. With capital mobility, the tax burden on capital income becomes a criterion in the investment decisions of firms.[5] National governments are thus concerned to lose their capital tax base when they set capital/ corporate tax rates without taking other governments reactions into consideration. Therefore, capital mobility is made responsible for potentially restraining the tax setting behavior of a national government. When taxing firms, a government risks losing companies to tax havens. A national government that seeks to avoid losing its tax base consequently takes this likely reaction of capital owners into consideration and finally adjusts its capital tax rate to the level of the low-tax country. In the extreme case, this approach will leave capital completely untaxed as the opponents of capital mobility usually argue.

The proponents of fiscal competition however point out, that economic integration forces governments to strengthen their tax policies by implementing efficient tax instruments like imposing user fees on residents for public goods provision and turning away from source-based taxes.[6] Besides, fiscal competition is assumed to effectively reduce the power of governments, thereby 'taming the Leviathan'.[7]

The analysis of the interaction of public sector activity and economic integration is a vast research area that still occupies a large number of economists, esp. since the 1980s. It describes the competition between governments for production factors – mainly very footloose factors like capital. However, the issue of competition for mobile capital does not only spin around tax rate setting. Fiscal competition can affect all policy areas where governments interfere with the market system. Therefore, the subject of fiscal competition also comprises competition with non-tax instruments, like all forms of regulatory decisions (e.g., in

---

4 For a survey of the theoretical research in this area consult Wilson (1999) or Fuest et al. (2005) for a more recent survey, that puts the emphasize on multinational firms and the topic of financial arbitrage.

5 Devereux and Maffini (2006) extensively survey the empirical literature on the interaction of multinational firms' investment decisions and capital taxation. Ernst & Young (2007a) delivers survey results of selection criteria for investment decisions.

6 Cf. Fuest et al. (2005).

7 Cf. Fuest et al. (2005); for Leviathan consult e.g. Psalm 74, 13-14.

the banking or insurance sector, setting of environmental, health or safety standards) or government spending (e.g., social insurance, subsidies, public goods, infrastructure). However, the most predominant branches of this research area deal with the above mentioned (possible) consequences of economic integration – in terms of factor (capital) mobility – on government taxation behavior and in the more recent literature the taxation of multinational firms.[8]

In this chapter, we mainly focus on the interaction of globalization and capital taxation behavior of governments. The aim is to examine the strength and direction of these interaction forces by summarizing the main results delivered by tax competition theory and comparing them to empirical studies on this issue. Main emphasis is put on studies that empirically estimate the degree and magnitude of capital tax competition between independent governments. We thereby focus on the empirical results obtained by researchers who explicitly integrate agglomeration economies in their estimation models.

We would not come up with a statement whether fiscal competition is a 'good' or a 'bad' thing since such a statement very much depends on the (economic) point of view a person generally takes on government action, as indicated above.[9] Additionally, we do not analyze situations where governments compete for mobile production factors (esp. capital), by standards or regulation policy.[10] We also abstract from scenarios where independent governments compete by public expenditure, be it infrastructure as theoretically illustrated in chapter 2 or income redistribution as pointed out by the model used in chapter 1. Questions concerning the issue of taxing multinational firms were highlighted in a model used in chapter 3 and are therefore left aside as well as competition in the field of commodity taxation.[11] Furthermore, we do not discuss the tax harmonization efforts of the OECD or the European Union.[12]

8 Cf. e.g. Fuest et al. (2005).

9 Cf. Oates (2001).

10 Pflüger (2001) provides a theoretical model that deals with the topic of ecological dumping.

11 Theoretical considerations about international commodity taxation are presented in Haufler and Pflüger (2004).

12 The OECD, for example, installed a "Forum on Harmful Tax Practices" which set forth guidelines for "Dealing with Harmful Preferential Regimes in Member Countries" and adopted a series of "Recommendations for Combating Harmful Tax Practices". Within the European Union, for instance, there are harmonization efforts for indirect taxes, for the company tax base and proposals to introduce a common consolidated tax base for multinational firms, as illustrated in Schratzenstaller (2007). Nicodème (2009) presents an extensive overview on international efforts to control tax evasion.

In accordance with Wilson and Wildasin (2004) we use a narrow definition of (capital) tax competition throughout this chapter. Tax competition is defined "as non-cooperative tax [rate] setting by independent governments, under which each government's policy choices influence the allocation of a mobile tax base among 'regions' represented by these governments"[13]. This notion solely focuses on horizontal tax competition, where independent governments that belong to the same level are competing over a mobile tax base (primarily mobile capital).

The remainder of this chapter falls into two sections. In the first part of section 2 the theoretical background of capital tax competition in an open economy setting is presented. The second part of section 2 turns to the results that were obtained by the empirical assessment of the interaction of economic integration and public policy. The main focus here is put on empirical studies that formalized the insights of new economic geography models to empirically test the influences of agglomeration forces on the degree of fiscal competition. Section 3 concludes this chapter.

## 5.2 Economic Integration and Fiscal Competition

It has already been explained that analyzing the fiscal implications of economic integration among independent governments occupies a large number of researchers today. The elementary roots for this research area, however, date to the late 1950s. Today, many of the implications of fiscal federalism discussed in the earlier time are merged with the research area of international economics to highlight the various facets of the organization of the public sector in an open-economy. The following section presents the most prevalent and influential theories on this topic and subjects them to empirical assessments.

### 5.2.1 Theoretical Considerations

The extensive theoretical and empirical research on the potential effects of globalization (in terms factor mobility) on fiscal policy has its origin mainly in the research that has been done on the question of public good provision in a federal

13 Cf. Wilson and Wildasin (2004, p. 1067).

state, developed by Tiebout (1956).[14] In his work, independently acting (regional) governments compete for mobile households by offering local public goods financed by local head taxes. The mobile households vote with their feet by settling down in the region where the government best responds to the households' preferences for local public goods. The model obtains efficient results on migration decisions: tax payments made by each resident are equal to the cost of providing the local public good (i.e. marginal-cost-pricing rule).[15]

Zodrow and Mieszkovski (1986) depart from Tiebout's setting by formalizing the ideas developed by Oates (1972) who reckons that there is a 'fiscal externality' at work that promotes inefficient migration decisions when manipulations in the tax rate of mobile factors in one country affect the tax receipts (and thus the welfare) in another region.[16] In accordance with the above given definition of tax competition, the model of Zodrow and Mieszkowski (1986) is usually addressed as the basic tax competition model.

Zodrow and Mieszkowski (1986) model a world in which independently acting governments provide a public good financed through taxes on capital income. Internationally mobile capital and immobile land, which is fixed in supply, are used to produce a good under perfect competition. Using this model they can show that capital mobility deters the optimal capital tax setting behavior of governments so that finally governments choose inefficiently low capital tax rates which in turn indicate an inefficiently low level of public good provision.

In the following we will use the graphical illustration in figure 5.1 to get a quick and easy access to the main idea developed in the basic tax competition model.[17]

Figure 5.1 illustrates the effects of introducing a source based capital tax in a small country.[18] The economy modeled in figure 5.1 will be labeled home and it produces a costless tradable good with internationally mobile capital $K$ and labor, which is immobile and inelastic in supply. The negatively sloped line labeled $F_K$ describes the marginal product of capital which is equivalent to the

14 Wellisch (2000) applies Tiebout's theory to a setting where independent governments compete for mobile firms.

15 Cf. Tiebout (1956) and Wilson (1999).

16 Cf. Wilson (1999).

17 The following considerations refer to Fuest (2001).

18 Capital demand in a small country does not influence the world return on capital income. We thus abstract from pecuniary externalities which would exist when countries are large enough to influence product or factor prices. This could also lead to inefficient tax policy decisions with a misallocation of factors as will be see later, cf. Wilson (1999).

demand for capital invested in home. Home is economically integrated with the countries that make up the rest of world and which are denoted foreign. The return of capital on the world capital market is $r$, which cannot be influenced by the home economy (i.e. small country assumption). Capital will be invested in home up to the point where its marginal product $F_K$ is equal to its marginal cost $r$. In a situation without a source tax on capital income, the amount of capital invested in home is $K_0$. The output is the sum of the areas $a, b, c, d$ and $e$. The total output consists of capital income $d+e$ (earned in home) and labor income $a+b+c$.

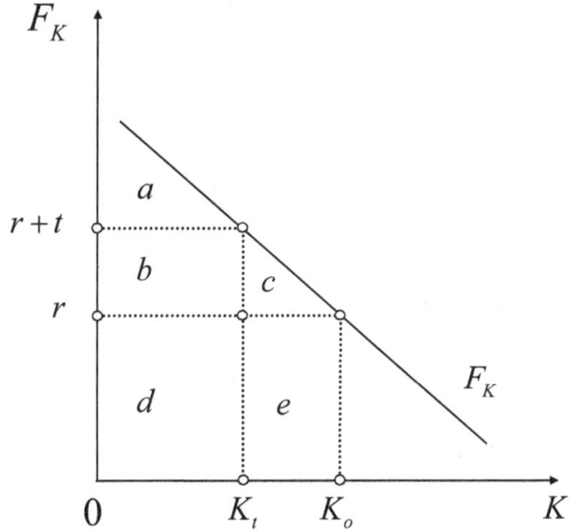


*Figure 5.1: Effects of a source based capital tax in a small open economy; Source: Fuest (2001)*

The government of home now introduces a capital source tax so that the return of capital invested in 'home' is now subject to a tax rate $t$. The tax increases the cost of capital. Under the source tax capital will be invested in home up to the point where the marginal product of capital $F_K$ is equal to the marginal cost of capital $r+t$. So now the amount of capital invested in home is $K_t$. The decline of invested capital in home $\overline{K_0 - K_t}$ implies a decline in output in this economy by the areas $c$ and $e$. The income received by workers is $a$, tax receipts by the government are denoted by the area $b$. Capital owners receive income on capital invested in the home economy $d$ and on capital invested in foreign $e$. Note that there is now a net loss in welfare in the economy of home: since the additional taxes reaped by the government $(b)$ are smaller than the total loss of income for workers $(b+c)$ the area $c$ denotes the net loss of welfare that occurs when a source based tax is introduced in a small open economy.

In this simple model the installation of a source tax on capital income in a small country comes with welfare losses. Since capital is mobile across countries, the incidence of the capital source tax will be borne by the immobile factors of production (here: only labor). Capital owners always demand the world capital return $r$ and therefore the capital source tax distorts the (efficient) allocation of capital across the economically integrated countries.

In the final analysis, the simple model on the welfare effects of introducing uncoordinated capital source taxes shows, that capital source taxes will eventually disappear. Due to capital tax competition governments will systematically outbid each other in lowering their capital source taxes up to the point where capital income will be left untaxed. Consequently, the above presented model predicts – in its most radical view – a race-to-bottom, an unintentional harmonization of government spending and social policy efforts (i.e. mostly the prevention of an autonomous public policy), since governments competing for the mobile tax base persistently undercut tax rates for mobile factors and also face strong restrictions on manipulating revenues of immobile factors and setting their own labor and social standards. The erosion of the mobile tax base finally wipes out differences in the level of governmental interference with the market system through the tax system and equalizes the shape and scope of social programs across integrated countries.[19] Note that this line of argument does not only apply to the changes in overall government spending but also to the structure of a government's budget.

Since the formalization of the ideas developed by Oates (1972), there have been many contributions to the basic tax competition model, relaxing the original assumptions with the aim to get more detailed answers on the interaction of economic integration and fiscal policy. However, the basic intuition can be understood fully by referring to the simple model illustrated in figure 5.1.

There is also a branch in the tax competition literature that challenges the above presented main argument of inefficient low government spending as a result of tax competition. The so-called Leviathan Models convey the idea that tax competition is a proper device to curb excessive government spending, the so-

19 Navarro et al. (2004) describe such a scenario in their 'convergence hypothesis'. According to Rodrik (1997) the convergence will also comprise labor and safety standards.

called “Taming of the Leviathan”.[20] Note that these models also come to the conclusion that tax competition reduces the size of governments. The sole difference between the basic tax competition model and Leviathan Models is that the former attaches negative welfare implications to this reduction while the latter see positive welfare implications. We abstract from a more detailed illustration of the Leviathan Models and turn to a fairly new way of analyzing the implications of capital mobility on public policy in an open economy setting.

Recognizing that industry tends to regionally cluster or agglomerate[21], a formal treatment of agglomeration economies has been developed which served many researchers in the recent past as a foundation to analyze implications of fiscal competition in the framework of the so called new economic geography. Primarily, the new economic geography literature delivers a systematic and rigorous explanation for an endogenous industry location. The initial formalization of models that deliver an explanation for endogenously clustering firms of the same industry has been done by Krugman (1991a) with his core-periphery-model with mobile (qualified) workers and by Venables (1996) who models vertically linked industrial production. The main feature of these models is that they can explain spatial industrial agglomeration apart from referring to exogenously given characteristics of a region like resources (e.g., oil, coal, etc.) or special geographic features (e.g., harbor, lowland plains, etc.). These models consider transportation costs for traded goods and exhibit increasing returns on the level of each firm, implying imperfect competition (monopolistic competition for the most part of the literature). As a result, these models can describe and explain geographical agglomeration of industry by the interaction of three forces: demand linkages (i.e. mobile firms/ workers tend to settle down where the demand is large) and supply linkages (i.e. mobile workers/ firms are inclined to settle down where supply (e.g. for firms using intermediate inputs) is large so that they save shipping costs) which both tend to accentuate agglomeration and the competition effect (i.e. increased competition among firms in agglomerated regions induces firms to spread over the regions) that works against agglomeration. The relative strength of these forces which can work non-monotonically varies with the different level of trading costs, consumer preferences for variants of an industrial good and the share of the industrial sector in the whole economy. An important message of these models for analyzing questions on taxing mobile

20 For a short overview consult Oates (2001) or Wilson and Wildasin (2004): the idea of Leviathan Models has been developed by Brennan and Buchanan (1980); a formal treatment is, for instance, presented by Rauscher (1998).

21 Cf. Combes and Overman (2004) for a survey article on the spatial distribution of industry sectors across Europe.

production factors is hysteresis of industrial agglomerations. Once full industrial agglomeration has been established in a country/ region which is then addressed the 'core', the demand and supply linkages ensure that industry will get stuck in its cluster. The reason for this observation is that there is an agglomeration rent accruing to the firms located in the core (i.e. the return of capital in the core is higher than in the periphery so that pure economic profits occur). The existence of agglomeration rents implies that governments can now tax away parts of this agglomeration rent without triggering a relocation of capital.

Thus, researchers began to analyze tax competition in the presences of agglomeration economies by integrating aspects of fiscal competition in the framework of economic geography.[22] Taking agglomeration forces and location hysteresis into consideration the economic geography framework could disclose additional channels and forces that influence the interaction between economic integration and public policy. A formalization of tax competition in this class of models (i.e. variants of new economic geography models) has, for example, been done by Ludema and Wooton (2000), Kind et al. (2000), Andersson and Forslid (2003), Baldwin and Krugman (2004), Ottaviano and van Ypersele (2005) as well as Borck and Pflüger (2006). To outline the main findings of this theoretical literature on tax competition in the presence of agglomeration forces we take the results obtained by Baldwin and Krugman (2004) and Borck and Pflüger (2006) in the following. We then compare them to the major results of the basic tax competition model and its variants as, for instance, illustrated by Wilson (1999).

Table 5.1 summarizes the main results of the basic tax competition model and the core-periphery tax competition model, where industry is already fully agglomerated in one region (i.e. the core) presented by Baldwin and Krugman (2004). Comparing the results seemingly indicates that the commonly cited conclusions obtained by the basic tax competition model are strongly opposed by the core-periphery tax competition results.

Due to agglomeration forces firms are inclined to 'lump' in one region for a certain range of transportation costs (agglomeration forces are strongest for intermediate levels of trade costs). Since the industrial core provides an agglomeration rent to firms, the region that owns the core has an advantage over the periphery region. Agglomeration rents manifest location hysteresis which gives the government in the core region the scope for taxing the mobile factor at a

22 Paty (2008) presents a short overview of the theoretical and empirical results of tax competition and agglomeration economies. However, her summary on the theoretical findings neglects the results obtained by Borck and Pflüger (2006), though she quotes this work.

higher rate as in the periphery region without triggering industry relocation, as long as the tax rate is not too high.

*Table 5.1: Results of basic tax competition and core-periphery tax competition; Source: cf. Wilson (1999) and Baldwin and Krugman (2004)*

| Basic Tax Competition | Core-Periphery Tax Competition |
|---|---|
| capital mobility and the capital tax rate should be negatively correlated | agglomeration forces can cause differences in the capital tax rate across regions |
| large countries (in terms of immobile factor supply) should maintain higher capital tax rates than small countries | differences in the capital tax rates between countries that may differ in their size depend on the level of goods' market integration (i.e. trade costs) and capital mobility |
| large countries should export capital to small countries | |
| capital tax rates and capital-labor-ratios $\left(\frac{K}{L}\right)$ should be negatively correlated | capital tax rates and capital-labor ratios $\left(\frac{K}{L}\right)$ can be positively correlated when agglomeration forces are strong enough |
| capital mobility depresses capital tax rates below the social optimum | in the presence of agglomeration forces capital tax rate harmonization would not be Pareto improving |
| capital tax rate harmonization can be Pareto improving | tax rate floors can improve the situation in the core without harming the periphery |

Since marginal changes in the capital tax rate may not cause industry relocation, the tax setting game modeled in Baldwin and Krugman (2004) eventually shows that the government in the core region chooses a tax rate that is higher than the tax rate of the periphery region and just low enough to prevent firms from leaving.[23] The difference in the capital tax rates across the regions thus depends on the level of trade costs and the mobility of capital. Since agglomeration forces are usually largest at intermediate trade costs, Baldwin and Krugman

23 Baldwin and Krugman (2004) refer to this setting as 'limit tax game'. To put it short: the tax gap has to be smaller than the agglomeration rent reaped by firms in the core.

(2004) can show that the tax rate differential takes the shape of a bell for declining trade costs: a decline in trade costs from relatively closed goods markets first enlarges the tax rate differential and then depresses it again. In the language of the tax competition literature this means that the degree of tax competition becomes first weaker with increasing goods market integration and then increases again. A tax rate harmonization (i.e. a cooperative choice of capital tax rates across the regions), which is proved to be welfare enhancing in the basic tax competition model, could be harmful in the core-periphery model. At a single tax rate firms would not relocate but stay in the core region due to agglomeration forces. Since industry sticks to the core region due to agglomeration forces, a downward harmonization of tax rates to the level of the periphery would not trigger any industry relocation into the periphery region (constant tax revenues in the periphery) but only decrease the tax revenues in the core region, implying Pareto deterioration in the core region. Increasing the periphery's tax rate to the maximum level of the core's tax rate would be welfare neutral in the core but welfare decreasing in the periphery since its initial tax rate was an efficient outcome of the Nash tax setting game that produced the differences in the tax rate prior to tax rate harmonization efforts. Thus, there would be no single tax rate the both regions would agree on since there is no mutual gain from a tax rate harmonization.[24]

However, Borck and Pflüger (2006) show that analyzing tax competition in the new economic geography framework has also to be done with caution. They generalize the results obtained by Baldwin and Krugman (2004) by using a model that also allows industry to be partially agglomerated in one region. Consequently, they present three different cases of tax competition that need to be distinguished in the new economic geography framework. Acknowledging that trade costs directly influence the strength of agglomeration forces Borck and Pflüger (2006) thus analyze tax competition for different levels of trade costs.

The findings of Borck and Pflüger (2006) qualify the strong results from Baldwin and Krugman (2004) to the extent that they also analyze cases where partial agglomeration occurs. They begin by replicating the results of Baldwin and Krugman (2004) for the core-periphery scenario. They can show that in their model the core region maintains a higher capital tax rate than the periphery. Besides, they can demonstrate that the tax rate differential between the core and the periphery is qualitatively the same as in Baldwin and Krugman (2004): with declining trade costs the tax gap first increases and then declines (i.e. a bell

24 The line of argument of the tax floor illustrated in Baldwin and Krugman (2004) will not be discussed here since there is no equivalent reasoning for the basic tax competition model. However, it is mentioned in table 5.1 for the sake of completeness.

shaped curve, the agglomeration rent also exhibits). For situations with high trade costs Borck and Pflüger (2006) illustrate that there is a deterring effect of tax differentials on industry location which is the same effect we already know from the basic tax competition model.

Whenever there is industrial agglomeration (full or partial) in one region, the government of this region can maintain a (constrained) tax rate differential on mobile factors without losing its entire industrial core.

However, agglomeration rents only occur in the core-periphery equilibrium. Consequently, under partial agglomeration the firms that are located in the partial core cannot reap an agglomeration rent which in turn cannot be taxed away. The analysis of Borck and Pflüger (2006) thus shows that there is a deterring effect on industry location due to an increase of the capital tax rate in the partial core, but the presence of agglomeration forces ensures that the region with the partial core can maintain a positive tax rate differential against the periphery (as long as it is not too large). Eventually, higher tax rates in a partial core relate to the fact that firms benefit from proximity due to agglomeration forces (e.g., market access, technology spillovers, etc.) however, there are no rents in the sense of pure economic profits.

With increasing trade costs the tax shield of agglomeration forces declines so that with high trade costs the results very much resemble the basic tax competition model. To sum up, Borck and Pflüger (2006) describe a tax competition game that rests in between the basic tax competition model and the core-periphery tax competition model.[25] Figure 5.2 presents a graphical summary of these results. Starting from high trade costs their results are equivalent to the BTCM. With declining trade costs agglomeration forces built up a tax shield that increases with a further decline in trade costs. Note, that the tax gap between the two regions exhibits a maximum and declines with a further decline in trade costs.

25 Borck and Pflüger (2006) can also show that there is a level of trade costs where the tax gap is not continuous. Since this does not play a role in the remaining course, we do not further deal with this issue, though we address the topic of non-monotony later on.

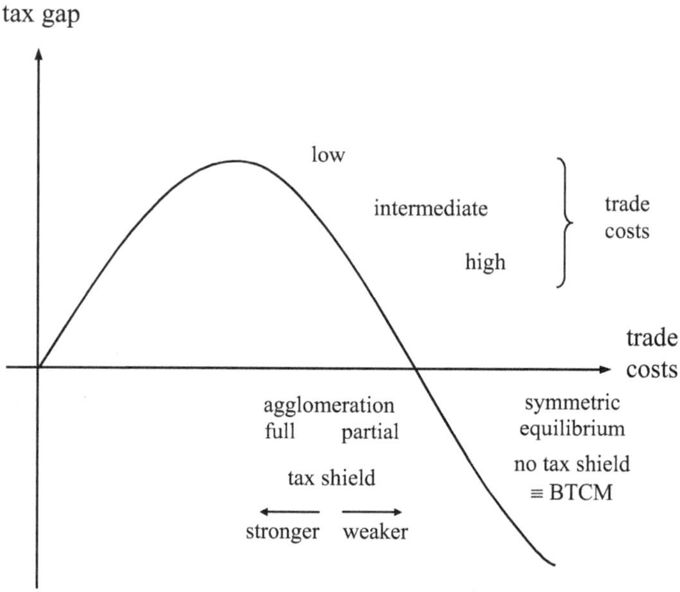


*Figure 5.2: Tax competition in the presence of agglomeration economies; Source: cf. Borck and Pflüger (2006)*

While the basic tax competition model points to the influence of the degree of capital mobility on the tax rate setting behavior of governments, the economic geography tax competition models stress the role of goods' markets integration on the choice of capital tax rates. Besides, Borck and Pflüger (2006) further point out the importance of considering differences in the economic structure when analyzing the implication of tax competition. Their results reveal that when there is tax competition between countries of equal economic structure, tax rate differentials can instantly trigger relocation effects which are stronger the stronger the agglomeration forces are. Therefore, theory expects different outcomes for tax competition between industrialized countries and for tax competition between an industrialized country and a developing country. In the economic geography framework, larger regions (i.e. the regions with the larger share of industry) maintain the higher tax rate, due to the presence of agglomeration economies. Though the basic tax competition model also reveals that larger regions maintain higher tax rates the economic geography defines size as share of industry the term 'large' in the basic tax competition means a large share of immobile factors (cf. table 5.1).

For the following we should keep in mind that it is important to thoroughly characterize the environment in which tax competition takes place. Besides the importance of the degree of trade integration, the economic structure of the countries competing for mobile production factors should be kept in mind. When talking about tax competition, it's crucial to distinguish between symmetric and core-periphery tax competition in the new economic geography setting.

### 5.2.2 Empirical Results

Theory showed that mobile factors of production (esp. capital) react to tax rate differentials across economically integrated countries. Besides, the brief summary of the theoretical models illustrated that the sensitivity of the interaction between taxation and location decision of mobile factors depends on the underlying assumption. Assuming that the intensity of tax competition between independent governments can be expressed by the degree to which mobile firms or capital react to tax rate changes, the topic of tax competition becomes therefore predominantly a question of magnitude. Hence, empirical research is needed to eventually quantify the degree to which mobile factors of production react to tax rate differentials.

In the last decade there have been numerous empirical studies that investigate the interaction of domestic public policy on international capital flows. During this time the availability of data has improved: while the earlier studies based on time series analysis, later research relied on panel and cross section analysis and the most recent studies use micro data on firm levels.

International capital flows are usually associated with Multinational Enterprises (MNE) and mainly related to foreign direct investments (FDI) in terms of real investments in plant and/ or equipment (i.e. investments in new plant and/ or equipment, plant expansions or mergers and acquisitions) and thus mostly associated to the allocation of real capital.[26] However, international capital flows also comprise financial resources in terms of portfolio capital and capital gains.

The remainder of this sections falls into two parts. The first part summarizes the results of a meta data analysis on various empirical studies investigating tax competition. The second part reviews the very recent empirical literature on tax competition that is based on new economic geography models.

---

26 Cf. De Mooij and Ederveen (2003).

### *5.2.2.1 A Meta-Analysis on Tax Competition*

There are numerous empirical studies on the interaction between domestic capital taxation and international capital flows. A recent survey on the main results of the empirical research on this issue has been done by Devereux and Maffini (2006) and can be found in De Mooij and Ederveen (2006).[27] However, due to the use of different data and methods empirical studies are usually very heterogeneous which makes it difficult to come up with a sound comparison of their results. This point has been made by authors of survey articles on empirical research about the interaction between economic integration and taxation policy like Schulze and Ursprung (1999) or Devereux and Maffini (2006). Therefore, this section takes a different approach and summarizes the outcomes of a meta analysis conducted by De Mooij and Ederveen. Meta-analysis is a statistical method to make the results of different empirical studies comparable by relating the different results of the empirical studies to their specific characteristics (e.g. type of data, estimation method and/ or estimation model, etc.). De Mooij and Ederveen generated several studies of this kind which primarily differ in their research subject, namely the focus on how different specific study characteristics explain variations in the obtained results of the underlying empirical research.[28] Each study of De Mooij and Ederveen shows the effects of specific study characteristics on the tax rate elasticity of capital relative to a benchmark set of characteristics (e.g., a time series model which uses all FDI flows, the statutory tax rate and does not make a distinction on how FDIs are financed etc.) which differ across their various studies.

To make the result of various empirical studies on this subject comparable, De Mooij and Ederveen firstly compute tax rate elasticities of capital for the available empirical studies to illustrate the degree to which foreign direct investments react on changes in the capital tax rate. They use the conceptual framework of semi-elasticity (defined as $\frac{\partial \ln(FDI)}{\partial t}$) which explains the percentage change in foreign direct investments $(FDI)$ in response to a one percentage

27 A survey on the more general issue of fiscal competition and national public policy is e.g. provided by Schulze and Ursprung (1999).

28 De Mooij and Ederveen (2006, 2008) are an extended version of De Mooij and Ederveen (2003). Further versions of their meta-analysis can be found in OECD (2007c) which is based on De Mooij and Ederveen (2005) which is closely related to De Mooij and Ederveen (2006).

point change in the capital tax rate $(t)$.[29] Finally, De Mooij and Ederveen construct a meta-sample consisting of the different tax semi-elasticity values for the available empirical studies. By additionally accounting for the specific characteristics of each underlying empirical study (i.e. specification of the estimation model and estimation method, type of data, etc.), the results obtained by their meta regressions are able to explain the variation of estimation results across the different empirical studies.

On the following pages the results of De Mooij and Ederveen will be presented. We thereby abstract from a general discussion of the virtues and the problems associated with meta analysis. These issues are outlined in De Mooij and Ederveen (2006). Furthermore, the estimation results of De Mooij and Ederveen (2003) are not summarized, since their later studies include a larger number of empirical research papers, extending the meta data base of the initial paper.[30] We therefore concentrate on the results presented in De Mooij and Ederveen (2006) which are closely related to De Mooij and Ederveen (2005). The former study gives more detailed information on estimation results than De Mooij and Ederveen (2008) discloses. Additionally, it reports effects of time and spatial dimensions, which would be interesting in anticipation of the following section on the empirics of tax competition on the background of new economic geography models.

The meta-sample of De Mooij and Ederveen (2005, 2006) consists of 427 observations on semi-elasticities.[31] The mean value of this sample is –3.72 implying that an increase of the tax rate in a certain location by one percentage point decreases foreign direct investments by 3.72 per cent. Since the distribution of semi-elasticities is skewed to the left, the median value is –2.91 and the standard deviation is 5.92. Referring to these aggregated figures on describing the impact of capital taxes on FDI behavior of firms neglects the variation in estimation results across different empirical studies on this subject. Consequently, De Mooij and Ederveen try to estimate the impact of specific features on the obtained empirical results of these studies.

29 Before running their meta-regression analyses De Mooij and Ederveen add a negative sign to all semi-elasticities so that positive meta-regression results for a dummy variable (e.g., capital data, tax data, etc.) as reported in their tables indicate a higher elasticity and thus a stronger reaction in absolute terms. A higher positive value of the semi-elasticity implies a stronger reaction of FDI to tax rate changes. However, they maintain the negative sign during the interpretation of their results.

30 Excluding 'extreme' results the number of observations increased from 351 to 427.

31 Severe outliners (i.e. observations that are plus minus two times outside the range of the standard deviation from the mean) in the sample have been removed, so that 95% of the total observation data are used.

To determine the impact of specific study characteristics on the variation of FDI-flows due to (capital) tax rate variations, De Mooij and Ederveen estimate the following equation in their studies: $y = \beta X + \varepsilon$, with $y$ denoting the vector of semi-elasticities which is explained by $X$ – the matrix of dummy variables which reflects the various characteristics of the empirical studies (e.g., type of capital data, tax data, time, source of finance, etc.) –, $\beta$ – the vector which measures the impact of each study characteristic on the semi-elasticity – and the error term $\varepsilon$.

The meta-regressions based on this estimation equation illustrate the impact of specific study characteristics on the tax elasticity results relative to a benchmark set of characteristics. This benchmark regression is a time series model which contains the country statutory tax rate and does not distinguish between different forms of financing FDI (retained earnings or transfer of funds) and between different features of the tax system (credit or exemption system) and with no further control variables.[32]

The results support the notion that the type of capital data (time series data on FDI, cross section data on the allocation of assets, discrete choice models which use count data on location choice or panel data on FDI) is important for the magnitude of the semi-elasticity. Studies using cross-section data obtain systematically higher semi-elasticities than other models.

The meta-regression also reveals that the semi-elasticities for specific forms of FDI (real investments, capital flows) systematically differ from each other. The semi-elasticities for new plants and plant expansions are larger than for other kinds of FDI (e.g., financial capital), i.e. real investments react more sensitive to tax rate changes than other forms of FDI. Since data on mergers & acquisitions exhibit smaller semi-elasticities, De Mooij and Ederveen conclude that ownership advantages are inversely related to the host country tax rate.

Various empirical studies on the impact of taxes on capital flows use different tax rates. The meta regression reveals that effective tax rates (marginal or average) produce larger and significant semi-elasticities than the country statutory tax rate.[33] Both tax rates have the expected sign (i.e. an increase in the tax rate induces a decline in FDI) and are significant. Concerning the impact of the marginal and average effective tax rates the regression results find that the latter exhibits a higher semi-elasticity in absolute terms than the former. This suggests

32 This benchmark equation is identical for De Mooij and Ederveen (2005) and De Mooij and Ederveen (2006).

33 Effective tax rates are computed referring to tax codes by determining the effective tax burden of a hypothetical and standardized investment project; cf. Elschner and Overesch (2007).

that effects of tax rate changes on the marginal investment (i.e. the amount of capital to be invested) are smaller than the impact of tax rate changes on the inframarginal investment (i.e. the location decision of a real investment). De Mooij and Ederveen (2006) thus conclude that the amount of invested capital responds more sensitively to changes in the tax rate than the location decision itself does.

Some empirical studies draw on implicit tax rates, which refer to (firm level or macroeconomic) data and are calculated by dividing the amount of (corporate or capital) taxes paid by the operating surplus of firms. In their sample only the macroeconomic implicit tax rate creates the significantly negative results. However, since implicit tax measures draw on the real amount of tax receipts of former periods there might be a problem of endogeneity: a firm may already have made the decision to settle in a different country which in turn has an effect on the amount of total tax receipts.

Concerning double taxation issues of foreign direct investments, the meta regression reveals that differences in the treatment of capital income from abroad (credit system or exemption system) do not significantly affect the semi-elasticity of the tax rate on FDI-flows. Furthermore, the meta-regression cannot identify significant impacts of different funding sources of FDI (retained earnings or financial transfers) on the semi-elasticity.

In a further regression, information on time and spatial dimensions is added. Referring to spatial impacts on the semi-elasticity the study cannot reveal systematic differences between groups of investing countries (EU investors, US investors, investors from small countries and investors from peripheral countries): none of the dummy variables on spatial dimensions for FDI delivers significant results so that the previous outcomes do not change. Note, that the 'spatial' dimension in De Mooij and Ederveen only accounts for the origin of invested capital but does not address any agglomeration forces featured by economic geography models illustrated before.

Integrating time dimensions in the regression analysis delivers less clear results. Accounting for time periods, the impact of the 1980s and 1990s on the semi-elasticities is significant. It supports the notion that semi-elasticities in the 1990s are higher than in the 1980s. However, De Mooij and Ederveen report relatively higher semi-elasticities before 1980 than after 1980. The regressions thus support the notion that changes in semi-elasticity values across time are non-linear. Theses results contribute to the observation that capital became more and more mobile over time.

The results of the meta-analysis by De Mooij and Ederveen (2006) finally suggest that the existence of a negative correlation between capital taxes and FDI-flows – as supported by orthodox theory – cannot be denied. Yet, the previous analysis showed that the average results on the semi-elasticities quoted at the beginning have to be handled with care. First, the authors report, that more than half of all the collected semi-elasticities (in total the meta sample consists of 427 observations) were insignificant. Besides, their study revealed that single study characteristics (i.e. variables and/ or statistical estimation methods) can be a substantial driver for the obtained overall results on semi-elasticities. Therefore the study highlights the importance of carefully considering the specific characteristics of empirical studies when estimating the influence of taxes on foreign direct investments (FDI) since these characteristics affect the extent to which capital flows react to tax rate changes. Hence, the analysis delivered an explanation for why the strength of the interaction between capital taxes and FDI-flows varies significantly across different empirical studies on this issue. Given the sensitivity of the interaction between capital taxes and FDI, it seems crucial to take further interaction forces into consideration suggested by theory. We therefore turn to empirical research that estimates this relationship by explicitly relying on the theoretical framework provided by the economic geography literature.

#### *5.2.2.2 Tax Competition in the Presence of Agglomeration Economies*

The meaning and the importance of agglomeration economies for location decisions of firms has been examined in several empirical studies by now. For example, a survey article by Combes and Overman (2004) illustrates the spatial concentration of industry across Europe. Head and Mayer (2004) did a survey on the empirical investigations of the main theoretical results supported by NEG models while Rosenthal and Strange (2004) evaluate the empirical literature on the characteristics and sources of agglomeration economies. However, the number of studies that empirically investigate the significance of agglomeration forces on the interaction between national corporate/ capital taxation and international capital flows is very small. In the following paragraphs we will thus concentrate on the following available studies by Devereux et al. (2007), Brülhart et al. (2007), Charlot and Paty (2007) as well as Jofre-Monseny and Solé-Ollé (2008). This section also refers to an essay of Koh and Riedel (2009a). The preliminary work of Jofre-Monseny and Sollé-Ollé (2009) is dropped since upon request the authors asked to not quote it.

As illustrated above, there is a considerable amount of literature that investigates and formalizes the benefits of agglomeration for firms. The source for this phenomenon can be traced back to Marshall's concept of externalities.[34] These 'Marshallian externalities' which positively affect the industrial productivity have been classified by Hoover (1937) in 'localization' and 'urbanization' economies. Urbanization economies relate to a general agglomeration of economic activity. Firms belonging to different sectors locate in proximity to other firms to benefit from general knowledge spillovers that increase productivity. Localization economies describe the spatial clustering of economic activity on the level of specific industries. Firms that belong to the same industry sector locate in proximity to each other to benefit from sector specific knowledge spillovers, labor market pooling effects or input-output linkages. Note that labor market pooling effects and input-output-linkages (i.e. advantage from easy access of firms to large labor markets, other input factors and to large sales markets) refer to pecuniary externalities that is, external economies that work through the price mechanism and do not directly affect a firm's productivity like knowledge spillovers do.

Charlot and Paty (2007) address urbanization economics by emphasizing the aspect of market access as a source of agglomeration economies. Devereux et al. (2007), Koh and Riedel (2009a) as well as Jofre-Monseny and Sollé-Ollé (2008, 2009) refer to urbanization and localization economies in their analyses, while Brülhart et al. (2007) focus on localization economies only.

The most striking result ahead: all studies could identify significant effects of agglomeration economies on governments' business taxation behavior in a way we would have expected from the theoretical considerations above.[35] The empirical studies of Brühlhart et al. (2007), Jofre-Monseny and Solé-Ollé (2008) and Koh and Reidel (2009a) are considered to be the closest in the spirit with the theoretical considerations on agglomeration and tax competition, illustrated in Borck and Pflüger (2006).

To take a closer look at the results of the single essays, we classify the empirical studies into two groups. The first group is made by Charlot and Paty (2007) and Koh and Riedel (2009a) who use the corporate tax rate as the dependent variable. Theses two studies mainly deal with the question whether jurisdictions take the existence of agglomeration economies (and its benefits for firms) into consideration for their choices of corporate tax rates. The second group contains the studies by Brühlhart et al. (2007), Devereux et al. (2007) and Jofre-Monseny and Sole-Ollé (2008) who use measures for economic activity

34 Cf. Krugman (1991b) and Fujita and Thisse (2002). See also Fujita and Thisse (1996) for a survey on theories of agglomeration.

35 Devereux et al. (2007) empirically investigate the interaction of firm births and government subsidies.

(the number of firm births for the first two and the aggregate employment for the latter) as the dependent variable. So these studies estimate how agglomeration economies influence the location decisions of firms on the background of differences in business tax rates across jurisdictions.

The remaining pages present the basic structure of the empirical essays and predominantly outline the results and the conclusions derived by the authors. In particular we are interested in the interaction of tax rates/ firm births and agglomeration forces. A table in the appendix summarizes the main features of each study.

#### 5.2.2.2.1 Dependent Variable: Corporate Tax Rate

Charlot and Paty (2007) and Koh and Riedel (2009a) use the business tax rate as the dependent variable. Thus these two studies assess the impact of agglomeration economies on the tax setting behavior of jurisdictions.

In their approach to analyzing the tax setting behavior of French municipalities, Charlot and Paty (2007) empirically asses the significance of urbanization economics in consumer dimensions. The estimation results confirm a positive and significant relationship between a municipality's tax setting behavior and consumer market access effects of firms.

Their basic considerations on the interaction of agglomeration economies and tax setting behavior of French municipalities are theoretically developed in an economic geography model – the so called linear footloose capital model – with fiscal interactions.[36] In this model, capital is mobile across two regions and due to the specific assumptions, common for new economic geography models (monopolistic competition under increasing returns on the firm-level, transportation costs for a manufactured good) firms benefit from locating where the consumer demand is relatively large (i.e. market access effect). In long-run equilibrium their model suggests that identical regions also maintain identical (business) tax rates, indicating that tax competition between the two regions increases the more similar the regions are. Besides, a higher local (business) tax rate relative to the (business) tax rate in the other region deters capital; an effect similar to the results of the basic tax competition model. However this deterring effect is conditional on agglomeration forces. Since firms benefit from location close to large markets, the deterring effect of taxes is smaller, the larger the market in the

36 Charlot and Paty (2007) rely on a model developed by Ottaviano and van Ypersele (2005).

region with the relatively higher tax rate is (respectively the smaller the transportation costs for shipping the good to other markets is, cf. figure 5.2).

The authors therefore conclude that agglomeration provides rents to firms due to the market access that counteract higher business taxes. In a Nash tax game between regions this will thus prompt governments of larger regions to set higher business tax rates than governments of smaller regions would chose. Empirical estimations should therefore deliver a positive relationship between the market access effect and the business tax rate.

To empirically assess their theoretical results that is to prove the existence of a market access effect in the tax setting behavior of French Municipalities, Charlot and Paty (2007) set up an estimation equation where a municipality's business tax rate is explained by an index reflecting the market access effect and a weight matrix that takes the tax rates set by neighboring jurisdictions into consideration to account for the possibility of a mimic behavior of jurisdictions in their tax rate choices. Market access is estimated by adding up the income of all other municipalities weighted by the Euclidean distance between the municipalities as a proxy for transportation costs. Additional explanatory variables are dummy variables that account for the political cycle in order to take strategic tax rate manipulations before elections into consideration. With regard to the special administrative characteristics of the French tax collection system further explanatory variables are constructed to allow for horizontal tax interaction among municipalities and vertical fiscal externalities.

Charlot and Paty (2007) use spatial panel data for 834 municipalities and cover the period from 1993-2003 to estimate their tax-setting equation. They use different approaches for the weight matrix that was introduced in the estimation equation to take into consideration that jurisdictions compete on the choice of the local tax rate setting: a geographical definition of neighborhood (Euclidean distance between the jurisdictional centers), a demographic interpretation of neighborhood (population size of a region) and a combined geographical and demographical definition of neighborhood. We now focus on the estimation results obtained by using a maximum likelihood approach with a spatially lagged dependent variable (business tax rate) and spatial fixed effects for the three different definitions of 'neighborhood'.

Their estimations produce positive and significant impacts of the market access effect on the (business) tax rate of a municipality. The authors thus conclude that French municipalities are aware of an agglomeration rent due to urbanization economies in consumer dimension and consequently choose higher tax rates with increasing market access. According to their calculations a 10% increase of market access leads to a 1.3% increase of the business tax rate. Besides, the authors show that the horizontal fiscal interaction (i.e. tax competition between municipalities) is fairly strong, i.e. municipalities imitate their geographical neighbors in choosing their business tax rates. The results imply that an average increase of the business tax rate of 10% in neighboring municipalities triggers an increase of the business tax rate of 5.5%. Note that Charlot and Paty (2007) do not incorporate any measures reflecting the similarity of municipalities. The theoretical results of the economic geography model by Borck and Pflüger (2006) would suggest that the mimic behavior of municipalities in the tax rate choice would primarily hinge on the question of municipalities' similarity with respect to the agglomeration forces. Addressing market access as agglomeration force the population/ market size of a municipality would be the determinant of similarity. The setup chosen in Charlot and Paty (2007) attaches different weights to the horizontal tax competition measure however the empirical model does not explicitly address differences in the market size of municipalities. Besides, agglomeration tax competition theory identifies the mimic behavior described by Charlot and Paty (2007) in the scenario of core periphery tax competition, where the core decides to set a tax rate just high enough not to lose the industrial core and the periphery would then follow the core.[37] Further aspects of vertical tax competition the authors deal with will be left out here, since the main aspect is directed to the interaction of agglomeration forces and tax rate setting behavior of municipalities.

Koh and Riedel (2009a) refer to localization and urbanization economies to empirically assess the impact of agglomeration economies on a municipality's tax rate choice (German local business tax). Thus, they distinguish between different agglomeration channels and estimate their impact on a municipality's tax rate choice. They find that both urbanization and localization economics exert a positive influence on the tax rate setting behavior of municipalities, i.e. in the presence of agglomeration economies municipalities choose higher business tax rates. This finding is quantitatively higher for localization economies. Furthermore the authors can show that the relative differences in the specific characteristics for industrial agglomeration across jurisdictions are an important prerequisite for municipalities to tax away agglomeration rents. This is an additional contribution, compared to Charlot and Paty (2007), for instance. Koh and Riedel (2009a) can empirically assess the role of a municipality's relative economic structure to its neighboring communities on the interaction of agglomeration economies and tax rate choice. The results support the notion that the relative strength of agglomeration economies across municipalities also matters for a municipality's tax rate choice, i.e. in municipalities that have relatively large firm agglomerations compared to neighboring jurisdictions or with a relatively

37 Cf. Baldwin and Krugman (2004).

large share of agglomerated industries that are underrepresented in neighboring communities, the business tax rate is also relatively higher.

To estimate the impact of agglomeration economies and the industrial structure of a municipality's business tax rate setting behavior, Koh and Riedel (2009a) set up testable hypotheses derived from theoretical considerations of a model based on Haufler and Wooton (2007). This model recognizes that firms react less sensitive to tax rate differentials across regions when agglomeration economies are prevalent. Koh and Riedel (2009a) thus derive two main hypotheses namely (1) that agglomeration economies positively influence the tax rate setting behavior of municipalities and (2) that the scope for a municipality to exhaust agglomeration rents by higher business tax rates depends on the characteristics of the neighboring communities.

The dependent variable in their estimation equation is the local business tax rate in a specific municipality at a certain point in time. The tax data used covers the years from 1999-2007 and only focuses on municipalities in Western Germany (a total of 8,464). The independent variables are several measures for urbanization and localization economies and a vector of control variables which should account for heterogeneous characteristics between communities. These are first nature characteristics that may also account for agglomeration (e.g., resources), public good provision, the community's financial situation, income per worker, the neighboring community's tax rate and a set of fixed effects. To account for possible reverse causalities between the tax rate and industrial agglomeration Koh and Riedel (2009a) employ an instrumental variables approach with long-lagged information on population and train connections as instruments.

As illustrated before urbanization economics can have a supply (e.g. common knowledge spillovers) and a demand (e.g. consumer market access) dimension. Koh and Riedel (2009a) refer to the number of employed workers in a municipality and construct two measures in accordance with their theoretical considerations. The first measure simply reports the number of employed workers in a municipality. The second measure incorporates information about the relative economic activity within a municipality. As outlined in their theoretical model, similar municipalities located in close neighborhood have a smaller scope for taxing agglomeration rents since firms can easily relocate in response to relative tax rate changes. This measure thus takes the employment and the geographic distance across different municipalities into consideration.

With regard to localization economics, Koh and Riedel (2009a) set up a localization index on the level of 4-digit industries by following an approach proposed by Duranton and Overman (2005) (DO index). This index can overcome a major problem inherent with discrete spatial measures, namely their sensitivity to changes in the size and the shape of the underlying spatial area. To adjust this index to their needs the authors first abstract from industries that do clearly not show any agglomeration patterns like retail companies. Then, they identify industries that are agglomerated at a distance of 0 kilometers and industries that are agglomerated at a distance of 10 kilometers. In the view of Koh and Riedel (2009a) an industry is assumed to be localized if it is significantly agglomerated at a distance of 0 kilometers and if the DO index is above the mean of the sample distribution. This guides the authors to construct a total of 4 localization indicators. The first is the number of employed workers in localized industries in a community. Since theory highlighted the importance to account for differences across jurisdictions in their economic structure, their second localization indicator mirrors the fraction of localized workers in a municipality. Their third localization measure combines these two measures to account for industrial cores that is large industrial agglomerations of localized industries in a community. This index reflects the number of employed workers in localized industries if the share of that industry within a certain municipality is larger than a specifically defined threshold. Finally, their last localization measure compares the number of employed workers in agglomerated industries between neighboring jurisdictions. This contributes to the theoretical consideration that differences in the economic structure between municipalities influence the tax rate setting behavior of them.

To empirically assess the influence of agglomeration economies, Koh and Riedel (2009a) run several regressions using the different localization measures explained above. They apply different empirical settings so that they can compare their empirical results for differences in the spatial scope (localization at a distance of 0 or 10 kilometers) and the degree of economic agglomeration (DO index larger than the mean or larger than the $90^{th}$ percentile). Generally speaking their results show that urbanization and localization economies have a positive impact on the local business tax rate choice of a municipality. The effect of localization economies is quantitatively larger than the effect of urbanization economies. Additionally, their various specifications concerning the spatial scope and the degree of economic integration reveal that localization at a smaller distance and at a higher degree respectively indicate a larger effect of agglomeration economies (i.e. urbanization and localization effects) on the tax rate setting behavior of municipalities. Referring to factors that determine the degree of a community's scope to set the local business tax rate, the authors' assessment reveals that municipalities with a relative larger industrial base (i.e. larger urbanization and localization economies) compared to neighboring communities can set higher business tax rates. Whenever localization economies occur at a larger scale (i.e. agglomeration spreads over community boarders) the scope for local business tax rate differentials is smaller.

Koh and Riedel (2009a) also quantify the effects of agglomeration economies on the tax rate setting behavior of municipalities. In a baseline regression, using the number of workers in significantly and above average localized industries as an indicator for localization economies the authors show that a ten percent increase in the number of total employment (i.e. a rise in the indicator for urbanization economies) induce an increase in the local business tax rate by 0.47 percentage points. A ten percent increase in the number of workers in localized industries (i.e. rise in localization economies) induce an increase in the local business tax rate by 0.58 percentage points. These results become stronger when the spatial scope of localization economies is chosen to be smaller (i.e. referring to industries that localize within a smaller geographic distance) and the focus is set on industries with a strong DO index (i.e. industries that are highly localized).

Substituting the previous localization measure by the sum of employment shares of localized industries within a municipality confirms the previous results. Re-estimating their empirical model by considering only agglomerations within a community that are based on a high share of the total industry's employment (i.e. industrial cores) also underpins the theoretical considerations and reveals higher quantitative impacts of agglomeration economies on the tax rate setting behavior. A ten percent increase in the number of total employment (i.e. rise in the indicator for urbanization economies) increases the local business tax rate by 0.6 percentage points while a ten percent increase in the number of localized workers in the core (i.e. a rise in the indicator for localization economies) induces an increase in the local business tax rate by 3 percentage points. This indicates that a community that hosts an industrial core has a distinctively larger scope for setting its business tax rate, implying that differences in the economic structure (also in the structure on agglomerated industries) play an important role for the tax rate setting behavior of a jurisdiction.

The authors can shed further light of the importance of relative differences in the economic structure by using the last measure for localization economies explained above. They use a measure for the relative employment in localized industries compared to neighboring municipalities. Again, their results confirm theory that larger urbanization economies and localization economies relative to neighboring jurisdictions exert a positive influence on the local business tax rate. Interestingly, the empirical estimations of Koh and Riedel (2009a) also indicate a mimic behavior in the local business tax rate choice of neighboring municipalities, similar to the results of Charlot and Paty (2007).

The robustness checks carried out by Koh and Riedel (2009a) refer to a companion paper Koh and Riedel (2009b) and confirm the previous results for a different index for localization economies developed by Ellison and Glaeser (1997). Employing a measure for market potential also doesn't alter the previous results.[38] Astonishingly, the sum of income in neighboring communities over the distance of the neighboring to the community of interest as a proxy for market potential only delivers a weak significance.

In their general empirical estimations the role of market potential on the tax rate choice does not play an important role in Koh and Riedel (2009a). The companion paper Koh and Riedel (2009b) deals with this issue and the empirical results are in line with the observation of Charlot and Paty (2007), though the regression results of the former are not always delivering statistically significant results.

Additionally, Koh and Riedel (2009a) can show that the similarity of the municipalities concerning their industrial structure and their size is an important determinant for differences of business tax rates across municipalities. This clearly supports the results received by the theoretical considerations above: agglomeration forces per se do not diminish the degree of tax competition between jurisdictions but differences across municipalities determine the influence of agglomeration economies on the tax rate setting behavior.

#### 5.2.2.2.2 Dependent Variable: Economic Activity of Firms

On the remaining pages we turn to three studies that use the number of firm births (startups) as dependent variable in the estimation equations, namely Brülhart et al. (2007), Devereux et a. (2007) as well as Jofre-Monseny and Solé-Ollé (2008). These three studies provide an empirical analysis on the question whether or not a firm's location decision is less sensitive to tax rate changes in the presence of agglomeration forces.

Brülhart et al. (2007) estimate a location choice model of firm setups across Swiss municipalities and support the hypotheses derived from theory that agglomeration forces can counteract differences in the corporate tax rate as a determinant for firms' location choice. Their empirical results could show for Swiss municipalities that the deterring effect of corporate income taxes for the location choice of new born firms is significantly weaker in sectors that are rela-

38 Using the sum of income in neighboring communities over the distance of the neighboring jurisdictions to the community of interest as a proxy for market potential only delivers a weak significant influence on the tax rate setting behavior.

tively more spatially clustered. Thus, they conclude that agglomeration economies can reduce the incentive for jurisdictions to compete for mobile factors by the strategic choice of tax rates.

To prove their hypothesis that the location choice of firms in more spatially concentrated sectors is less sensitive to tax rate differentials, they set up an intuitive baseline model derived from the profit function of a firm and a specific model that is based on the theoretical consideration of a firm's optimization problem. They estimate a conditional logit model via Poisson (sectors = grouping variables) with sector-level counts of the number of 'new born' firms being the dependent variable in both estimation equations. The principal difference between the two models is that the specific model does not contain an explicit interaction term between the tax burden index and the sector agglomeration intensity index.

The authors take the number of new firm counts (new entries by mergers, takeovers or breakups are not counted) per municipality and sector from 1999-2002 and empirically analyze two pooled waves of firm creations from 1999-2000, assigned to control variables from 1998 and from 2001-2002, assigned to control variables from 2001. In total they have 13,768 observations (firm counts) for the first period and 12,465 observations for the second wave. The explanatory variables are a tax index (a revenue-weighted average of consolidated municipal and cantonal profit and capital taxes) and an agglomeration index which is calculated according to Ellison and Glaeser (1997). The estimation further includes dummy variables to account for additional important location aspects namely prices of labor and real estate, household income taxes, public expenditures, proximity to same sector firms, the size of demand (i.e. market potential), distance to highways (i.e. accessibility to other markets), assisted municipality (eligibility of a municipality to allow tax exemptions for newly created firms) and area (to assure that only usable land is taken into consideration for firm location). The specific model contains a subset of these explanatory variables.

Both estimations, the baseline model and the specific model, support the results derived from theory. The baseline model can show that the tax index is statistically significantly negative (there is a deterring effect of taxes on industry location) and the interaction index which measures the interaction of the tax index and the agglomeration index is significantly positive. The additional explanatory variables are largely in line with expectations derived from theory: especially the market potential exerts a significantly positive effect on a firm's location decision. Besides, public expenditure, the proximity to same sector firms and availability of land has also a significantly positive location effect. Interestingly, their results about the interaction of wages and property prices with the EG index are in line with the reasoning for the interaction of agglomeration and taxation: with strong agglomeration economies the deterring effect of wages and property prices on location decisions is weaker for agglomerated industries. In the baseline model the authors are additionally able to quantify the importance of agglomeration economies on the sensitivity of firms' location decisions to tax rate differentials: an increase of a municipality's tax rate by one sample standard deviation decreases the count of firms in a sector with average agglomeration intensity in this municipality by 3.8 %. The deterrent effect of taxation on the number of firm births in a weakly agglomerated sector (18th percentile of the agglomeration index) is determined by –3.3 % respectively –6.8 % for an even more weakly agglomerated sector (20$^{th}$ percentile of the agglomeration index). Thus Brülhart et al. (2007) can show that the adverse effects of corporate taxation on firms' location decisions can considerably be mitigated by sector agglomeration.

The specific model is able to support the results of the baseline model. Furthermore the authors can quantify the effects of the interaction between sector agglomeration and corporate taxation: for firms belonging to sectors with the lowest agglomeration index (least agglomerated industries) the tax differential across regions is 2.5 times more important for their location decision than for firms belonging to sectors with the highest agglomeration index (most agglomerated industries).

Devereux et al. (2007) use a conditional logit model with fixed effects to empirically assess how government grants affect the location choice of firms for setting up new plants (greenfield investments). The authors use a discrete choice framework where the location decision is a function of characteristics of a region, the plant and the industrial sector as well as a discretionary regional grant which aims to promote setting up plants in economically deprived areas. Thereby specific interest is directed to the question whether potential benefits from spatial proximity to other firms reduces the effectiveness of these government grants (here: UK's program of Regional Selective Assistance – RSA). Their estimation results show that the existing industrial structure of a region has an important influence on the location decision of a firm. Therefore, a firm's response to government aid also depends on the number of plants that already exist in a certain region.

To come up with an estimation model the authors first construct a firm's location choice model. A firm's expected profit depend on a range of variables, reflecting demand and cost conditions and taking region-specific variables as well as factors that vary on the industry-region, firm-region and firm-industry level into consideration. The model further accounts for local demand conditions (variation in GDP, population and manufacturing employment), for differences in the size of a region and for differences in the ownership structure (foreign or domestic). Differences in the costs of production across the regions are captured by using information on skilled and unskilled wage rates, the unemployment rates and measures reflecting the industrial geographic concentration. Agglomeration economies occur in the form of both urbanization and localization economies. The authors account for agglomeration economies by including information on the number of 4-digit industry leveling each region-year and a measure containing information how localized or geographically clustered the employment in an industry is. Localization economies are taken into consideration by including measures of region size and information on the degree of diversification of manufacturing employment.

The authors then estimate a conditional logit model across 88 potential regions to set up a firm, where the above mentioned variables reflecting potential profits enter the estimation equation with a one-year lag so that expectations are derived from the information of the preceding period (i.e. extrapolative expectations). Besides, area fixed effects are used to control for unobservable characteristics of a region which are assumed to be exogenous, like infrastructure etc..

In addition to expected profits from establishing a plant in a specific region, a firm also has to account for the possibility of receiving a grant. This location subsidy is modeled as a lump sum payment to firms. It is conditional on a firm's application for the grant (which can only be made for one region) and the positive reply of the government agency (i.e. the actual payment of the grant). The level of the grant depends on various factors like expected employment, expected investment and the economic condition in the region the firm wants to set up a plant. The authors then estimate the grant equation to generate a measure for the expected grant for setting up a plant in each of the 88 location choices. Control variables are used to account for the various characteristics of the grant, including dummy variables to capture area characteristics.

The data used (firm setups and grant data) covers the time period from 1986-1992 and 88 location choices for plants. Agglomeration economies are taken into consideration by calculating a measure for industry-county localization and an industry-level measure proposed by Maurel and Sédillot (1999) which reflects the geographical concentration of employment within an industry. Furthermorre, the authors construct a Herfindahl index to determine the degree of industrial diversity in a county.

Devereux et al. (2007) then begin to estimate the factors that determine the expected grant offer and the amount of the subsidy and use this information to estimate the impact of expected grants and agglomeration economies on the location decision of setting up plants.

The estimations concerning the discretionary grant deliver significant results that plants belonging to high-tech sectors, chemicals, high-tech manufacturing and motor vehicles are more likely to apply for the grants. Concerning the size of the grant offer the results show that foreign-owned plants and those belonging to the high-tech manufacturing sector receive higher grant offers. The size of the firm or group that wants to set up a plant is not related to the likelihood of applying for a grant. However, the size of the group is positively related to the amount of the offered subsidy.

In the following, the authors take the obtained results on grant applications, offers and amounts to empirically assess the impact of subsidies and agglomeration economies on the location decisions of firms. They find a robust relationship between the location decision and the market access, i.e. firms tend to locate where demand (measured by regional GDP) is relatively high. Urbanization economies are an important criterion for the location decision since the estimations find a positive and significant relationship. Localization economies are positively and significantly related to a firm's location decision and even to a greater extent when the employment in that industry is highly agglomerated. Increasing the agglomeration index by 0.01 units doubles the marginal location effect of industries in this region. Since the data set distinguishes between greenfield investments from foreign-owned multinational firms and UK-based groups, the estimation results can additionally show, that a larger presence of foreign plants exerts a significantly positive influence on location decisions for new plants from foreign firms, though these effects are fairly low. The average probability of a foreign-owned plant to locate where foreign firms are already settled increases by 3% when the number of foreign-owned plants doubles in this region. Taking expected grant offers into considerations the estimations unveil a positive and significant influence on the location decision, which is, however, fairly small (increasing the expected grant by £ 100,000 also increases the location probability from 1% to 1.03%). More importantly, when the authors interact the expected grant offer with the measure of existing plants of the same industry the location effect of the grant further increases (increasing the expected grant under a higher number of firms by £ 100,000, increases the location probability to 1.032%). Devereux et al. (2007) consider that the grant offers need to be increased to encourage firms to set up plants in areas where benefits from agglomeration economies are smaller. They conclude that agglomeration externalities can potentially offset positive location effects of subsidies and infer that location grants work more effectively in counties where the industrial activity is higher.

Jofre-Monseny and Solé-Ollé (2008) empirically assess the effect of agglomeration economies on the sensitivity of firms' location decisions to differences in the local business tax. Their main focus is set on the employment effects of changes in the local business tax rate and the impact of the interaction between agglomeration forces and the degree of dissimilarity in municipalities' economic structure on this relationship.

They use a theoretical economic geography model described by Fujita and Thisse (2002) and modified it so that it can deal with local taxation issues to develop two empirically testable predictions: the deterring effect of corporate taxes on firm location in a municipality increases (decreases) with the strength of agglomeration economies if the industrial structure of this municipality is similar (dissimilar) to its neighboring jurisdictions.

The dependent variable in their empirical study is the growth rate of employed workers in a municipality, which according to the authors serves as proxy for the economic activity there. The explanatory variables are municipality fixed effects (i.e. availability of land, infrastructure accessibility, public goods and further amenities), year fixed effects to account for business cycles and variables that measure the interaction of agglomeration economies with the tax rate. These are an index that reflects the strength of agglomeration economies and a measure to comprise the degree of dissimilarity between municipalities. The former index comprises a measure for the concentration of economic activity within industries (i.e. localization industries) according to the proposal by Ellison and Glaeser (1997) (EG index). Besides, they also compute a co-agglomeration index according to Ellison and Glaeser (1997) to have a measure for the strength of agglomeration forces across industries (i.e. urbanization economies). Both measures are combined to quantify the strength of agglomeration forces. Thus a municipality is considered to have strong agglomeration economies, when it hosts a more than average number of industries with high agglomeration economies. Jofrey-Monseny and Solé-Ollé (2008) then build an index to reflect the similarity of neighboring jurisdictions with respect to size and industrial structure. It's assumed that municipalities are neighbors, when they draw their workforce from the same local labor market. The proposed dissimilarity measure than delivers the expected difference of the labor shares in two neighboring municipalities.

Since Jofre-Monseny and Solé-Ollé (2008) assume that the effects of taxes on the changes in employment are cumulative, the change in explanatory variables does not report the change to the proceeding period (i.e. one year) but the change to the proceeding three years.

To empirically assess the impact of agglomeration forces and the dissimilarity measure on the interaction of the municipal tax on business and changes in municipal employment, Jofre-Monseny and Solé-Ollé (2008) use a panel of municipality data from 1995-2002 for the region of Catalonia. Due to data availability they use two three-year periods (from 1995-1998 and 1999-2002) and pool them to run their regressions so that the overall number of observations is 675 (i.e. 256 municipalities in the first and 419 municipalities in the second period of observation).

To take into consideration that employment shocks may be correlated to tax rate manipulations (e.g., a firm passes away and lays off workers which in turn induces local authorities to cut down local business tax rates), the authors add different labor market and industry fixed effects to explain variations in the municipality's employment apart from agglomeration forces or dissimilarities in the size or economic structure.

In an OLS approach the authors compute the effects of the interaction of local business taxes with agglomeration economies and the interaction of local business taxes with combined agglomeration economies and the degree of dissimilarity on the change of employment in a municipality. The interaction term of taxes and agglomeration forces delivers statistically significant negative effects (i.e. an increase in the tax rate/ agglomeration forces depresses the employment). This supports the theoretical consideration that agglomeration forces alone do not manifest a tax rate setting advantage over neighboring municipalities. Besides, the interaction term of local business taxes, agglomeration forces and the dissimilarity measure has a significantly positive influence on the change in employment within a municipality, that is stronger agglomeration economies reduce the negative effect of taxes on employment whenever municipalities are dissimilar in their size and economic structure. This is also in line with the theoretical consideration of above. The authors can quantify the point of dissimilarity, from which on agglomeration economies can offset the negative effects of business tax rate changes on employment. This is the case when the dissimilarity measure is at least 1.5 standard deviations larger than the mean value. 14% of the municipalities in the sample data have a dissimilarity measure over this point, indicating that the municipalities are generally identical concerning size and industrial structure and therefore in general the presence of agglomeration economies increases the location effect of taxes so that tax competition is intensified.

Since the OLS estimate of the 'plain' tax effect on employment change is biased due to institutional characteristics of the Spanish business tax system, the authors use an instrumental variables approach to recalculate this effect.[39] Therefore the authors use an instrumental variables approach to estimate the effect of changes in the business tax rate on the municipality's changes in employment.

39 In Spain there are legal constraints (upper bounds) for municipalities in setting their business tax rate, which depend on the population size of a municipality.

Their estimations deliver a statistically significant negative effect of taxes on employment growth. Thus, a decrease of a municipality's business tax rate of one standard deviation below the average increases the employment in that municipality by 5% over the period of three years.[40]

The tax rate effects on employment changes support the theoretical results of Baldwin and Krugman (2004) and Borck and Pflüger (2006). The more similar the municipalities are, the more intense are the tax effects on the employment growths in the presences of agglomeration forces. Increasing the agglomeration forces in this setting emphasizes the deterring effect of taxation on the location decision of firms (cf. tax competition around the symmetric equilibrium). On the other hand, agglomeration forces offset the deterring effect of business taxation on employment growth, when municipalities are different in their size and economic structure (cf. tax competition in the core-periphery setting).

Hence, the results obtained by Jofre-Monseny and Solé-Ollé (2008) finally support our previous observations and conclusions gained from theoretical and empirical research that the results of tax competition are very sensitive to the underlying assumptions and especially the specific context.

## 5.3 Conclusion

The objective of this chapter has been to integrate the recent theoretical and empirical contributions of the economic geography literature in the broad field of tax competition literature. For this, the fundamental insights provided by the basic tax competition model have been graphically and verbally illustrated. Then, the major theoretical implications of the basic tax competition model have been compared with the main findings of the economic geography models which deal with fiscal interactions. Thereby, two important issues already became visible: when talking about the interaction of international factor flows and national tax setting behavior for mobile factors, it is very important to (1) distinguish between the underlying assumptions and to (2) closely keep the specific characteristics and thus the context in which jurisdictions use tax rates to compete for mobile factors in mind. The ensuing discussion of the most recent empirical studies on this issue could support these theoretical conclusions.

40 Jofre-Monseny and Solé-Ollé (2008) also report the results of an instrumental variable estimation over the entire empirical setting described above. Theses results confirm the results above but they come with a loss in efficiency and are therefore not discussed here.

While the basic tax competition model supports the notion of a race-to-bottom scenario, namely a world in which jurisdictions continuously cut down tax rates for mobile production factors (esp. capital) so that they will not lose their mobile tax base to other jurisdictions, further research could show that these strong results have to be qualified, for instance, by considering differences in the size of jurisdictions. The economic geography models with fiscal interactions could now disclose additional channels that work against the looming scenario of a race-to-bottom. Considering agglomeration forces delivers an additional explanation that strongly qualifies an impending doom attached to capital mobility in the course of European economic integration. In the presence of agglomeration forces, benefits from agglomeration may become visible and with closer economic integration, leading to further clustering of economic activity. This leaves scope for corporate income taxation which finally result in a 'race to top', a situation where jurisdictions can increase their corporate or capital tax rates without losing their industrial base. This scenario is illustrated in Baldwin and Krugman (2004), who use the core-periphery model with fiscal interactions to explain the development of the average corporate tax rate across the European Union.[41]

Thus, there are additional forces at work that influence the location decisions of firms or other forms of investment capital. The tax sensitivity of capital depends on various factors which may mitigate the deterrent effects of tax rate differentials across jurisdictions. What is more, agglomeration forces may offset the deterring effect of capital taxation indicated by the basic tax competition model. But caution has to be exercised: the conclusion that agglomeration forces alone will offset the deterring effect of capital tax rate differentials across jurisdictions rests on an import premise namely on differences in the industrial structure and the size of a jurisdiction. This insight has been delivered by theory and confirmed by empirical research.

When talking about capital tax competition in an economic geography framework it is therefore crucial to distinguish between different scenarios on which tax competition may take place. In a symmetric tax competition setting, the theoretical results of the tax competition literature deliver similar results than the basic tax competition model does: marginal changes in the capital tax rate of a jurisdiction instantly trigger relocation effects of mobile capital. This may be the case when tax competition between similar countries is considered. In a 'core-periphery' tax competition setting (i.e. when firms in the core receive an agglomeration rent) capital tax rates can be set in a certain range without trigger-

41 Note that Baldwin and Krugman (2004) take the total corporate tax revenues and divide them by the GDP.

ing relocation effects of capital. This case may be applicable when analyzing tax competition between countries with strong differences in the industrial structure. Eventually in a 'partial core-periphery' tax competition setting the partial core can maintain a tax rate differential without losing industry due to agglomeration forces. This may be the case when there is tax competition between countries with intermediate differences. The comparative analysis of empirical studies about the interaction of agglomeration economies with the tax rate choices of jurisdictions confirmed these theoretical findings illustrated e.g. in Borck and Pflüger (2006). Jofre-Monseny and Solé-Ollé (2008) therefore rightly point to this issue when they conclude, that the results of tax competition are very sensitive to the underlying assumptions and especially the specific context.

Finally, the strong support for the theoretical results delivered by the empirical research may quickly inspire policy makers to salvage the treasure hidden behind agglomeration rents. But this conclusion may turn out to be premature. The theoretical considerations showed that the effects of agglomeration are non-monotonic what makes it extremely difficult to assess the effect of tax rate changes in the sense of making full use of agglomeration rents. Tax rate manipulations may be too large so that 'all in a sudden' industry will relocate. And then, hysteresis will make it very difficult and expensive for a jurisdiction to win back industrial activity. Therefore, the above illustrated results carry the wisdom of composure in public policy: neither an overhasty increase of capital tax rates to exploit agglomeration rents nor frantically cutting down capital tax rates in the fear of losing the mobile tax base proved to be a sound fiscal policy.

# Appendix 5.A Tabular Arrangement of Empirical Results

*Table 5.A.1: Comparison of empirical results I*

| | Charlot and Paty (2007) | Koh and Riedel (2009a) |
|---|---|---|
| Objective | impact of agglomeration economies on the tax rate setting behavior of municipalities<br>existence of a 'market access effect in the tax setting behavior of French municipalities | impact of firm agglomeration on jurisdictional tax setting behavior of municipalities<br>differentiation from neighboring jurisdictions (industry structure and size) positively impacts on a municipality's tax rate choice |
| Results | positive and significant relationship between tax rates and market access effect<br>mimic behavior in tax rate setting across neighboring municipalities | agglomeration economies exert a positive influence on a municipality's tax rate choice<br>tax rate positively depends on agglomeration economies relative to neighboring communities |
| Country | Municipalities in France | West German municipalities |
| Theory | economic geography model by Ottaviano and van Ypersele (2005) | a model derived from Haufler and Wooton (2008) |
| Agglomeration economies | urbanization economies (market access effect) | localization and urbanization economies |
| Agglomeration measure | market access ( income of all other municipalities weighted by trade costs) | four measures based on Duratorn and Overman (2005) |
| Dependent variable | local (business) tax rate in a municipality | tax rate (German local business tax) |
| Explanatory variables | index of local (business) tax rate of other municipalities, index of market access effect (income of all other municipalities weighted by trade costs), political variables (election dates), demand for public goods, measures to account for vertical and horizontal tax competition | measure for urbanization economies, four measures for localization economies, first nature characteristics, level of public good provision, financial situation of a community, income per worker, neighboring communities' tax rate, fixed effects for heterogeneity between jurisdictions, year fixed effects |
| Time Period | 1993-2003 | 1999-2007 |
| Empirical method | maximum likelihood (with spatially lagged depend variable and spatial fixed effects) | instrumental variables (IV) |

*Table 5.A.2: Comparison of empirical results II*

| | Brülhart et al. (2007) | Devereux et al. (2007) |
|---|---|---|
| Objective | influence of agglomeration economies on firms' sensitivity to tax rate differentials in their location choice | influence of government grants on the location decision of new firms interaction of agglomeration economies with public policy instruments for industry location |
| Results | high corporate income taxes are deterrent to location of firm start-ups this deterrent factor is weaker for sectors that are spatially clustered | the existing industrial structures of a region have an effect on the location decision of a new entrant firms are more responsive to subsidies when there are plants of the same industry in the neighborhood |
| Country | Municipalities in Switzerland | assisted areas in the United Kingdom |
| Theory | Baseline model: general profit function (intuitive) Specific model: firm's optimization problem proposed by Crozet et al. (2004) | location choice model (function of firm's expected profits and expected grant) |
| Agglomeration economies | localization economies | localization and urbanization economies |
| Agglomeration measure | Ellison and Glaeser (1997) | number of plants in each region and each county-year; industry level agglomeration according to Maurel and Sédillot (1999); Herfindahl index of industrial diversification |
| Dependent variable | number of new firms per municipality and sector | sector firm births in assisted areas |
| Explanatory variables | tax index (local corporate taxes), agglomeration index, interaction index for taxes and agglomeration (in baseline model), several dummy variables (prices of labor and real estate, household income taxes, proximity to same sector firms, demand size, distance to highways, eligibility to tax exemptions, available land) | expected grant , local demand conditions (variation in GDP, working age population and manufacturing employment), size of a region (number of plants), costs of production (skilled and unskilled wage rates, unemployment rates), measures on industrial geographic concentration, diversification measure, localization measure, owner structure of a firm (foreign or domestic) |
| Time Period | 1999-2002 | 1986-1992 |
| Empirical method | conditional logit model via Poisson (with sector and location fixed effects) | conditional logit model (with area fixed effects) |

*Table 5.A.3: Comparison of empirical results III*

| | Jofre-Monseny and Sollé-Ollé (2008) |
|---|---|
| Objective | impact of agglomeration economies on the tax rate setting behavior of municipalities<br>variations in the impact of local business tax on the employment in a municipality<br>analyzing the variation in the effect of local business tax on employment subject to agglomeration economies and dissimilarity across municipalities |
| Results | a municipality with stronger agglomeration economies experiences lower tax effects if it is sufficiently dissimilar to its neighboring community (in terms of size) |
| Country | municipalities in Catalonia, Spain |
| Theory | economic geography model by Fujita and Thisse (2002) |
| Agglomeration economies | urbanization economies (knowledge spill overs) |
| Agglomeration measure | Ellison and Glaeser (1997) |
| Dependent variable | employment in a municipality |
| Explanatory variables | local business tax rate, municipality fixed effects (land availability, infrastructure accessibility, public goods, further amenities), year fixed effects (to account for business cycle), interaction index between agglomeration and tax rate |
| Time Period | 1995-2002 |
| Empirical method | ordinary least squares (OLS), instrumental variables (IV) |

# 6 Conclusions

## 6.1 Concluding Remarks

Global economic integration in general and the expansion of the European Union in particular fosters widespread concerns about the declining power of national governments in the area of fiscal policy. The preceding pages illustrated four different approaches to draw up a comprehensive view of the various impacts of economic integration on the scope and content of national public policy. The results showed that the alarming scenario of a race-to-bottom in the course of economic integration as for example pointed out by Rodrik (1997) or Sinn (2003) has to be qualified from the theoretical as well as the empirical perspective. There is no doubt that economic integration makes factors of production more footloose and sensitive to differences across countries that are tied up to each other by integration of their product and factor markets. Capital in particular has become a very mobile factor of production in recent decades and the existence of multinational firms tends to increase the mobility of jobs as well. However there are mechanisms and forces that have to be taken into consideration when consequences from economic integration on public policy should be derived.

The simple perfect competition model illustrated in the first chapter put the focus on labor mobility to develop an analysis on the welfare effects of economic integration on independent income redistribution policies. Economic integration, no matter how it articulates (e.g., factor mobility, free goods market access), puts aside market restrictions which allowed governments to easily exercise their national tax and social policies. In the case of the simple perfect competition model explained in the first chapter, economic integration enabled the factor labor to move freely. With open boarders a system of independent income redistribution in one region induces welfare losses compared to a closed economy situation. It negatively influences the migration behavior of workers so that finally inefficiently high numbers of workers move into the region that offers income redistribution. These results hinge on the inefficiencies that are carried into the model by the implementation of redistribution systems. The inefficiencies are not explicitly addressed since it is acknowledged that these redistribution systems usually have manifest themselves over decades and are eventually the outcome of political decision making processes. In this simple setting the only way to prevent welfare losses that come along with migration, not just for one region but also for the entire economic union, is for entities within the economic union to cooperate and establish a common system of income redistribution within the entire economic union. When this approach is pursued an independent economic policy by each member of the region becomes impossible. If each state sticks to its own income redistribution system welfare losses come along with economic integration and governments will finally be forced to adjust their welfare systems thereby sacrificing their fiscal independence. Whenever the member countries of the economic union cannot agree on a common redistribution system, a race-to-bottom can easily be unleashed, with the well known negative effects.

Major concerns, however, are usually linked to capital mobility that has been overwhelmingly enforced by economic integration. Capital or corporate tax rates are usually assumed to be the primary deterrents to investment location decisions of firms. However, tax rates alone are not the only criteria for the location decisions of firms, a fact which has been regularly proven by surveys among firms like Ernst & Young (2007a), for instance. There are numerous other factors that determine the 'right spot' to invest in production facilities. The model in the third chapter on taxes, public infrastructure and industry location was used to draw the attention to this point. A distinctive feature of this model is the prevalence of agglomeration forces due to market size effects. Local public infrastructure that facilitates setting up firms is provided through taxes levied on immobile labor income and mobile capital income at different rates. Economic integration is modeled by capital mobility and openness of goods markets denoted by transportation costs for shipping goods between two regions. The model strongly qualified the notion of declining fiscal power in the course of economic integration since corporate income taxes are no longer the only ingredients that determine the location decision of firms. Besides, differences in the market size, differences in the tax rate on labor income as well as the level of economic integration all together influence a firm's location decision. Even though the model clearly emphasizes the influences of economic integration on the fiscal behavior of a government, the notion of a strong decline in fiscal power of a regional government due to economic integration turns out to be an exaggeration. The model acknowledged that countries trading with each other are not the same in all respects and to move the model closer to reality, the model further took market imperfections into consideration. This reveals that the race-to-bottom results presented in the second chapter are very sensitive to the underlying assumptions and have to be qualified. Differences in the market size or the degree of public infrastructure provision for example, allow governments to maintain a certain degree of independence in their fiscal decisions. Therefore, there are several more items that make up a business environment allowing firms to develop and prosper which are far reaching and comprise not only a sound physical or 'hard' infrastructure like roads, bridges, railways or telecommunication wires but also 'soft' elements like property rights, a properly functioning legal and administrative system, skilled workforce as well as social consensus of a society. Since this broad infrastructure lowers the costs of setting up and running a business, the burden of taxes used to finance the infrastructure is qualified and only taking capital taxes into consideration when talking about industry location is therefore misleading.

Capital mobility does not only affect foreign direct investments (FDI), i.e. the allocation of real investment capital (i.e. investments in new plant and/ or equipment, plant expansions or mergers and acquisitions). International capital flows also comprise the transfer of financial resources like portfolio capital and capital gains. Multinational firms (i.e. firms with several affiliates located in different countries) have become a distinctive characteristic of economic integration, especially in the recent two decades. While operating several affiliates in different countries, multinational firms can use transfer pricing (i.e. crediting input of services and primary products) to shift their profits between the various affiliated companies from high-tax to low-tax countries in order to lower the aggregate tax burden of the whole company. Since this may only be a bookkeeping issue which does not involve the transfer of real funds or invested assets, it is a very easy and reasonable way to optimize the tax bill of a multinational firm. Since profit shifting hinges on the different corporate/ capital tax rates among the member states of the European Union (EU), the scenario of a wasteful while welfare decreasing tax competition over these tax rates again becomes obvious with a race-to-bottom scenario looming. So, finally, firms' attempts of reducing the tax burden through transfer pricing has lead to public efforts to harmonizing the taxation of multinational firms in the EU by introducing a common consolidated tax base to prevent firms from profit shifting through transfer pricing. Therefore, the fourth chapter used a simple model to illustrate the implications on transfer pricing by modifying the tax code for multinational firms. Considering that multinational firms are usually large corporations that are able to exercise substantial market power in the countries where they operate and sell their products, the transfer price consists of two parts: (1) a strategic component that allows the multinational firm to reap additional profits due to market power and (2) a taxation component that is used to shift the tax base. Again, the tax rate is not the only determinant of a company's behavior in choosing its optimal transfer price.[1] Increased economic integration was expressed in a declining spatial product differentiation in one region. The model showed that due to the strategic

1 Cf. Ernst & Young (2007b).

effect, the incentives for transfer pricing in response to tax rate differentials remain under a common consolidated tax base. With increasing economic integration, the market power of the multinational firm declines and so the strategic effect of transfer pricing declines in both tax schemes. However, with increasing economic integration the incentives for transfer pricing remain stable under the scheme of a common consolidated tax base (i.e. formula apportionment), while they decline under the current taxation scheme (i.e. separate accounting) that treats the profits of the affiliates separately. The logic behind this observation can be found in the way the common consolidated tax base is set up. The apportionment factors, used to distribute the overall profits (i.e. tax base) of a multinational firm to the countries in which it operates affiliates are directly linked to the output of each affiliate and the main office/ headquarter. Thus, the multinational firm can adjust its production to optimally reply to changes in the tax rates by influencing the return in each country and thus indirectly manipulating its average tax rate. This is not possible under a tax scheme that treats profits from different affiliates separately so that the current system offers lower incentives for transfer pricing with increasing economic integration. Instead, the model could show that economic integration can mitigate the issue of tax competition and, ignoring other strategic aspects of entrepreneurial behavior, for instance, may miss the aim of a cooperative public policy on corporate tax issues.

The objective of chapter 5 has been to augment the preceding theoretical considerations by empirical results on the interaction of capital/ corporate income taxation with economic integration. It therefore summarized the recent theoretical and empirical contributions of the economic geography literature in the broad field of tax competition literature. While the basic tax competition model supports the notion of a race-to-bottom scenario, namely a world in which jurisdictions continuously cut down tax rates for mobile production factors (esp. capital) so that they will not lose their mobile tax base to other jurisdictions, further research could show that these strong results have to be qualified, e.g., by considering differences in the size of jurisdictions. Comparing the major theoretical implications of the basic tax competition model with the main findings of economic geography models which deal with fiscal interactions revealed two important issues: when talking about the interaction of international factor flows and national tax setting behavior for mobile factors, it is very important to (1) distinguish between the underlying assumptions and to (2) closely keep the specific characteristics and thus the context in which jurisdictions use tax rates to compete for mobile factors in mind. The ensuing discussion of the most recent empirical studies on this issue could support these theoretical conclusions. Economic geography models with fiscal interactions could disclose additional channels that work against the looming scenario of a race-to-bottom.

Taking agglomeration forces into consideration delivers further explanations that strongly qualify an impending doom attached to capital mobility in the course of European economic integration. In the presence of agglomeration forces, benefits from agglomeration may become visible and with closer economic integration may lead to further clustering of economic activity. This leaves scope for corporate income taxation which finally may result in a race-to-top scenario, a situation where jurisdictions can increase their corporate or capital tax rates without losing their industrial base.

Thus, there are additional forces at work that influence the location decisions of firms or other forms of investment capital. The tax sensitivity of capital depends on various factors which may mitigate the deterrent effects of tax rate differentials across jurisdictions. Besides, agglomeration forces may offset the deterring effect of capital taxation indicated by the basic tax competition model. But it needs to be cautious: the conclusion that agglomeration forces alone will offset the deterring effect of capital tax rate differentials across jurisdictions rests on an important premise namely on differences in the industrial structure and the size of a jurisdiction. This insight has been delivered by theory and confirmed by empirical research.

When talking about capital tax competition in an economic geography framework it is therefore crucial to distinguish between different scenarios on which tax competition may take place. In a 'symmetric' tax competition setting, the theoretical results of the economic geography tax competition literature are similar to those delivered by the basic tax competition model: marginal changes in the capital tax rate of a jurisdiction instantly trigger relocation effects of mobile capital. This may be the case when tax competition between similar countries is considered. In a 'core-periphery' tax competition setting (i.e. when firms in the core receive an agglomeration rent) capital tax rates can be set in a certain range without triggering relocation effects of capital. This case may be applicable when analyzing tax competition with strong differences in the industrial structure. Eventually, in a 'partial core-periphery' tax competition setting the partial core can maintain a tax rate differential without fully losing industry due to agglomeration forces. This may be the case when there is tax competition between countries with intermediate differences. In this respect, the results of tax competition are very sensitive to the underlying assumptions and especially the specific context. The strong support for the theoretical results delivered by the empirical research may quickly inspire policy makers to salvage the treasure hidden behind agglomeration rents. But this conclusion may turn out to be premature. The theoretical considerations showed that the effects of agglomeration are non-monotonic which makes it extremely difficult to assess the effect of tax rate changes in the sense of making full use of agglomeration rents. Tax rate manipulations may be too large so that 'all in a sudden' industry will relocate. And then hysteresis will make it very difficult (i.e. expensive) for a jurisdiction to win back industrial activity. Therefore, the above illustrated results carry the wisdom of composure in public policy: neither an overhasty increase of capital tax rates to exploit agglomeration rents nor frantically cutting down capital tax rates in the fear of losing the mobile tax base proved to be a sound fiscal policy.

## 6.2 Outlook

Eventually, the approach used for this thesis points out that the effects of economic integration on the fiscal policy deliver a far more intricate picture that partly qualifies the commonly used term of a race-to-bottom scenario. This, however, does not mean that economic integration will have no impact on fiscal policies, but that fears about an erosion of capital tax receipts and public spending due to enhanced tax competition can largely be relaxed. Political institutions still play an important role in the design and the scope of public spending indicating that the political consensus still constitutes the fundament of fiscal policy. Additionally, solely focusing on capital tax rates may be misleading since these are not the only determinants of investment decisions but just one item among others that contribute to a proper business environment.

# References

Andersen, Torben (2003). European Integration and the Future of the Welfare State. *Journal of Population Economics*, 16 (1), 1-19.

Andersson, Fredrik and Rikard Forslid (2003). Tax Competition and Economic Geography. *Journal of Public Economic Theory*, 5 (2), 279-303.

AsylbLG. Asylbewerberleistungsgesetz in der Fassung der Bekanntmachung vom 5. August 1997 (BGBl. I S. 2022), zuletzt durch Artikel 2e des Gesetzes vom 24. September 2008 (BGBl. I S. 1856).

Baldwin, Richard, Rikard Forslid, Philippe Martin, Gianmarco Ottaviano and Frederic Robert-Nicoud (2003). *Economic Geography and Public Policy*. Princeton: Princeton University Press.

Baldwin, Richard and Paul Krugman (2004). Agglomeration, Integration and Tax Harmonization. *European Economic Review*, 48 (1), 1-23.

Barba Navaretti, Giorgio and Anthony Venables (2004). *Multinational Firms in the World Economy*. Princeton: Princeton University Press.

Bénassy-Quéré, Agnès, Nicolas Gobalraja and Alain Trannoy (2007). Tax and Public Input Competition. *Economic Policy*, 22 (50), 385-430.

Bernard, Andrew, Bradford Jensen and Peter Schott (2006). *Transfer Pricing by U.S. Based Multinational Firms*. NBER Working Paper No. 12493.

Bester, Helmut (1992). Bertrand Equilibrium in a Differentiated Duopoly. *International Economic Review*, 33 (2), 433-448.

Boadway, Robin (2005). Income Tax Reform for a Globalized World: The Case for a Dual Income Tax. *Journal of Asian Economics*, 16 (6), 910-927.

Borck, Rainald and Michael Pflüger (2006). Agglomeration and Tax Competition. *European Economic Review*, 50 (3), 647-668.

Brander, James and Barbara Spencer (1985). Export Subsidies and International Market Share Rivalry. *Journal of International Economics*, 18 (1-2), 83-100.

Brennan, Geoffrey and James Buchanan (1980). *The Power to Tax. Analytical Foundations of a Fiscal Constitution*. Cambridge: Cambridge University Press.

Brülhart, Marius, Mario Jametti and Kurt Schmidheiny (2007). *Do Agglomeration Economies Reduce the Sensitivity of Firm Location to Tax Differentials?* CEPR Discussion Paper No. 6606.

Charlot, Sylvie and Sonia Paty (2007). Market Access Effects and Local Tax Setting: Evidence from French Panel Data. *Journal of Economic Geography*, 7 (3), 247-263.

Choi, Yoon and Theodore Day (1998). Transfer Pricing, Incentive Compensation and Tax Avoidance in a Multi-Division Firm. *Review of Quantitative Finance and Accounting*, 11 (2), 139-164.

Clausing, Kimberly (2003). Tax-motivated Transfer Pricing and US Intrafirm Trade Prices. *Journal of Public Economics*, 87 (9-10), 2207-2223.

Clausing, Kimberly (2009). Multinational Firm Tax Avoidance and Tax Policy. *National Tax Journal*, 62 (4), 703-725.

COM (2005). *The Contribution of Taxation and Customs Policies to the Lisbon Strategy*. Ed.: Commission of the European Communities, 532.

COM (2007a). *Communication from the Commission to the Council, the European Parliament, the European Parliament, the European Economic and Social Committee and the Committee of the Regions. Modernizing Social Protection for Greater Social Justice and Economic Cohesion: Taking Forward the Active Inclusion of People Furthest from the Labour Market.* Ed.: Commission of the European Communities, 620 final.

COM (2007b). *Proposal for a Decision of the European Parliament and of the Council on the European Year for Combating Poverty and Social Exclusion (2010)*. Ed.: Commission of the European Communities, 797 final.

COM (2007c). *Implementing the Community Programme for Improved Growth and Employment and the Enhanced Competitiveness of EU Business: Further Progress during 2006 and next Steps towards a Proposal on the Common Consolidated Corporate Tax Base (CCCTB)*. Ed.: Commission of the European Communities, 223.

COM (2009). *Taxation Trends in the European Union. Data for the EU Member States and Norway*. Ed.: Commission of the European Communities. Office for Official Publications of the European Communities, Luxembourg.

Combes Pierre-Philippe and Henry Overman (2004). *The spatial Distribution of Economic Activities in the European Union.* In: Henderson, Vernon and Jaques-Francois Thisse (Eds.). Handbook of Regional and Urban Economics, vol. 4, Amsterdam: Elsevier, 2845-2909.

Cremer, Helmuth and Pierre Pestieau (1996). Distributive Implications of European Integration. *European Economic Review*, 40 (3-4), 747-757.

Cremer, Helmuth and Pierre Pestieau (2003). Social Insurance Competition between Bismarck and Beveridge. *Journal of Urban Economics*, 54 (1), 181-196.

Cremer, Helmuth and Pierre Pestieau (2004). *Factor Mobility and Redistribution.* In: Henderson, Vernon and Jacques Thisse (Eds.). Handbook of Regional and Urban Economics, vol. 4, Amsterdam: Elsevier, 2529-2560.

CVT (2002). *Consolidated Version of the Treaty Establishing the European Community*, C 325/33, 24.12.2002, Official Journal of the European Communities.

Devereux, Michael (2004). Debating Proposed Reforms of the Taxation of Corporate Income in the European Union. *International Tax and Public Finance*, 11 (1), 71-89.

Devereux, Michael, Rachel Griffith and Alexander Klemm (2002). Corporate Income Tax Reforms and International Tax Competition. *Economic Policy*, 17 (35), 450-495.

Devereux, Michael and Rachel Griffith (2003). Evaluating Tax Policy for Location Decisions. *International Tax and Public Finance*, 10 (2), 107-126.

Devereux, Michael and Giorgia Maffini (2006). *The Impact of Taxation on the Location of Capital, Firms, and Profit: A Survey of Empirical Evidence.* Oxford University Centre for Business Taxation Working Paper 07/02. http://www.sbs.ox.ac.uk/centres/tax/papers/Pages/PaperWP0702.aspx

Devereux, Michael, Rachel Griffith and Helen Simpson (2007). Firm Location Decisions, Regional Grants, and Agglomeration Externalities. *Journal of Public Economics*, 91 (3-4), 413-435.

Dixit, Avinash and Joseph E. Stiglitz (1977). Monopolistic Competition and Optimum Product Diversity, *American Economic Review*, 67 (3), 297-308.

Duraton, Gilles and Henry Overman (2005). Testing for Localization Using Micro-Geographic Data. *The Review of Economic Studies*, 72 (4), 1077-1106.

Eaton, Jonathan and Gene Grossman (1986). Optimal Trade and Industrial Policy under Oligopoly. *Quarterly Journal of Economics*, 101 (2), 383-406.

Egger, Hartmut and Joseph Falkinger (2006). The Role of Public Infrastructure and Subsidies for Firm Location and International Outsourcing. *European Economic Review*, 50 (8), 1993-2015.

Eggert, Wolfgang and Bernd Genser (2005). *Dual Income Taxation in EU Member Countries*. CESifo DICE Report 1, 41-47.

Ellison, Glenn and Edward Glaeser (1997). Geographic Concentration in the U.S. Manufacturing Industries: A Dartboard Approach. *Journal of Political Economy*, 105 (5), 889-927.

Elschner, Christina and Michael Overesch (2007). Trends in Corporate Tax Levels in Europe. *Intereconomics*, 42 (3), 127-132.

Elschner, Christina, Jost Heckemeyer and Christoph Spengel (2009). *Besteuerungsprinzipien und effektive Unternehmenssteuerbelastungen in der Europäischen Union*. ZEW Discussion Paper No. 09-034. ftp://ftp.zew.de/pub/zew-docs/dp/dp09034.pdf

Ernst & Young (2007a). *European Attractiveness Survey 2007*. Ernst & Young Global Ltd., June 2007.

Ernst & Young (2007b). *2007-2008 Global Transfer Pricing Survey*. Ernst & Young Global Ltd., December 2007.

Forslid, Rikard (2005). Tax Competition and Agglomeration: Main Effects and Empirical Implications. *Swedish Economic Policy Review*, 12 (1), 113-137.

Fuest, Clemens (2001). *Europäische Steuerpolitik: Zwischen Harmonisierung und Wettbewerb*. In: Ohr, Renate and Theresia Theurl (Eds.). Kompendium Europäische Wirtschaftspolitik. München: Verlag Vahlen, 468-499.

Fuest, Clemens, Bernd Huber and Jack Mintz (2005). Capital Mobility and Tax Competition. *Foundations and Trends in Microeconomics*, 1 (1), 1-62.

Fujita, Masahisa and Jaques-Francois Thisse (1996). Economics of Agglomeration. *Journal of the Japanese and International Economies*, 10 (4), 339-378.

Fujita, Masahisa and Jaques-Francois Thisse (2002). *Economics of Agglomeration. Cities, Industrial Location, and Regional Growth*. Cambridge: Cambridge University Press.

Grosse, Robert (1985). An Imperfect Competitions Theory of the MNE. *Journal of International Business Studies*, 16 (1), 57-80.

Grubert, Harry (2003). Intangible Income, Inter-company Transactions, Income Shifting, and the Choice of Location. *National Tax Journal*, 56 (1), 221-242.

Haufler, Andreas (2001). *Taxation in a Global Economy*. Cambridge: Cambridge University Press.

Haufler, Andreas (2006). *Die Besteuerung multinationaler Unternehmen*. Manuskript für die Tagung des Finanzwissenschaftlichen Ausschuß des Vereins für Socialpolitik in Gießen, 8.-10. Juni 2006.

Haufler, Andreas and Michael Pflüger (2004). International Commodity Taxation under Monopolistic Competition. *Journal of Public Economic Theory*, 6 (3), 445-470.

Haufler, Andreas and Ian Wooton (2007). *Competition for Firms in an Oligopolistic Industry: Do Firms or Countries Have to Pay?* Münchener Wirtschaftswissenschaftliche Beiträge (VWL) 2007-13. http://epub.ub.uni-muenchen.de/1399/

Head, Keith and Thierry Mayer (2004). *The Empirics of Agglomeration and Trade*. In: Henderson, Vernon and Jaques-Francois Thisse (Eds.). Handbook of Regional and Urban Economics, vol. 4, Amsterdam: Elsevier, 2609-2669.

Hellerstein, Walter and Charles McLure (2004). The European Commission's Report on Company Income Taxation: What the EU can Learn from the Experience of the US States. *International Tax and Public Finance*, 11 (2), 199-220.

Helpman, Elhanan and Paul Krugman (1985). *Market Structure and Foreign Trade*. Cambridge: MIT Press.

Helpman, Elhanan and Paul Krugman (1989). *Trade Policy and Market Structure*. Cambridge: MIT Press, Cambridge.

Hines, James (2005). *Corporate Taxation and International Competition*. University of Michigan: Ross School of Business Paper No. 1026.

Hoover, Edgar (1937). *Location Theory and the Shoe and Leather Industries*. Cambridge: Harvard University Press.

Hotelling, Harold (1929). Stability in Competition. *Economic Journal*, 39 (159), 41-57.

Jofre-Monseny, Jordi and Albert Solé-Ollé (2008). *Which Communities should be afraid of Mobility? The Effects of Agglomeration Economies on the Sensitivity of Firm Location to Local Taxes*. CESifo Working Paper No. 2311.

Jofre-Monseny, Jordi and Albert Solé-Ollé (2009). *Is Agglomeration Taxable?* Paper presented at the XVII Encuentro de Economía Pública in Murcia 2010. http://www.um.es/dp-hacienda/eep2010/comunicaciones/eep2010-77.pdf

Kind, Hans, Karen Midelfart Knarvik and Guttorm Schjelderup (2000). Competing for Capital in a 'Lumpy' World. *Journal of Public Economics*, 78 (3), 253-274.

Knirsch, Deborah (2007). *Finding a New Tax base for German Companies after the Abolishment of the One-Book System*. Mimeo. Paper presented at the 63rd Congress of the IIPF in Warwick.

Koh, Hyun-Ju and Nadine Riedel (2009a). *Taxing Agglomeration Rents: The Importance of Being Different*. Mimeo. Paper presented at the 6th Norwegian-German Seminar on Public Economics in Munich. http://www.cesifogroup.de/portal/page/portal/CFP_CONF/CFP_CONF_2009/Conf-ng09-Koethenbuerger/Conf-ng09-papers/ng09_Riedel.pdf

Koh, Hyun-Ju and Nadine Riedel (2009b). *Taxing Agglomeration Rents: The Importance of Being Different*. Mimeo. Paper presented at the III Workshop on Fiscal Federalism: Financing Sub-Central Governments in Barcelona. http://www.pcb.ub.es/ieb/aplicacio/fitxers/WS09Riedel.pdf

Krugman, Paul (1991a). Increasing Returns and Economic Geography. *Journal of Political Economy*, 99 (3), 483-499.

Krugman, Paul (1991b). *Geography and Trade*. Cambridge: MIT Press.

Krugman, Paul and Anthony Venables (1995). Globalization and the Inequality of Nations. *Quarterly Journal of Economics*, 110 (3), 857-880.

Ludema, Rodney and Ian Wooton (2000). Economic Geography and the Fiscal Effects of Integration. *Journal of International Economics*, 52 (2), 331-357.

Maurel, Françoise and Béatrice Sédillot (1999). A Measure of the Geographic Concentration in French Manufacturing Industries. *Regional Science and Urban Economics*, 29 (5), 575-604.

Martin, Phillippe and Carol-Ann Rogers (1995). Industrial Location and Public Infrastructure. *Journal of International Economics*, 39 (3-4), 341-359.

Mahoney, Joseph (1992). The Choice of Organizational Form: Vertical Financial Ownership Versus Other Methods of Vertical Integration. *Strategic Management Journal*, 13 (8), 559-584.

Markusen, James (2004). *Multinational Firms and the Theory of International Trade*. Cambridge: MIT Press.

McLure, Charles and Joann Weiner (2000). *Deciding Whether the European Union Should Adopt Formula Apportionment of Company Income*. In: Cnossen, Sijbren (Ed.). Taxing Capital Income in the European Union. Oxford: Oxford University Press, 243-292.

Mintz, Jack (2004). Corporate Tax Harmonization in Europe: It's all about Compliance. *International Tax and Public Finance*, 11 (2), 221-234.

Mintz, Jack and Alfons Weichenrieder (2005). *Taxation and the Financial Structure of German outbound FDI*. CESifo Working Paper 1612.

Monopolkommission (1998). *Marktöffnung umfassend verwirklichen*. Zwölftes Hauptgutachten der Monopolkommission 1996/ 97, Ed.: Monopolkommission.

Monopolkommission (2000). *Wettbewerbspolitik in Netzstrukturen*. Dreizehntes Hauptgutachten der Monopolkommission 1998/ 99, Ed.: Monopolkommission.

Monopolkommission (2002). *Netzwettbewerb durch Regulierung*. Vierzehntes Hauptgutachten der Monopolkommission 2000/ 01, Ed.: Monopolkommission.

Monopolkommission (2004). *Wettbewerbspolitik im Schatten „Nationaler Champions“*. Fünfzehntes Hauptgutachten der Monopolkommission 2002/ 03, Ed.: Monopolkommission.

Mooij, Ruud de and Sjef Ederveen (2003). Taxation and Foreign Direct Investment: A Synthesis of Empirical Research. *International Tax and Public Finance*, 10 (6), 673-693.

Mooij, Ruud de and Sjef Ederveen (2005). *Explaining the Variation in Empirical Estimates of Tax Elasticities of Foreign Direct Investment.* Tinbergen Institute Discussion Paper, TI 2005-108/3. http://www.tinbergen.nl/discussionpapers/05108.pdf

Mooij, Ruud de and Sjef Ederveen (2006). *What a Difference does it make? Understanding the Empirical Literature on Taxation and International Capital Flows*. European Commission Economic Papers No. 261. http://ec.europa.eu/economy_finance/publications/publication_summary586_en.htm

Mooij, Ruud de and Sjef Ederveen (2008). Corporate Tax Elasticities: A Reader's Guide to Empirical Findings. *Oxford Review of Economic Policy*, 24 (4), 680-697.

Navaretti, Giorgio Barba and Anthony Venables (2004). *Multinational Firms in the World Economy*. Princeton: Princeton University Press.

Navarro, Vincente, John Schmitt and Javier Astudillo (2004). Is Globalization Undermining the Welfare State? *Cambridge Journal of Economics*, 28 (1), 133-152.

Nicodème Gaëtan (2009). On Recent Developments in Fighting Harmful Tax Practices. *National Tax Journal*, 62 (4), 755-771.

Nielsen, Søren Bo, Pascalis Raimondos-Møller and Guttorm Schjelderup (2003). Formula Apportionment and Transfer Pricing under Oligopolistic Competition. *Journal of Public Economic Theory*, 5 (2), 419-437.

Oates, Wallace (1972). *Fiscal Federalism.* New York: Hartcourt Brace Jovanovich.

Oates, Wallace (2001). Fiscal Competition and European Union: Contrasting Perspectives. *Regional Science and Urban Economics*, 31 (2-3), 133-145.

OECD (2005). *OECD Handbook on Economic Globalisation Indicators*. Ed.: Organisation for Economic Co-Operation and Development, Paris: OECD Publications.

OECD (2007a). *Staying Competitive in the Global Economy: Moving up the Value Chain*. Ed.: Organisation for Economic Co-Operation and Development, Paris: OECD Publications.

OECD (2007b). *Globalization and Regional Economies. Can OECD Regions Compete in Regional Industries?* OECD Reviews of Regional Innova-

tion. Ed.: Organisation for Economic Co-Operation and Development, Paris: OECD Publications.
OECD (2007c). *Tax Effects on Foreign Direct Investment. Recent Evidence and Policy Analysis*. OECD Tax Policy Studies No. 17. Ed.: Organisation for Economic Co-Operation and Development, Paris: OECD Publications.
OECD (2009). *OECD Transfer Pricing Guidelines for Multinational Enterprises and Tax Administrations*. Ed.: Organisation for Economic Co-Operation and Development, Paris: OECD Publications.
Ottaviano, Gianmarco and Tanguy van Ypersele (2005). Market Size and Tax Competition. *Journal of International Economics*, 67 (1), 25-46.
Paty, Sonia (2008). Tax Competition and New Economic Geography. *Urban Public Economics Review*, 8, 69-83.
Pflüger, Michael (2001). Ecological Dumping under Monopolistic Competition. *Scandinavian Journal of Political Economy*, 103 (4), 689-706.
Rajan, Madhav and Stefan Reichelstein (2004). A Perspective on "Asymmetric Information, Incentives and Intrafirm Resource Allocation". *Management Science*, 50 (12), 1615-1623.
Rauscher, Michael (1998). Leviathan and Competition among Jurisdictions: The Case of Benefit Taxation. *Journal of Urban Economics*, 44 (1), 59-67.
Rodrik, Dani (1997). *Has Globalization gone too far?* Washington D.C.: Institute for International Economics.
Rosenthal, Stuart and William Strange (2004). *Evidence on the Nature and Source of Agglomeration Economies*. In: Henderson, Vernon and Jaques-Francois Thisse (Eds.). Handbook of Regional and Urban Economics, vol. 4, Amsterdam: Elsevier, 2119- 2171.
Sachverständigenrat (2005). *Die Chance Nutzen - Reformen mutig voranbringen*. Jahresgutachten 2005/2006 des Sachverständigenrates zur Begutachtung der Gesamtwirtschaftlichen Entwicklung, Wiesbaden.
Schindler, Dirk and Guttorm Schjelderup (2006). *Company Tax Reform in Europe and its Effect on Collusive Behavior*. CESifo Working Paper No. 1702.
Schjelderup, Guttorm and Lars Sørgard (1997). Transfer Pricing as a Strategic Device for Decentralized Multinationals. *International Tax Public Finance*, 4 (3), 277-290.
Schratzenstaller, Margit (2007). Company Tax Coordination in the EU - Status Quo and Perspectives. *Intereconomics*, 42 (3), 116-120.
Schulze, Günther and Heinrich Ursprung (1999). Globalisation of the Economy and the Nation State. *The World Economy*, 22 (3), 295-352.
SGB II. Sozialgesetzbuch (SGB) Zweites Buch (II) - Grundsicherung für Arbeitsuchende - (Artikel 1 des Gesetzes vom 24. Dezember 2003, BGBl. I

S. 2954), zuletzt geändert zuletzt durch Artikel 2 des Gesetzes vom 14. April 2010 (BGBl. I S. 410).

SGB XII. Sozialgesetzbuch (SGB) Zwölftes Buch (XII) - Sozialhilfe - (Artikel 1 des Gesetzes vom 27. Dezember 2003, BGBl. I S. 3022), zuletzt durch Artikel 4 des Gesetzes vom 30. Juli 2009 (BGBl. I S. 2495).

Sinn, Hans-Werner (2003). *The New Systems Competition.* Cambridge: Blackwell Publishers.

Sinn, Hans-Werner (2004). *Migration, Social Standards and Replacement Incomes.* NBER Working Paper No. 10798.

Sørensen, Peter Birch (2004). Company Tax Reform in the European Union. *International Tax and Public Finance*, 11 (1), 91-115.

Sørensen, Peter Birch (2005). Dual Income Taxation: Why and How? *Finanzarchiv*, 61 (4), 559-586.

Swenson, Deborah (2001). Tax Reforms and Evidence of Transfer Pricing. *National Tax Journal*, 54 (1), 7-25.

Tiebout, Charles (1956). A Pure Theory of Local Expenditures. *Journal of Political Economy*, 64 (5), 416-424.

Treaty on the Accession of the Czech Republic, Estonia, Cyprus, Latvia, Lithuania, Hungary, Malta, Poland, Slovenia and Slovakia, L 236/46, 23.09.2003, Official Journal of the European Communities.

UNCTAD (2007). *World Investment Report 2007: Transnational Corporations, Extractive Industries and Development.* Ed.: United Nations Conference on Trade and Development. United Nations, New York and Geneva.

Venables, Anthony (1996). Equilibrium Location of Vertically Linked Industries. *International Economic Review*, 37 (2), 341-359.

Wellisch, Dietmar (2000). *The Theory of Public Finance in a Federal State.* Cambridge: Cambridge University Press.

Wellisch, Dietmar (2003a). Internationale Verrechnungspreismethoden, Neutralität und die Gewinne multinationaler Unternehmen (Transfer Pricing, Neutrality, and the Profits of Multinational Firms). *Jahrbücher für Nationalökonomie und Statistik (Journal of Economics and Statistics)*, 223 (3), 332-359.

Wellisch, Dietmar (2003b). Internationale Verrechnungspreismethoden, Neutralität und die Gewinne multinationaler Unternehmen (Transfer Pricing, Neutrality, and the Profits of Multinational Firms). *Jahrbücher für Nationalökonomie und Statistik (Journal of Economics and Statistics)*, 223 (4), 464-478.

Wellisch, Dietmar (2004). Taxation under Formula Apportionment - Tax Competition, Tax Incidence, and the Choice of Apportionment Factors. *Finanzarchiv*, 60 (1), 24-41.

Wildasin, David (1991). Income Redistribution in a Common Labor Market. *American Economic Review*, 81 (4), 757-772.

Wildasin, David (1994). Income Redistribution and Migration. *Canadian Journal of Economics*, 27 (3), 637-656.

Wildasin, David (2000). State and Provincial Corporate Income Taxation: Current Practice and Policy Issues for the United States and Canada. *Canadian Tax Journal*, 48 (2), 424-441.

Wildasin, David (2003). Fiscal Competition: An Introduction. *Journal of Public Economic Theory*, 5 (2), 169-176.

Wilson, John (1999). Theories of Tax Competition. *National Tax Journal*, 52 (2), 269-304.

Wilson, John and David Wildasin (2004). Capital Tax Competition: Bane or Boon. *Journal of Public Economics*, 88 (6), 1065-1091.

Zodrow, George and Peter Mieszkowski (1986). Pigou, Tiebout, Property Taxation, and the Underprovision of Local Public Goods. *Journal of Urban Economics*, 19 (3), 356-370.

# Abbreviations

| | |
|---|---|
| BTCM | Basic Tax Competition Model |
| CCCTB | Common Consolidated Corporate Tax Base |
| CES | Constant Elasticity of Substitution |
| DIT | Dual Income Tax (-ation) |
| EC | European Commission |
| EU | European Union |
| FA | Formula Apportionment |
| FDI | Foreign Direct Investment |
| GDP | Gross Domestic Product |
| GATT | General Agreement on Tariffs in Trade |
| MNE | Multinational Enterprise(s) |
| OECD | Organization for Economic Development |
| SA | Separate Accounting |
| WTO | World Trade Organization |

# List of Tables

# List of Figures

Kolibri 360 GmbH
Ferdinand-Jühlke-Straße 7
99095 Erfurt, Deutschland
produktsicherheit@kolibri360.de